Global Exchanges and Gender Perspectives in Africa

This book is a product of the CODESRIA Gender Institute

Global Exchanges and Gender Perspectives in Africa

Edited by

Jean-Bernard Ouédraogo
Roseline M. Achieng'

CODESRIA

COUNCIL FOR THE DEVELOPMENT OF SOCIAL SCIENCE RESEARCH IN AFRICA
Dakar

FOUNTAIN PUBLISHERS
Kampala

Council for the Development of Social Science Research in Africa
Avenue Cheikh Anta Diop, Angle Canal IV
P. O. Box 3304 Dakar, 18524, Senegal
Website: www.codesria.org

In association with:

Fountain Publishers
P. O. Box 488
Kampala, Uganda
E-mail: sales@fountainpublishers.co.ug
            publishing@fountainpublishers.co.ug
Website: www.fountainpublishers.co.ug

ISBN: 978-2-86978-488-8 (CODESRIA)

ISBN: 978-9970-25-109-4 (Fountain)

Typesetting: Daouda Thiam
Cover Design: Ibrahima Fofana

The Council for the Development of Social Science Research in Africa (CODESRIA) is an independent organisation whose principal objectives are to facilitate research, promote research-based publishing and create multiple forums geared towards the exchange of views and information among African researchers. All these are aimed at reducing the fragmentation of research in the continent through the creation of thematic research networks that cut across linguistic and regional boundaries.

CODESRIA publishes *Africa Development*, the longest standing Africa based social science journal; *Afrika Zamani*, a journal of history; the *African Sociological Review*, the *African Journal of International Affairs*; *Africa Review of Books* and the *Journal of Higher Education in Africa*. The Council also co-publishes the *Africa Media Review*; *Identity, Culture and Politics: An Afro-Asian Dialogue*; *The African Anthropologist* and the *Afro-Arab Selections for Social Sciences*. The results of its research and other activities are also disseminated through its Working Paper Series, Green Book Series, Monograph Series, Book Series, Policy Briefs and the CODESRIA Bulletin. Select CODESRIA publications are also accessible online at www.codesria.org.

Contents

Notes on Contributors

Roseline M. Achieng' is a sociologist. After studies in Kenya, she got her PhD from the Sociology of Development Research Centre, University of Bielefeld, in Germany. Achieng' is currently in charge of developing the academic and research components of the sociology unit of the School of Arts, Monash South Africa, a campus of Monash University, Australia. She is also an associate researcher with the Centre for Refugee Studies at Moi University, Kenya. She won the 2006 Young Researcher Prize from the German Association for African Studies (VAD) for her thesis defended in 2005, entitled "Home Away from Home: Internally Displaced and Their Translocal Ethnic and Gender Cooperation in Reconstructing the Meaning of Place". Achieng' has published many articles on issues of development and methodology in the social sciences. Between 2006 and 2009, she worked as a Programme Manager, first in the Research Programme, and later in the Office of the Executive Secretary, Council for the Development of Social Science Research in Africa (CODESRIA).

Béatrice Faye holds a PhD in Philosophy. She teaches Analytic and Oriental Philosophy at the Inter-Institute Philosophy Consortium, Saint Augustin Centre, and the Spirituality and Theology Institute (IST). Her research interests include the theology of religiosity, particularly the enculturation of consecrated life in the African context, the philosophical questions related to Gender for the promotion of the 'Women's Genius' concept in Africa. Dr Faye was a laureate of the 2002 CODESRIA Gender Institute, and a beneficiary of the CODESRIA Small Grants for Thesis Writing in 2005.

Edward N. Waswa Kisiang'ani is a scholar and political commentator. He is currently the Director of Alumni Programmes at Kenyatta University, Nairobi, where he has taught Political History for many years. In 2002, Dr Kisiang'ani was a Fulbright scholar at the Boston College, U.S.A., and in 2006 a North-South Cooperation resident scholar at the University of Nantes, France, where he carried out research on "The African Youth, Globalization and Postnational Identities". He has published in the fields of gender, biotechnology, political theory and the youth.

Zachary Arochi Kwena holds an MA degree in Geography from Kenyatta University. He joined Kenya Medical Research Institute (KEMRI) in May 2002, and has risen through the ranks to become a Study Coordinator of the Male Microbicide Safety, Acceptance and Efficacy against STIs/HIV project based in Kisumu, Kenya. Most of Kwena's research and publications revolve round social aspects of STIs/HIV and community health.

Mathias Marie A. Ndinga is a professor of Economic Sciences at University Yaoundé II, Cameroon. And also teaches at University Marien Ngouabi, Brazzaville. He is a member of the technical branch of the National Committee against Poverty at Cameroon's Ministry of Territorial Planning and Management. His research interests are in the fields of governance, poverty, labour economics, gender and international trade. Prof Ndinga is an active member of the African Economic Research Consortium (AERC) and the Council for Development of Social Science Research in Africa (CODESRIA). He was also a laureate of the CODESRIA 2002 Gender Institute.

Samwel Ong'wen Okuro is a medical historian based at Bondo University, Kenya. He has vast research experience on HIV/AIDS and agrarian processes in Africa. Dr Okuro's most recent article: "Daniel Arap Moi and the Politics of HIV/AIDS in Kenya" was in the African *Journal of AIDS Research* Vol. 8, Issue 3, 2009.

Iwebunor Okwechime is a lecturer in the Department of International Relations, Obafemi Awolowo University, Ile-Ife, Nigeria. He has published in reputable local and international journals. He was a laureate of the CODESRIA 2000 Governance Institute and the 2002 Gender Institute

Jean Bernard Ouédraogo is a professor of Sociology. He is Director of Research at CNRS, LAIOS, IIAC, CNRS/EHESS, Paris, France and Director of the Research Group on Local Initiatives (GRIL) at the University of Ouagadougou, Burkina Faso. From 2002 to 2008, he was Deputy Executive Secretary of CODESRIA,where he also headed the Department of Training, Grants and Fellowship. He is the author of *Violences et communautés en Afrique noire [Violences and Communities in Black Africa]*, Paris: Éd. L'Harmattan, 1997 ; *Arts photographiques en Afrique. Technique et esthétique dans la photographie de studio au Burkina Faso [Photographic Arts in Africa: Technic and Aesthetics in Studio Photography in Burkina Faso]*, L'Harmattan, 2003; *Identités visuelles en Afrique [Visual Identities in Africa]*, Amalthée 2008. He is the editor of Norbert Elias' *Art Africain [African Art]*, Kimé, 2002. He has published many articles on the city, migration, labour, photography and the methodology of social sciences.

Zo Randriamaro is a sociologist and human rights and gender activist with extensive experience on gender and economic issues. She has presented papers on these issues at different meetings of academics and activists at regional and global levels. +She was Manager of the Gender and Economic Reforms in Africa (GERA) Programme of the Third World Network, based in Accra, Ghana. She is author *inter alia* of "African Women Challenging Neo-liberal Economic Orthodoxy: The Conception and Mission of the GERA Programme", in *Gender & Development*, Volume 11, Issue 1, 2003, "Gender and Trade: Overview Report" in *Bridge, Development-Gender*, 2007 and "Financing for the Poor and Women: A Policy Critique" in B. Herman, F. Pietracci, K. Sharma (eds) *Financing for Development: Proposals from Business and Civil Society*, United Nations University, Policy Perspectives 6, UNU Press: New York, 2001. She has also served as expert at UNIFEM Regional Office in Dakar, Senegal. Randriamaro is member of Women environment and Development Organization (WEDO) board and Development Alternatives with Women for a New Era (DAWN).

Gérard Tchouassi is a professor of Economic Sciences at the University of Yaoundé II-Soa, Cameroon. Winner of both Agence Universitaire de la Francophonie (AUF) and Grand Lyon (France) scholarchips, he has been a visiting professor to many universities. He has worked as a resource person and research consultant with many national and international organisations, particularly the United Nation's Women's Fund (UNIFEM). His research areas include women's entrepreneurship, microfinance, fair trade, regional integration, cross border trade, gender analysis, migration, development aid, formal and informal financial systems, pro-poor analysis, economic governance, economic attractiveness, social and economic solidarity.

1

Introduction
Gender in a Global Market Society

Jean-Bernard Ouédraogo & Roseline M. Achieng'

We linked hands in solidarity. We refused to vindicate those responsible for this tragedy. Some people spoke of settling of scores…others talked of war…But why did it have to be our market? What had our street done? Did our market really have anything to do with that terrible tragedy which transformed children into assassins? How could they have borne a grudge against our market? Nobody understood why this market had become the target of such violence, such wanton acts of vandalism and the scene of all those horrors. Nobody!

Ghislaine Sathoud, *Le marché de l'espoir*, 2005

The classical liberal ideology does not seem to draw any significant distinctions between men and women when they engage in commercial transactions that sanction the unevenness of the product without really factoring in the social status of the trading partners. It apparently does not consider that the individual, *homo oeconomicus*, whose conduct, viewed from the standpoint of the minimum 'human' referent, maximizes its utility based on a stable scale of preferences whose history is never recorded; such interest, which is at the root of trade, is constantly discounted by an individual reduced solely to his or her economic activity. Within liberal theory itself, the contradictions highlighted by the growth of real capitalism as practiced, which clash with the tenets of liberal thought, have always led to a conceptual readjustment of some of its classical tenets and a review of the system of ideological legitimization of the quest for profit. However, we have recently been witnessing a resurgence – after a long Marxist contestation – of this vision of rational economic agents who pursue their own goals, free from all institutional influence, and whose actions automatically regulate their social sphere of action. In light of the progress achieved so far in the social sciences, this idea is again being strongly challenged by the new economic sociology; some researchers (Wacquant and Calhoum 1989; Boltanski and Thévenot 1991) assert that the practices and representations of actors are the product of their specific historical and cultural background; the identity of individuals is neither natural nor vested with 'ahistorical' permanence, but it is exclusively informed by the general social ties that bind and mould society as a whole. Such major issues, which are at the centre of the dynamics of capitalism, are transposed and updated in areas that have recently come under the influence of the market economy. However, such issues have been reformulated differently because they echo problems raised in a specific contemporary context and addressed, therefore, by new theoretical approaches in tune with the characteristics of the host society.

It is worth noting that this phase of rapid expansion of market relations, after a very long period of social maturation, is predicated on the dismantling of geographical boundaries of the economy which outpaces the requisite emergence of nation-states as a form of political emancipation from the powerful religious forces that are dominant in the Judeo-Christian West. Adam Smith (Rosanvallon 1979) understood that the geographical sphere of influence of the politician was reduced to small zones, whereas in that era, trade zones were already expanding and opening up on a quasi-global scale. The dismantling of national frontiers is preceded by a huge wave that destroys weaker social entities, and by the reconstruction of a broader and relatively homogenous social environment. It is easy to understand why the objective of building a market society – a social structure superior to the market economy – entails the elimination of all barriers to free movement of individuals and trade to foster the building of a 'fluid and homogenous space structured exclusively by the geography of prices' (Rosanvallon 1979). This historical re-shaping of social relations jolts one of the pillars of the social order, namely the extended family, viewed as a place of captivity and immobility. The nuclear family is an offshoot of the market society. This social unit is, indeed, the tentative consequence of an extreme form of individual distinctiveness proposed by liberal ideology as the social and economic completion point of the model. The domestic economy soon becomes a target, as do all the non-market and intra-communal exchanges. This social model, as a preferential context, is based on the smart distinction it makes between 'formal rationality' and 'material rationality', vying with one another for the historical establishment of conventional trade. Formal rationality is defined as that which is based exclusively on accounting assessments, with no consideration of the social conditions of participants in trade, while material rationality is that which integrates ethical and moral requirements into economic activity.

Admittedly, the analysis of gender identity on the market cannot elude such a conflict of 'values' which logically involves a controversial re-definition of the scale of social values governing various forms of social belonging and egalitarian considerations. Max Weber makes a very accurate analysis of the break-up of the domestic community (Weber 1995) caused by the expansion of 'commercial relations' coupled with 'increasing calculability' in the social environment. The Weberian analytical model takes for granted the set-up of a relatively autonomous economic order, free from the moral injunctions of Protestantism and independent of its religious roots. It is easy to imagine the consequences of this historical confrontation between the market order and the peculiar history of relations that are social constructs between the two sexes; as Weber points out:

> When the market is left to its own legal devices, it only considers commodities, and not individuals nor natural human relations, which are peculiar to people-oriented communities. All these relations are obstacles to the development of a truly communal market, and the specific interests of such a market are tempting for all (Weber 1995).

The term 'domestic economy' does not only pertain to the management of the home or domestic units that are more or less large, but also includes all communities established on the fringes of capitalism. Fernand Braudel, in his analysis (Braudel 1985) inspired by the work of Karl Marx,[1] presents the capitalist as an 'evening visitor' who arrives just in time and uninvited to partake of the evening meal without having contributed to it. The capitalist takes all the credit for social structures of which he is not the creator. The age-old project of restructuring the domestic economy, the market society as it has developed in the West – whence it has set out to conquer the whole wide world – places at the very centre of the current capitalist expansion the challenge of imperatively reshaping gender identity, *inter alia*,[2] in market relations.

Globalization, as a product of a global environment of interdependent market relations, is not a new phenomenon. The effects of this general expansion of the market society, whose principles alone dominate Western societies, quickly influenced discussions in the social sciences, well before the confirmed advent of globalization. Ester Boserup's pioneering book (Boserup 1970) revealed the changing role of women in the production system streamlined by the internationalisation of capital and division of labour on a global scale. In the book, Boserup already castigated the globally harmful effects of 'modernisation' in the countries of the South on women, and highlighted the gender division of agricultural and industrial labour as well as the various effects of development strategies on men and women. In her view, colonialism and the voluntarist policies of modernization have considerably transformed the status of the woman. However, this perspective remained clearly development-oriented and did not place the change in the status of the woman in a historical perspective linked to the metamorphosis of capitalism itself.

In light of Immanuel Wallerstein's research (Wallerstein 1980) on the 'global system', globalization can be defined as 'the spatial expansion of capitalism' and accordingly as a 'process of circumventing, razing to the ground and, ultimately, dismantling the physical and regulatory borders that obstruct the accumulation of capital at the global level' (Adda 2006:7). The old norms that had hitherto governed the identity of individuals and hierarchical relations between them are now undergoing a decisive and unprecedented transformation. The spread of ideologies advocating the return to the market (liberalisation, privatisation and deregulation of labour), which accompanies global financial integration, growth of multinational firms and technological innovations (revolutions in the Information Technologies), are the main drivers of this new capitalism, liberated from the fetters and constraints imposed by the old States and communities.

The dissemination of this hegemonic capitalist model called 'westernization of the world' by some scholars (Latouche 1988) reflects a 'category that is both analytical, that is, indicative of an economic phenomenon, and normative, in the sense that it prescribes rules of conduct, defines and justifies the content of norms and institutions' (Talahite 2000:121). The globalization process is, therefore, based on the establishment of a hierarchy and competing social entities that are part of the process to build a market society at the global level.

A careful perusal of initial studies on relations between globalization and gender reveals that special attention is paid to the social consequences of Structural Adjustment Programmes (SAPs). Christiana Gladwin (1991) in her study of African peasants shows that the SAPs imposed by the IMF and World Bank – both of which are institutions inspired by the neo-liberal model – affected households by triggering variations in income (salaries and commodity prices), food prices and public expenditure (increases in school fees and cost of medication). Bisilliat notes that Structural Adjustment Programmes have only 'reinforced, hardened, and aggravated structural inequalities between men and women, as development projects since the 1950s had already done, according to the cumulative logic of the double patriarchy: that of decision-makers of both the South and the North' (Bisilliat 1998:100). The patriarchal relationship is resolutely destroyed or reformulated in a peculiar context of reformulated secular ties between men and women involved in the ongoing context of social reproduction. However, everyone is well aware that condemnation of gender inequalities does not always reflect a clear understanding of a phenomenon as complex as formulation of a global market society; reducing this historical process to its simple economic expression blinds one to the influential reciprocal relations between the patriarchy and peripheral capitalism, which is in turn subject to an unbalanced relationship with the hard core of capitalism. Like Karl Marx and Fernand Braudel, Claude Meillassoux (1975) has shown that the main objective of capitalism, as concerns 'domestic forms of production', is not necessarily to destroy them but to subject them to economic exploitation. This stranglehold on domestic production seems to affect the cultural identities of women and modulate their statutory rights in the new system of social relations called modernity.

There is hardly anything new in the assertion that the crisis of development theories and practical models in Africa is closely related to the contestation of theories spearheaded by the liberal school which is dominant in contemporary social sciences. The new conception of 'the rational economic individual' has sparked several criticisms. Since this vision, which is both academic and political, increasingly seemed to focus on technical aspects based on 'precision' and 'rigour', and became distanced from the daily reality of social actors, a protest movement gradually developed, giving birth to circles of opposition to the dominant model. The growth of this movement was accompanied by a proliferation of alternative schools of thought and political action that proposed alternative frameworks for analysis. These schools of alternative thought professed a 'heterodox' vision at variance with the ongoing 'conservative subversion'. Feminists, who emerged as an epistemological force in the early 1970s and who passed themselves off as a ramification of the heterodox economy, tried to anchor the falsely rational reasoning in social and political processes with a firmly established historical perspective. The lack of historicity is indeed the kingpin of the liberal vision of the rational actor who is presented as an individual without any social weight and who is constantly reduced to his or her productive and consumerist function. Feminist economists, who have been largely inspired by some Marxist theories such as the critical study of social division of labour, forms of production, their inherent power relations as well as the institutional frameworks for economic and social relations, have collectively sought to explain the processes and mechanisms sustaining exploitation and inequalities between the individuals, in particular, between men and women. In fact, as Beneria (2003:43) asserts, feminist economists have not merely focused their work on a social construct of the economy, but have consistently called into question the central role played by individual choice, as opposed to the insurance principle of individual and collective wellbeing. They focus their analyses on processes ushered in by capitalism and on the emerging inequalities in new power relations observed at various levels of society. The process of capitalist expansion which shapes and moulds the social identity of participants in the new global market society firmly anchors the characteristics of belonging and their functions in the new social order.

Meanwhile, such a global perspective ought not to be locked in sterile linearity which within the process of globalization would fail to perceive the irreversible opening up of the worlds of the south. There is the need within the framework of the analyses presented here to quite cogently define the sense of the notion of the market. The market here does not refer to saving or the localized exchange of goods, a perspective which is imposed by normative perceptions. In fact, a strictly materialistic reading of exchange would be included, since every social practice and interaction implies a communitarian transaction; meanwhile the exchange system under study here broadens to root out the obligation of the maximization of mercantile profit from the cycle of exchange. Trade here would have a meaning closer to those of old, one of human interaction, in a way that one could refer to 'good trade' between humans. In an acclaimed study, Mauss elaborated a broader vision of social exchanges:

> What they trade is not exclusively goods and wealth, furniture and buildings, economically useful items. They are before all else, courtesies, feasts, rituals, military services, women, children, dances, parties, fairs of which markets are only a part and where the movement of wealth is only one of the terms of a much more general and more permanent contract (Mauss 1978).

In one way, trade places itself at the heart of social exchanges and is carried along by a multitude of social interactions. Certainly, the reader is called upon to take into account the major mercantile formations of the social trade system, without forgetting the diversity of exchange routes as well as the varying modalities of social construction, at the margins and within market logics – those of implicit value in trade between humans – which the texts herein also seek to review. The globalization process which is at issue here cannot be reduced to simplistic analyses of movement of materials, but ought to be considered in the globalization of interactions through the broadening and the intensification of contacts on the planetary scale which create a clash between cultures, objects, techniques and values in the constant forging of innovative social relations under the influence of major global currents, while remaining determined to local historical frameworks. In order to grasp such a complex phenomenon, the encounter of different disciplinary perspectives allows for the elucidation of contradictory facets of this social dynamic, many of whose characteristics continue to remain hidden and rarely explored.

In discussing the subject of International Trade Dynamics and Gender Perspectives in Africa, the 2002 session of the Gender Institute of CODESRIA, from which the articles of this volume emerge, showed how different kinds, at different scales, of globalization can hold different meanings and trigger social, economic and technical strategies among contemporary African women. These manifestations of globalization are even, of course, perceptible on the smallest social relational scale. It should be pointed out that globalization has been described and analysed as a protest ground or a vast strategic chessboard that does not leave enough leeway for time marking or capitalization in the face of life's adversities. As such, the supposed winner – the powerful market network – always carries the day. The presentations contained in this volume reveal two parallel and paradoxical trends. On the one hand, while globalization has liberalized and opened up some domains – the most important being the economic sphere – it has, paradoxically, ushered in other forms of 'liberties' and this same dual process has also led to a new enslavement of marginalized social groups whose boundaries do not always square with those defined by the identity-based groupings of the former social regimes.

The analyses arising from these different presentations address the issue of the social construction of these reconstituted entities and the economic bases of factors giving rise to various forms of social and gender inequality, in the context of the changes and adjustments triggered by the globalization process. Equally scrutinized are the gains that eclipse the increasing isolation of, and withdrawal of all responsibility from women, which came with the advent of financial and commercial policies informed by the new values of globalization.

It must be admitted that the debate sparked off by the analysis of the systematic strategy of *homo oeconomicus* hinges directly on the collective component in the definition of the rationality of social agents, thereby questioning the function of utility and social identity, belonging to a given group, like those relating to sexual identity.

It is quite understandable that the theory of social identity considers gender categorization as a 'salient categorization' in the repertoire of possible identities for a group of individuals. However, although the economics of conventions has clearly shown the fundamentally limited nature of rationality and *ipso facto* the performance of social and institutional referents, the competition in situations of action existing between 'self-stereotyping' and external institutional taxonomic operations, the historical test of social reality places women at a constructive and argumentative disadvantage, a critical process that limits depersonalization and increases the oneness of women.

The expansion of the global trend in the sphere of influence of capitalism contains theoretical and technical principles that underpin liberal thought, the paragon of this economic and social order which is expanding rapidly today. The studies presented in this volume lay, from the perspective of trade, a historical framework for understanding the phenomenon of globalization while also seeking to show multiple modes of construction of feminine identities and the dynamics of their confrontation with major trends of the globalization process. For, contrary to the justifications proffered for this expansion, the various aspects examined here show quite clearly that the market order, even at global level, bears major contradictions which portray the level of involvement of the societies considered in globalization and consequently, the reflection of the degrees of contradiction that it engenders and reformulates to portray social identities still resistant to the imposed standardization. It is thus interesting to note that a practice so often presented as general, human and, therefore, socially neutral and only subject to principles of overcoming the material or symbolic lack of fulfilment, is strongly informed by the expression of social identities. The upholding of feminine identities in the global market begins, as Béatrice Faye shows, with its encroachment on economic theories developed in a male chauvinist intellectual context.

Béatrice Faye breaks new ground in her study of historical philosophy which seeks to capture the implications of gender and the interpretative frameworks that have made this concept a central category – highly favoured by international organisations – for analysis. Basing her analysis on interpretations of ancient philosophers such as Anaxagoras, Socrates, Plato, or those of philosophers of a more recent epoch such as Thomas Aquinas, Rousseau, Machiavelli, Aristotle through Hobbes, Pufendorf, Locke to the most recent such as Adam Smith and John Stuart Mill, the author chose to discuss the dialectics of the intellectual and social transition from the economics of gender to the gender of economics.

Thus, she is defending an incomplete thesis which directly asks the following question: 'If women were in control of the economy, would ethics, economic policies and the choice of priorities be the same?' To answer this crucial question, one needs to return to the biological origins of inequality between man and woman and, in so doing, retrace the process of confiscation of power by man to the detriment of woman, an extension of the primary physical dichotomy. By considering gender, not as a biological, natural fact but as a social construct, it becomes possible to rethink the epistemology of philosophy and that of the social sciences while releasing them from the grip of essentialism. One of the aims of this critical review of the intellectual history of the West is to refuse the blindness imposed by dominant philosophical concepts and economic theories, the latter having considered for a long time the economics of gender relations as relations between market values without underlining the historically constructed identities conflicting therein.

The sustained silence over issues of gender equality was powerfully covered by the search for equality for the citizen, who had become sacred. Paradoxically, this policy fostered the development of metaphysics of gender which launched a radical counter-offensive to vindicate womankind confronted by the domineering phallic order. The author constantly raises the problem of the exclusion of women from some areas of knowledge and, concurrently, the silence of theoreticians of economics who have brought about a rethinking of the integration of women into market relations today as well the manner in which this process is addressed by the dominant liberal thought. The chapters in this volume explore, each in its own way, the difficult circumstances surrounding this encounter between the gender order and the order of contemporary substantive and symbolic economics.

In the same critical vein, the article by Edward Kisiangani draws from the French theoretician, Michel Foucault, to show through a study of fashion, the media and music, the manner in which the new liberal movement – height of irony – has contributed to the imprisonment of the body. It shows how global trade in fashion and music, driven by the media, has stripped the feminine body of all power while increasing the authority of men and, by the same token, the subordination of women. The author maintains that in the global village, African women have become subjects who keep watch over themselves according to the panoptic principle, an expression he borrows from Foucault. Kisiangani advocates a critical analysis of disciplinary practices – in terms of the control Michel Foucault gives to this concept – introduced by the globalization process, which seems to have punished the feminine body by imprisoning it and making it inferior while emancipating and liberating the masculine body.

Such relegation to inferior status, although considered more in its economic sense, is the theme addressed in the chapter by Iwebunor Okwechime. Through his analysis, the author shows how the changing political and economic environment has deprived women of their 'traditional economic spaces'. He goes on to state that the local economy has been eroded by the opening up of markets to free trade. However, he shows how women have been able to benefit from feminine movements both at local and international levels by availing themselves of their power, and also how, through such ties, they have succeeded in raising their voices and triggering change. The salient points of this study concern the means of action employed by women at the grassroots to fight petroleum multinationals, as well as the way in which – thanks to their union and their activism – grassroots women have succeeded in overcoming the barriers imposed on them by global exploitation structures.

Samuel Ong'wen Okuro's article explores the theme of alternative economic spaces. He portrays parallel processes engendered by globalization. Whereas this process has opened up national borders in Africa and ushered in the free movement of money, goods and persons, coping strategies on the fringes have, paradoxically, developed. Take, for instance, the increase in fraudulent movement of goods across borders as well as growth in the ranks of smugglers swelled mostly by women. The fact remains that despite the relative success of these women's strategies, the positions they still occupy in society have always taken a toll on them due to such economic and social liberalization.

From a local standpoint, using the case of Cameroon, Gérard Tchouassi examines the conditions for building a new trade model – termed equitable – at the global level. Designed as an alternative to the current domineering system which is unfavourable to producers of the South, this equitable trade seeks to combat the degradation of global terms of trade and to transform the power relations wrought by the global economy. However, this alternative is based on the desire to subvert the market order, dominated by the principles of economic rationality, through the application of ethical and moral principles with a view to building a world where social inequalities – including gender-related ones – would be banished. Observing a relatively strong presence of women in the equitable trade system, Tchouassi questions the effectiveness of this mode of access to world trade.

Although it would be illusory to apply a single market model, he observes the limits of this utopia in the increasingly evident influence of the rules of the dominant order that compel 'local', 'personalized', markets to abide by the logic of economic calculation, far from the ethical imperatives of 'fair trade'.

Two articles, one written by Ndinga and the other by Zachary Arochi Kwena, discuss the innovative aspects of the expansion of market relations to African societies. Ndinga in his presentation describes the use of new means of communication by women in Brazzaville in their business activities and shows clearly how they adapt to the new world and how mobile phones do not seem, for anything in the world, to disturb a non-egalitarian system dominated by men. The author examines the incidence of ICTs and their unequal use in the trade in loincloth practiced by both men and women. Against the backdrop of globalization and transformation of relations between genders, Ndinga's economic analysis attempts to explain this gender-based differential integration in the economic and technical environment of globalization. He equally portrays an influence that varies with gender as well as the position of each player in the loincloth business, which itself is subject to the vicissitudes and opportunities of globalization. Henceforth, communication technologies have taken centre stage.

Studying the role of social capital in small enterprises, Kwena shows how women put social belonging to good use. Such is the case with the 'tontines' where access is closely linked to the capacity to mobilize the requisite social capital. He concludes that in the era of globalization social capital as expressed in associations, rules and networks of all types, is indispensable to the creation and sustainability of women-owned micro enterprises.

Zo Randriamaro's article underscores the permanence of a global division of intellectual labour which is reflected in issues of relations between gender and global trade liberalization. She observes that although cognizance is given to the place of gender in policies and institutions governing world trade, African women are still very poorly represented in these debates. Radriamaro proposes a critical review of existing literature on relations between gender and trade after laying down the general framework represented by GATT and the WTO. She moves on to state the causes of Africa's predicament in the current world trade system. This debate that she launches enables her to figure out the modalities for creating and maintaining inequalities in the global order as a major prerequisite for understanding the structural discrimination that affects both women and the poor. In this critical perspective, the interaction between gender, social class, race and ethnic group should be constantly borne in mind by whoever seeks a profound understanding of the inequalities engendered by the global market order. She then underscores the need for a radical transformation of the interpretative paradigms that condition the transforming action of advocates of a balanced global order and an equitable position for African women.

It is evident that the market order, in spite of the strength of the social forces imposing it, faces resistance that calls into question the theoretical legitimacy and the social justice of its practices. The consistency of the social identity of this capitalist expansion, this global market society, depends on the resolution of these contradictions, some aspects of which are unveiled in this volume. This is a prerequisite for the building up of a utopia, a world of equality which the history of humanity also enjoins us to work for.

Notes

1. Marx writes 'Capital did not inaugurate the world but found at its disposal production and products that it made a point of duty to subject to its process'. *Karl Marx, Foundations of the Critique of Political Economy*, T 2, Paris: Anthropos, p. 191.
2. These, of course, should include forms of captive belonging such as religious and ethnic groups.

Bibliography

Adda, J., 2006, *La mondialisation de l'économie : genèses et problèmes*, [1996], Paris : La Découverte.

Beneria, L., 2003, *Gender, Development, and Globalization: Economics as if All People Mattered*, New York & London: Routledge.

Bisilliat, J., 1998, 'Les logiques d'un refus. Les femmes rurales africaines et les politiques d'ajustement structurel' in H. Hirata and H. Le Doaré (eds.), *Les paradoxes de la mondialisation*, Cahiers du Gedisst, No. 21, Paris: L'Harmattan, pp. 93-109.

Boserup, E., 1970, *Women's Role in the Eeconomic Development*, London: Earthsean Publications Ltd.

Boltanski, L. and Thévenot, L., 1991, *De la justification. Les économies de la grandeur*, Paris: Gallimard.

Braudel, F., 1985, *La dynamique du capitalisme*, Paris: Arthaud.

Gladwin, C. (ed.), 1991, *Structural Adjustment and African Woman Farmers*, Gainsville: University of Florida.

Latouche, S., 1988, 'Contribution à l'histoire du concept de développement in Coquery',
    Vidrovitch C. *et al.* (eds.), *Pour une histoire du sous-développement. Etats, sociétés, développement*,
    Paris: L'Harmattan, pp. 41-60.

Marx, K., 1967, *Fondements de la critique de l'économie politique*, T 2, Paris: Anthropos.

Mauss, M., [1925] 1978, 'Essai sur le don. Forme et raisin de l'échange dans les sociétés
    archaïques', in *Sociologie et Anthropologie*, Paris: PUF, p151.

Meillassoux, C., 1975, '*Femmes, greniers et capitaux*', Paris: Ed. Maspero.

Rosanvallon, P., 1979, *Le capitalisme utopique. Critique de l'idéologie économique*, Paris: Seuil.

Talahite, F., 2000, Mondialisation in H. Hirata *et al.* (ed.), *Dictionnaire critique du féminisme*,
    Paris: PUF, pp. 120-125.

Wacquant, J.D.L. and C.J. Calhoum, 1989, 'Intérêt, rationalité et cultures. A propos d'un
    récent débat sur la théorie de l'action', *ARSS*, No.78.

Wallerstein, I., 1980. *Le système du monde du XVème siècle à nos jours*, Paris: Flammarion.

Weber, M., 1995, *Economie et société*, Plon, T 2, Paris.

2

The Difference in the System of the Self: A Philosophical Contribution to the Gender Approach

Béatrice Faye

Introduction

The place given to the difference between the sexes is a 'blind spot' in the teaching of philosophy, as it is in the history of ideas in general. Philosophical language is the language most strongly marked by the masculine. The 'major writers' or the 'major systems' are studied, but no attention is paid to the positions they have taken on questions concerning this matter. With many philosophers, an unquestioned hiatus is left between reflections on man in general and any reflection on the sexual division concerning the place and role of women, and also their cognitive, moral and aesthetic capacities. The power that men have over them is explained in terms of a balance of force (physical force) that is inherent in nature, which the making of laws may organize and regulate, or even change, but never abolish. This involves the belief that since the beginnings of mankind, men have had the biological privilege of regarding themselves as the only sovereign subjects. For Francoise Héritier, 'There is little doubt that masculine physical superiority and above all the burden women have to bear, and their forced immobilization and weakening during the greater part of their life, have been the basic causes of the origins of humanity' (Héritier 1978:387). In other words, the dualism of the sexes is based on the reality of the body. Later on, ideologies took over this original dichotomy and extended it to every part of life and to every distinct aspect of knowledge.

There are thus two main aspects in the relationship between women and knowledge, the first a socio-historical one, which studies the mechanisms by which women were kept away from knowledge or from certain areas of knowledge, or were only admitted to them as simple executants or disseminators, but never as creators. The second aspect concerns the use made of this knowledge. Does an examination of scientific knowledge from the parameter of sexuation transform one's understanding of it? This approach has certainly been fruitful in the field of human sciences, since these sciences have human reality as a whole as their object, and because dealing with this by making a distinction between men and women and by analysing their relationships can throw fresh light on the subject matter. As Collin tells us:

> It is a decisive step to start considering a society, whether a traditional one or a Western one, by asking oneself about the place particular individuals occupy in it, by studying the structure of the family in the same way, including that form of the family modestly described as 'one parent,' or by introducing this parameter into the statistics. Philosophy, history, sociology, and even economics can be enriched or even transformed by this (Collin 1992:19).

In a well-known schema that is inscribed in psychoanalytical thought, masculine knowledge can have affinities with detachment, cutting off or with separation, while feminine knowledge has affinities with the global. Men can thus isolate one element of reality, project it away from themselves, and then devote themselves to it, while forgetting or ignoring whatever is connected with it. Women on the other hand do not consider detachment to be anything but a passing moment. 'In this perspective, which can be called holistic, there is no hiatus between knowledge and thought, any more than there is between thought and love' (Collin 1992:21).

The invisibility or occultation of women in public activities demonstrates the privilege enjoyed by the masculine actor and his historically central position. In a more specific way, it can be noted how economic theories have generally nothing to say on how social relations affect economic development. There is nothing surprising in this, since conventional economics is poorly equipped to deal with the most fundamental questions about development. It is little better equipped to explain social relations between men and women. It represents more of an obstacle to any analysis of these relations than an instrument for carrying it out.

This is why feminist thinking, which is accustomed to endless deconstruction and reconstruction, can use gender as an analytical tool. Let us briefly recall that gender (*genre* in French) appears to be one of the last of the hermeneutical concepts introduced by Western feminism (Collin 1992).[1] It was not invented by us. We can find the inspiration for it in anthropological, sociological or cultural studies of literature, particularly Anglo-Saxon literature, which is devoted to relations between the different roles and functions of men and women in our societies. This mediation was particularly introduced by American feminists in the 1980s and taken up a little later by feminists in France and Quebec.[2] If we start off from the point of view that gender is not simply the biological fact of being a man or a woman, then we can envisage it as 'a social construct, a way of being in the world, a way of being educated, a way too of being perceived, which conditions the way we are and the way we act' (Gebara 1999:94). In other terms, the concept of gender, over and above the biological reality of two sexes, encompasses the whole business of being and acting in the world, of creating relationships, and thus marking differences, and of claiming rights, of emphasising potentialities, and of making policy.

The mediation of gender as an instrument or tool gives us a better understanding of the place of woman in the economy. Without making this mediation an absolute, it does provide us with an important tool for understanding the complexity of human relations from a different point of view. It provides us, therefore, with a tool that can transform social relations in both the public and domestic areas of our life. Its usefulness lies in its providing a new way of looking at social realities and in its relevance for dealing with any situations characterized by inequalities, whether these are due to sex, race or to age.

The gender approach enables us to discern the special position of women in the economy and to make a link between this and social dynamics. This leads us to the possibility of understanding 'something' more certain about the 'fate' of women. The gender concept shows us that not only is the masculine the norm in language and science, but that an understanding of the economy or of trade, and of the forms put forward to understand them, is based on masculine models. We have here a bit of 'globalization' of knowledge and of power as it exists in a patriarchal world, whose ill effects on the history of women and indeed of all humanity call for denunciation. If we are against totalitarian approaches, we cannot set up a single key that explains everything. We always have to keep the dialectic of relations between men and women, since human life is carried on by continual interaction between the two sexes.

We have to accept that gender is an abstract concept. It can sometimes be a source of confusion, since it does not only signify woman, it also refers to man. The fact of using the two terms interchangeably is a conceptual error. The term gender is used for discerning sexual roles. It defines the values and attitudes which a community or a society regards as appropriate for one or the other sex. It follows, therefore, from a process of socialization in which different roles are given to men and women at the level of production or distribution of responsibilities. Despite the similarities that exist among different feminist currents of thought, it has to be emphasized that there has never been complete agreement on understanding the role of the difference and the power of the difference.

Discussions based on opposition between men and women have not indeed helped us to make much progress at the theoretical level. Difference of gender is, however, one difference among many. There are differences between men and women, between men and men, and between women and women. And these differences are counter-pointed by the differences of age, culture, religion and many others.

Even if it is accepted that a headlong rush towards globalization, to which the 'single' neo-liberal thinking is propelling us, is a basically masculine way of looking at things, the concept of gender, particularly when it is applied to the economy, is essentially a critical way of looking at the organization of society. It makes us question things at every level, personal or global. The onset of globalization provides an opportunity for our gender approach. It is in this sense that Yvonne Gebara says:

> Today more than ever, the challenges that call on us to rethink epistemology are presented to us by the increasing mix between cultures, the globalization one can call it of cultures, which is imposed on us by the globalization of the economy, through the means of communication and, more particularly, by the awakening of conscience among women, who are looking to be accepted as complete historical subjects (Gebara 1999:107).

When one introduces the mediation of gender into the economy, it is necessary to adopt a different way of looking at social relationships. To think of human beings in a different way seems to be an absolutely necessary challenge for today. We need to develop relations that are more just and to build a widespread solidarity throughout the world, in order to construct a world system that is ethically sustainable. It is against such a background, which can disturb us and can invite us to change our traditional guiding principles, that we are embarking on this lengthy questioning process.

Our first line of consideration concerns the conceptual evolution of approaches on women, in order to show the 'blindness' of philosophical, sociological and economic conceptualizations of women. This will enable us to challenge and interrogate them through the gender approach.

Gender in questions of economic theory forms the second line of our work. A question with an (S) is to be understood in two ways. First as a questioning of the economy, and then as a tool for analysis and reflection. The gender approach[3] goes on from this enquiry to rethink what could provide humanity with new reasons for life, belief and hope.

We have attempted to limit the very wide and complicated field of 'globalization, gender and trade' to the following questions: Why do people want what they do want, and how do rational beings, who concern themselves with their personal interests, look for what they want? What is the sexual dimension of the traditional definitions of such concepts as welfare, choice, wealth and exchange? We shall attempt in this way to understand and to explain the complexity and even the disorder of any process of change and of any form of accelerated mutation, intensified by unbridled liberalism and irresistible globalization.

Conceptual Evolution of Approaches to Gender

A long Tradition of Inequality: The Metaphysics of the Sexes

The metaphysic of the sexes, which one can also call essentialism, affirms that there is an essential or natural difference between men and women and it defines their respective specificities. How was the question of women and the difference between the sexes first considered and how has it changed its basis in philosophical schemes up to the present time? Its exclusion goes back to the beginnings of philosophy with Anaxagoras, Socrates, Plato, Aristotle and Thomas Aquinas. Because of their nature, women were also deemed incapable of progress. Several philosophers, selected for the clear way they express themselves on this question, tried to demonstrate this point: Pufendorf, Locke and Kant. If they could not completely eliminate the feminine principle, they all tried to devalue it in one way or another.

The Equality of Women Connected with the Future of Men

For Anaxagoras, the determination of the sex came from the father. The concepts which Plato and Aristotle (Aristotle 1961) used to describe the world already reflected with equal clearness 'the laws of physics, the equality of citizens, and the inferiority of women, children and slaves.' Their claim to universal validity already expressed the balance of forces that existed in the agora.

In the *Meno*, we see how ironic Socrates was over the idea, put forward by one of the group, that there were virtues proper to each sex, since virtues came from the soul and the soul had no sex. On the other hand, in the *Timaeus*, a certain inferiority in the feminine powers of reasoning is suggested, compared with masculine powers of reasoning. Thus those who look for procreation of the body turn to women, while those who look for wisdom look to the procreation of the spirit and turn to men. On can see, appearing at various points, the Platonic doctrine of affirmations, according to which women had a tendency that leads them to lower activities or they had the same qualities as men, but to a less pronounced degree. One could imagine that this involved natural faults: the law was made to contain them and to reveal feminine ability basically equal to that of men.

In going through the various dialogues, one can see that any egalitarian statements that are founded on a supposed identity and that minimize anything that could dispute this are often challenged. Equality derives from identity and an identity based on the masculine model relegates to the shade any feminine characteristics, while keeping in view those of men chosen as models. In the *Timaeus*, Plato argues that men, who in their first life 'were cowardly and who passed their time in injustice, would be changed into women in their second life,' (Plato 1984, T II:521) implying that to be a woman was a punishment of fate. The equality of women seems linked to their becoming men. While putting forward the principle of equality of men and women, Plato spoils it by his statement that 'However, woman is in every way inferior to man' (Plato 1984:VII, 454).

In the *Republic*, where the distinction between public and private is abolished, children being brought up in common, women are called to undertake the same public duties as men.

> Music and gymnastics have been given to men. It follows that this double discipline should be provided to women also, and as for war, it is necessary that they should be enrolled under the same conditions (Plato 1984:I, 1021-1028).

So, the same capacities of the soul are present in both men and women. Both deserve the same education. However, nowhere is it envisaged that women should decide things for themselves, any more than their general subordination to men is questioned.

On the theme of the generation and the determination of sex, Aristotle worked out one of the finest explanatory models: a complete, justified and fully reasoned philosophical model. The question asked was: Who is superior? The earth which receives the seed, or the seed which fertilizes the earth? Several answers were given, including a purely genetic one by Aristotle, which we shall examine.

The Genetic Difference: The Hypothesis of Aristotle and Thomas Aquinas

Two main lines of questioning emerge from Aristotle's thinking: if the distinction between form and matter characterized not only human beings but also everything that existed in the cosmos, how could this be applied to the distinction between the sexes? Further, if all human beings shared the same form and were similar from a metaphysical point of view, how could females be regarded as a monstrous deviation from the perfect human being?

In a long exposition, Aristotle, unlike his predecessors, showed how he regarded this essential difference as one of quality between hot and cold, which implied and justified the anatomical difference between the organs.

> Some claim that this difference has always existed, in seeds, for example. Anaxagoras and other naturalists argued that the sperm came from the male, while the female provided the place. The male came from the right, the

female from the left, just as males in the uterus are on the right and females on the left. Others, like Empedocles, argued that the difference was determined in the womb. According to him, the seeds that penetrated into a warm uterus became males but females in a cold uterus. The cause of this heat or cold he attributed to the menstrual flow and depended on whether it was colder or warmer or old or more recent. Democritus stated that the differentiation of the male from the female took place inside the mother, but that it was not the warmth or the cold that made a male or a female, it was rather the predominance of the sperm from one of the parents, this sperm coming from the parts that characterized the female and the male (Aristotle 1963:136-146).

The movement was what came from the man and characterized his genetic and individual potency. The matter was what came from femininity. On principle, there had to be a prime mover, whether the activity was carried out within itself or in another being. For Aristotle, therefore, the 'congenital weakness' of the woman 'touched the soul itself,' and she had neither the faculty of 'deliberating' nor that of 'deciding' (Aristotle 1963:I, 1260a). Man and woman were also unequal in procreation: it was the male that transmitted humanity, bearer of the divine principle, the woman only brought the matter (Aristotle:I, 1, 421a). The active principle of life was the male seed; the woman was only a passive receptacle.

Apart from the fact that the principle of matter introduced corruption[4] and death into the universe, it was also the cause of deformity. The maternal responsibility for deformity is put very clearly. Deformity correctly defined applied to the case where what had been engendered was not of the same species as the progenitor. A simple lack of resemblance was enough to define a monster in a general sense. 'The first deviation of a genetic kind was the birth of a female instead of a male' (Aristotle 1963:Book IV, 2). Aristotle argued in vain that the monster that was the female was necessary to maintain the difference between the sexes; the woman was still presented as a failure of humanity.

> Females are by their nature feebler and more cold, and one has to regard their nature as a natural deformity. It is also a monstrosity when a male child resembles his mother (Aristotle 1963:Book IV, 6, 775a).

Thomas Aquinas later borrowed from Aristotle the idea that men and women were opposed in the same way as form and matter. He was prolix on the difference between the sexes. His originality came from his attempt to adapt Aristotle's teaching and make it compatible with that of the Church Fathers. His rehabilitation of nature and reason gave his theology a particularly open and 'liberal' character. It is precisely because he tried to rehabilitate human reason that the fact that woman did not have any produced such serious consequences. Thomas Aquinas distinguished between the subjection of the slave and that of the woman. The first was simply the consequence of sin, and if the second was natural, it was because order would have been lacking to the multitude of humans, if some had not been governed by others who were wiser. It was precisely because of this kind of subjection that, in nature, woman was in submission to man, since by nature, man was more greatly provided with discernment and reason. All this was written with a political and social vision, which posterity developed further.

Invisibility and Over-exposure in Social Institutions from Hobbes to Rousseau

Forged in the seventeenth century by the theoreticians of the natural law, the idea of the social pact was very widespread in the eighteenth century. The theory of the social contract, in its classical form of a pact of submission, held sway. It had almost become part of received wisdom. Locke and Rousseau gave it a new meaning. We know, however, that this idea had a very different meaning with Hobbes and with Pufendorf. In one way, you could study all the political philosophers of the seventeenth and eighteenth centuries from their theories of the social compact. However, this is not in itself the subject of our enquiry.

Nevertheless, it seems important to us to show how these differing concepts of the social contract were in the last analysis based on different views of women. One can thus understand Hobbes, Pufendorf, Locke and Rousseau in a unified way. Their approach is the same: they ask the question about the place of women in the social pact.

Equality in the State of Nature and Domination in the Political State

Hobbes considered that in the state of nature, women were equal to men, since between the two sexes, there was no difference of power or foresight that could determine this right, *without war*. No doubt, Hobbes was not much concerned with the freedom of women. The force of his subversive comment lies elsewhere: he wanted to establish that domination, any kind of domination, was of political origin, contractual, voluntary, and emerging from consent. He envisaged therefore equality in the state of nature and domination in the political state. This leads us to consider women in this sphere.

The point of departure for Hobbes's major work, *Leviathan* (Hobbes 1999), published in 1651, is that man, a bodily individual, is ruled by the strength of his passions. The approach by which he puts into man's natural state the obligation to 'choose' subjection is meant to be completely logical and scientific. In the state of nature, human animals are machines ruled by an impulse towards accomplishing their desires. Their only relationship is that which brings them into conflict with those who want the same thing. Hence, the need for a voluntary act, by which these individuals/wolves who are nevertheless provided with the power of reason, can create a *second nature*, a *single* expression of will, and give up *definitively* their freedom and their *natural rights*, in order to benefit from the all-powerful monster, Leviathan, who is at one and the same time machine and 'artificial man', and who 'by the terror he inspires', unites them and protects them (in spite of themselves) against the ravages of that other biblical monster, the Behemoth of civil war.

In keeping with the scientific knowledge of his time, Hobbes did not deny that man was the 'principal agent of his generation'. However, he insisted that God had given him woman as a 'helpmate', but one who naturally possessed the same ability to kill. And who, as well, enjoyed the exclusive privilege of knowing who the child's father was. If power flowed from the act of generation, it would be the mother who would naturally possess it.

> From which it follows that, by the same right, a child is under the immediate domination of whoever is the first to have control over it. But the child who is just born is in the power of its mother, before it finds itself in anyone's else's power, so that the mother can bring it up or expose it, as seems best to her, without being responsible to anyone (Hobbes 1996:157).

Hobbes seems here to follow the logic: the father can only have power over the child, if the mother agrees to give it to him. It is not the act of generation, but consent that creates domination. He also seems to concede that the family, just like the state or any other human association, is based on a contract, an act freely consented, by which individuals submit voluntarily to a power that is one and indivisible, as is underlined in the following lengthy extract:

> Domination is acquired in two ways: in begetting or by subjugating. The right of domination that flows from generation is that which a parent has over his children; one thus speaks of parental authority. This right does not derive from the act of generation, in the sense that it might appertain to the parent to dominate his child, from the sole fact that he has procreated it. It derives from the consent of the child, explicit or manifested by sufficient proofs. Indeed as for what concerns the act of generation, as God has given man an auxiliary, there are always two parents, who are equally so, one and the other. Domination over the child should therefore belong equally to both of them, which is not possible, because no one can be made subject to two masters. Doubtless, some have attributed domination to the father alone, alleging the superiority of the masculine sex, but this is a false reasoning. Indeed, there does not always exist between the man and the woman a distinction in force or foresight, which the law could determine without conflict. This case is dealt with by the civil law; and in most cases (not always, however), the verdict is in favour of the father, because in most cases, Republics have been founded by fathers and not by the mothers of families (Hobbes 1999:208-209).

In exposing so radically the artificial and conventional nature of all political domination, Hobbes broke with the earlier metaphysical naturalists. Nevertheless paradoxically, in thus claiming to make absolutism more firmly based, he weakened it. Whoever speaks of convention speaks of instability: whatever man does, he can undo. Concerning women, Hobbes did not succeed in fully assuming his break with naturalism. Abandoning here the logical hypothesis and replacing it with an historical hypothesis, he rewrote in the nature of things an institution that was manifestly incompatible with the hypothesis of one nature for men/ mushrooms. There remains therefore a lasting doubt over the validity of his construct of human nature and political artifice. If families were, as he insisted, 'little kingdoms', already existing in the state of nature, there would be individuals who would be naturally subject to 'little sovereigns'. Furthermore, if these little sovereigns had created the artifice of the Republic, this would not have been the voluntary product of free and equal individuals, but would have been composed *already* of organic pre-political groups.

As a consequence of this, if the demonstration of the artificial and conventional character of power for women left room for custom, for the state of fact, or for the natural order of things, this must be because they had not voluntarily participated in the creation of the state. The argument turns against Hobbes, because if women are not, unlike men, the true authors of Leviathan, why should they be under any obligation to obey it? Pufendorf and Locke provide some enlightenment on this question through the pact of subjection.

The Pact of Subjection: From Political Rights to Domestic Rights

Pufendorf saw a double contract in the origin of the setting up of the state: first of union than of submission. Men united themselves by a first convention for the sake of mutual defence. However, this pact of union did not guarantee peace. Man did not, indeed, have a natural inclination that was sufficiently strong to bring him spontaneously to 'will' a political society. So one had to imagine that a second convention was made, to complete the work of the first, a convention of submission, a pact of subjection. By insisting on the 'reciprocity' of the contract, Pufendorf tried to establish the 'moral' nature of legal and political relations. Leading on from this, the contract infused itself everywhere, taking over not only political and international law, but also domestic law. This arizes from the equivocal nature of the idea of the contract of submission, which has a tendency to legitimize authority and the privileged few. In addition, this second contract derived its obligatory character from the fact of the divine will. So consecrated, the contract acquired all its absolutist consequences and in particular forbade any possibility of a right of resistance.

That is why one can find traces of this ambiguity or even of the incoherence of his ideas in the status accorded to women by Pufendorf. He did indeed call in question the divine or natural bases for marital authority and insisted on the contractual nature of marriage. The control of man over man, as a moral reality, could not exist without some positive human act. However, no woman was obliged to obey her husband before agreeing to submit herself to her husband's will. Pufendorf basically proceeded here as he did for the state. He subtly made a natural order of reality acceptable by means of consent and then gave it its own legal basis. He did not claim that a feminine 'nature' existed, in distinction to that of man's, but introduced other considerations than that of the rights of individuals: the finality of marriage, the good order of society, patriarchal traditions, according to which it was the woman who entered into the family of the man, and not the other way round. In short, in the light of these considerations, the woman could only wish to be dominated by the man.

To base the distinction between private and public, which Locke introduced, on the natural subjection of women, sets out as we shall see, the perimeter within which the freedom of women as political subjects was to be contained.

General Superiority of Every Man over Every Woman

A place of private liberty for the proprietor-head of the family, the domestic area became for the woman the place where she was deprived of that first liberty, which consisted of property, and which Locke made the 'beginning and end of every republic'. It thus 'deprived' women of the ownership of their bodies and of the fruits of their labour, which were at their husband's disposal. It also deprived them of the right to 'leave their fortune to whomsoever it pleased them', and thus of the authority, which this power to transmit goods as a legacy, would have given them. Locke certainly did not specify the exclusion of women from politics, as Machiavelli had done. However, by relying on nature to provide a base for conjugal authority, he affirmed the general superiority of *every* man over *every* woman, both within and outside the family. His distinction between private and public removed from women not only the autonomy necessary for any active participation in political life, but also the 'reasons' for which men had agreed to the institution of political society. As they belonged neither to the category of independent proprietors nor to that of workers who could 'freely' sell their labour, they enjoyed neither the necessary freedom nor the 'reasons' to sign that contract on which was based the obedience of the majority of the masculine population to the civil laws. Inferior by nature, but still authorized to do business, women became, through the 'inconsistency' of this theory of Locke's, an anomaly in the modern political community. By implying the superiority of 'all' men, the basis on which Locke founded conjugal authority implied the subjection of 'all' women, even those who were not married. In this case, who should the spinsters and widows obey? Doubtless not every single man, unless all the men could agree to give them the same instructions. In view of his enormous influence, one can see how damaging the consequences of his misogyny were.

'In Anything that is not Sex, Woman is the Same as Man'[5]

In this dictum is contained all the ambiguity of Rousseau. For many years, his work has been the subject of interpretations both passionate and contradictory. There is no room here to discuss this diversity of view. Let us simply retain the point that at the origin of his most disturbing questionings, one finds the complex and disconcerting status that Rousseau gives to nature. Looking into the sources of inequality among men, he asks us brazenly to 'forget all the facts'. Man is free just as the animals are, apart from the slight difference that nature programmes every action of an animal, while man does things 'as a free agent'.

In brief, no external necessity can influence the choices and wishes of a man, whose senses perfect themselves by the exercise of reason. It is, therefore, 'only an accidental collection of outside causes' that can make him evil as well as civilized. A set of accidents and contingencies can lead to corruption, competition and inequality. In the face of such unhappy circumstances, men choose to organise their security and to protect their property.

Because nature speaks more clearly about women, it would be absurd, according to Rousseau, not to let her speak and to contradict her by educating girls just like boys. From the point of view of her sex, a woman is a woman, but for the rest, she belongs, just like man, to the human race. In other words, a woman is more a *'true' woman:*

> The male is only a male at certain moments, but the female is female all her life or at least through all her youth. Everything keeps on reminding her of her sex, and so that she can fulfil her role, she has to have the constitution that goes with it (Rousseau 1966:470).

In short, the enclosing of women in the Rousseau family formed a part of the effort to reconcile the individualism of natural law with the values of the community, liberty and individual autonomy with the solidarity and reciprocity that are necessary for life in society. This is why,

> Woman has more wit and man greater genius; women observe, and men reason: from this conjunction results the clearest enlightenment and the most complete science that the human spirit is capable of acquiring by its own efforts, the most certain knowledge in one word of oneself and of others that can be obtained by our species. And see how art can constantly improve the instrument given us by nature (Rousseau 1966:466).

So when Rousseau tries to define the ideal couple, Emile and Sophie, he deliberately 'makes' the woman the complement of the man. Having described Emile at length as an active, impetuous, strong, courageous and intelligent creature, the philosopher gives the portrait of a wife who is passive, timid, weak and submissive:

> Made specially to please a man, Sophie was brought up to be a coquette, not very intelligent and happy to play secondary roles... Such is her nature, not to have been created for her own sake, but in order to be dominated by a man... is what she wants... to yield to him and even put up with him when he is unjust (Rousseau 1966 V:693-731).

In other words, a woman and a man are made for each other, but their mutual dependence is not an equal one:

> Men depend on women because they want to; women depend on men both because they want to and because they need to; we can more easily exist without them than they can without us. For them to have what is necessary to them, and for them to be satisfied, we have to give it to them, we have to want to give it to them, and we have to regard them as worthy of being given it; they are dependent on our feelings, on how much we value their worth, of what we make of their charms and their virtues (Rousseau 1966 V:731).

To prepare her, therefore, for her 'vocation' as wife and mother, it is necessary to *give* her a soft character, to *make* her practise restraint, and to make her *learn* that 'dependency is a state that is natural to women' (Rousseau 1966 V:731).

With the help of a table we have summarized the views of men and women on each other. When one looks carefully at these stereotypes (Rocheblave-Spenle 1964), one is struck by the eternal opposites marked with the *plus* or the *minus* sign.

Table 1: Social Stereotypes by Sex

Masculine Stereotypes	Feminine Stereotypes
Emotional Stability	
Decisive, firm, poised, calm.	Capricious, hysterical, sensible, fearful, childish, frivolous.
Control Mechanisms	
Disciplined, methodical, organized, rigid, grasp of organization, discreet, frank.	Talkative, incoherent, stylized, secretive, thoughtless, cunning.
Autonomy, Dependence	
Patriotic, risk-taking, independent.	Need to confide in someone, need to please, coquette, submissive.
Domination, Self-assertiveness	
Need for power, need for fame. Ambition, taste for command, domination, self-sufficient, sure of himself, need of push, need for assertion.	Weak.
Aggressiveness	
Combative, cynical, taste for fighting.	Cunning.
Level of Activity	
Impetuous.	Passive.
Acquisitiveness	
Egoist, materialistic.	Curious.
Intellectual Qualities, Creativeness	
Creator, lucid, objective, keen on theories. Aptitude for science, mathematics. Sceptical, reasoner.	Intuitive.
Affective Orientation, Sexuality	
Obscene.	Caressing, sympathetic, soft, modest, keen on dressing, need to have children, need for love.

It seems important to us to take account of the stereotypes we use. It appears from the table that in the difference between the genders, there is something of biology, and much that is cultural. Thus, the woman is brought up to be seductive and pleasing to the other; the man to dominate, to intervene, to act and be himself. The feminine or masculine personality is defined by the values and behaviour of the gender to which they belong. Traits of personality that are not innate but acquired are attributed to women. All human beings, from the moment of their birth, undergo an endless cultural apprenticeship on how to behave that is in keeping with their cultural condition. The boy is brought up as an autonomous person and the girl as a function of the other, and her love and desire is built up by emphasizing her dependence. She is not to talk or to ask, but to weep, implore, dissemble or keep quiet. She does not gain much self-assurance, and in the last resort, her preoccupation is limited to wanting to please others. In short, women are made to be wives.

A brief review of the theories about social institutions leads us to the conclusion that women are made invisible in two ways: as social actresses, and even as human beings, and as a group that is socially constructed. This is the correlative of their over-exposure as beings supposed to be more natural then men. This construct of the inequality that exists between men and women reflects the different way they are treated in society. The domination of the head of the family, for example, is one of the most problematical points of the classical theory of natural law. The idea of a natural difference or even of a disparity between the sexes, more or less explicitly interpreted in the sense of hierarchy, is sustained or considered as part of the evidence, even if specific qualities are recognized as existing in women. What is in the theories of economists?

From the Economy of Sex to the Sex of the Economy

The history of ideas demonstrates that the different traditional categories (nobility, bourgeoisie, clergy, etc.) no longer correspond with the new view that society takes of itself. The assumption of wealth encourages us to consider social organization with new categories. For the physiocrats, indeed, the nation was reduced to three new classes of citizen: the productive class, the owner class and the sterile class. The productive class was made up of cultivators, farmers, and agricultural workers. The owner class included the sovereign, the landowners and those who benefited from the tax (dime).[6] The sterile class was made up of artisans, manufacturers, traders and more generally all the citizens who were engaged in work other than agriculture.

The same approach is to be found in Smith. It is the economic categories of people that define the social classes. For him, however, agriculture is not the only source of wealth. He divided the annual product of the nation into three parts: rent from land, profit from capital and wages from work. This product thus provided income of three different kinds: there were those who lived from rent, those who lived from wages, and those who lived from profits. It is these three kinds of income that defined social classes. To provide an economic base for sociology implied regarding society as mobile. Smith introduced three modifications to what the physiocrats had put forward, and these had important consequences:

1. First of all, he rejected their analysis of the sources of wealth; for him, the land was simply one source of wealth among others.

2. He then worked out a kind of sociological dialectic. There was a separation of social classes at the point of production, but a unity of classes at the point of consumption.

3. Smith took over from the physiocrats the distinction between productive and unproductive. However, he gave it a new meaning. He did not put it within the sphere of wealth, but as a line of separation between the state and civil society.

John Stuart Mill, the famous political economist and liberal feminist of the 19th century, was a dominant figure of philosophy and economics. He argued that the doctrine of free trade had a basis as solid as the basis for the principle of individual liberty. From this flowed the need to dissociate the legitimacy of the liberty of the individual from that of economic liberty. He thought of the fulfilment of the individual in a perspective of the development of civil society. The development of the individual, which was a necessary condition for social development, depended on the freedom for each individual to cultivate his faculties to the highest possible degree. The analysis of the subjection of women as one of the main obstacles to the progress of mankind had its roots in this liberalism.

This economic description of society implied a profound sociological transformation. Such a reversal of traditional analysis, which I have sketched too briefly and schematically, was so far-reaching that I cannot claim to cover it satisfactorily in so few pages. The questions it raises are highly complex. Is there room for woman in this reversal? Without claiming to compose a treatise on economic sciences, let us see how these theories have contributed to the economy of sex in economic knowledge.

The Economy of Sex in Economic Theories

The Object of Economic Knowledge

Material Resources

Adam Smith's work, *The Wealth of Nations*, suggests a first definition of the object of economic knowledge. Why should there not be a science of wealth, as there is a science of light, of the stars or of vegetables? The difficulty is in knowing what wealth is. Material goods, first of all, but also the services needed for existence or for welfare. We can already see that wealth is what satisfies a need, and this act of satisfaction defines utility, which is a key word in the language of economics. However, while a length or a weight has an objective reality, there is no such thing as utility alone, something that has an absolute value. The idea of wealth is a relative and subjective one. It is not sufficient to constitute a science. A woman's practical needs, for example, are often linked to difficult living conditions and to a lack of resources.

Exchange

The concept of the market changed its meaning with Adam Smith. It was no longer simply a particular place where goods were exchanged. Society as a whole became the market. It was not just a way of allocating resources through a free determination of prices: it was a mechanism for social organization, more than a mechanism for economic regulation. The market, for Smith, was a political and sociological concept, and it was from this that it derived an economic dimension. In effect, he conceived of relations between men being like the relations between goods, in the sense that the nation was defined as a system of needs. He considered the economy to be the basis of society and the market to be what made the social order work. Even if reciprocal benevolence between men did not exist, the social bond was not broken because of this. It continued to be maintained for 'economic' reasons. Adam Smith wrote about this:

> Society can thus exist among men, as it exists among merchants, by a sentiment as to its utility, without any bond of sympathy: although no man is tied to another by duty or by the bonds of gratitude, society can still be sustained, by the help of an interested exchange of mutual services, to which are assigned an agreed value (Smith 1776:97).

However, goods and services have no intrinsic value in themselves; their value only arises when they are traded. What is economic is precisely what is capable of being traded. An economic act only shows itself as such when there is a movement or transfer of goods between persons. It is essentially social in character. And because the simplest transfer requires the presence of two people, the economic act is a dichotomized act. There has to be a hand that gives and a hand that receives, an entry and a departure, a debit and a credit. It follows from this that an act that does not involve payment is not one that forms part of the science of economics, although it is possible that an act that is free today may give rise, sooner or later, to some return.

In short, relations between persons are regarded in the same light as relations between the value of goods that are traded. The economic tie that links people as producers of goods for the market is regarded as the real pillar that holds society together. Society exists because everyone says, 'Give me what I need, and I will give you what you need yourself' (Smith, cited in Rosanvallon 1979:69). The result of an exchange expresses itself as a price, that is to say a relationship between the quantities that are transferred from one person to another, which this price expresses either in goods (a relative price, the price of rice in terms of groundnuts, for example) or in money (an absolute price, the price of rice expressed in terms of Francs).

In our social order, women are 'products' that are used or traded by men. Their status is that of 'goods'. This status obeys the laws of the market, a market that has its own logic, connected to the logic of a system of exclusion and oppression by one group for the benefit of another group. How can this object of use and of trade claim a right to speak, and more generally, to participate in trade? What is the concept of the feminine body? We believe that this specific situation of oppression may give women the possibility of working out a 'critique of political economy', since they are in an external position as regards the laws of the market, while at the same time being included in it as being 'goods' themselves. One can see that the science of trade comes down to being a science of prices. Everything that can be expressed in terms of price is an economic good. However, to know how to calculate the price, we have to get to the bottom of the problem. A third line of research indicates itself.

The Choices

A significant idea exists at the birth of the economic problem: that of limitation or disequilibrium. Man carries inside himself a need for the infinite, and he is constantly confronted with the finite nature of creation. This antithesis expresses itself first of all in the idea of *scarcity*. Needs appear to be endless, but the means of satisfying them are limited. It can also happen that the means are sufficient, or sometimes even excessive. Another idea then makes its appearance, that of disequilibrium. Goods are not necessarily present where they are needed or when they are needed. If they are lacking, they have to be produced, or if there are too many of them, their number has to be reduced. It is necessary to speed up or to slow down their arrival. The economic act then seems to be above all an act of adjustment. If the notion of *adjustment* encapsulates the essence of economics, and if in the final analysis, economics is the science of adjustment, then economics should ensure both the knowledge of the adjustment and the way to realize it, knowledge and realization being always linked together in mutual support. In any case, to adopt an economic attitude is to know how to make choices, and first of all, to choose which end to pursue in preference to another. Once you have chosen the end, you have then to decide the best way to achieve it out of all the possible ways. It may be possible to list all the ends in order of preference, but if the ways of achieving them are limited and capable of being diverted to other applications, and if, finally, the time available for the realization is also limited, your behaviour takes the form of a choice. This is the essential economic act. However to whose benefit should one apply the principle that 'the end justifies the means'?

Looked at more closely, one can see that conventional economics regards everyone's norms and standards as given, and it never considers the question why people want what they want and how rational beings, who look after their own personal interests, look for what they want. Economics then concentrates on individuals and underestimates the role of collective action. Lastly, it concentrates on the value of production for the market and of productive work. Here, the distinction between productive work and non-productive work can help us to situate the place of the woman in the transformation of traditional presentations of hierarchies and social utility.

To quote Adam Smith:

> The work of several of the most respectable classes of society, such as that of domestic servants, produces no value. The monarch, for example, as well as all the other civil and military authorities who serve under him, all the army and the fleet, they are all non-productive workers. They are servants of the state, and they are maintained with part of the annual production of others. The work they do, However honourable, However useful, However necessary it may be, produces nothing which can then be used to buy a similar quantity of services. Some of the more frivolous professions can be placed in the same category, such as actors, comedians, musicians, singers, ballet dancers, etc (Smith 1776:414).

One can deduce that government officials, soldiers, priests and judges are to be considered, economically, to be the parasites of others. Women are, once again, concealed in all this. We have to wait for John Stuart Mill, known for being not only the great philosopher of British liberalism, but also the only important philosopher of liberalism to have made the subjection of women a constitutive part of his philosophical work.

'Subjection': The Real Manifesto of Women's Rights

John Stuart Mill was very soon convinced that the idea of equality between the sexes was a well-founded one. In the light of this, he published *The Subjection of Women* in 1869, a veritable manifesto of women's rights. The subjection of women was not solely the result of their exclusion from public life; it was rooted in the family and the power relationships that were exercized there, which harmed the deepest part of women's individuality, by depriving them of financial autonomy, because everything they possessed belonged to their husbands.

Mill indeed argues that women should be free to choose whatever career they find suitable, without being obliged to marry in order to meet their needs. Equal access to education and to paid work should ensure their financial autonomy, transform the marriage of necessity into one of choice, something that might also contribute to solving the problem of overpopulation. However, if they chose marriage, women should accept the division of labour, which 'according to established custom, expects the man to earn a living and the woman to organize domestic expenditure' (Mill 1992:94-98).

It seems to us that we need to emphasize the failure to take 'gender' into account and therefore also the power relationships between the genders, since this demonstrates particularly well the rudimentary nature of the orthodox economic approach. This perspective calls for a change of outlook. It is not a matter of 'Add the women and stir', or in other words, simply extending the field of analysis to women, without asking oneself about the sexually charged dimension of the traditional definitions of such concepts as welfare, trade and economic choices. By now taking up a position, not on the basis of a contest (as a preliminary to any construction), but on that of a positive orientation, might not gender provide a revolutionary leaven that could create a civilisation based on solidarity, not a mere termite heap, but a community freely consented to by responsible people? This is the object of feminist economics.

The Sex of the Economy

Faced with the question of what women have brought or what they could bring to the economy, it is interesting to turn the question round and ask what is it that economic activity has brought to women, and what have they found in it for themselves? Put another way, is there a specific contribution that women could make to the economy? Better still, if women were in control, would the ethics and policies of the economy – the choice of priorities, for example – remain the same?

Currents of Thought in Women's Movements

The existence of inequality and social injustice determines the main orientations of the demands made by feminist movements across the world. There have been various efforts made, either by women alone or with the help of men, to organize themselves, in order to demand the principle of equality and justice for all. The same determination to make women the subjects and not the objects of the language of politics; the same social and political demands for equality. It is against the background of these analogies that the differences from earlier attempts can be noted. A difference of economic analysis: on the one hand, the criterion of financial independence is used to mark not only the social autonomy of the female worker, but also the autonomy, as a family, of a salaried individual; on the other, the status itself of women's work is considered to be part of the totality, where domestic work is not separated from social work, or where the reproductive function is not separated from the system of production.

Feminism can be defined as the movement of ideas and actions that aims to produce actions and renewable knowledge, which can both contribute to the elimination of the androcentric perception, which still dominates the humanities, and at the same time, define new relationships between men and women. Closer examination enables us to identify three main currents that have marked women's movements.

Radical Feminism
In this current, the primary division between the classes lies in the biological difference connected with reproduction. It does not see how nature could serve as an explanation of the inferiority of women and argues that this has arisen more from the oppressive system of relationships of the patriarchal system. It has as its aim the abolition of these relationships. It proposes, therefore, to redefine social relationships outside any biological constraints.

Egalitarian or Reformist feminism
This relates inequality to the models of socialization based on sex, which reduce women to a situation of inferiority. It calls for a more egalitarian situation between men and women by means of reforms to improve the social, economic and legal status of women. It excludes from its strategy any break with the established order.

The Feminist-Marxist Approach
In the economics of Karl Marx, the analysis of what was produced for sale and for profit out of paid labour showed that this surpassed the profits that capital and the family could obtain from the non-traded domestic production of women. This is why Karl Marx and Engels did not regard the emancipation of women as a consequence of the emancipation of the proletariat. Associating moral criticism with a scientific analysis of injustice, exploitation and class domination in capitalist-industrialist society, they launched a universal appeal (beyond cultural, national or religious frontiers) for the abolition of this domination.

The interest of the works of Marx and Engels lies less in their analysis of the situation of women in modern society than in the conceptual and political tools they provide for feminist analyses of society. A great number of feminist currents of thought have closely followed their thinking, but at the same time subjected it to criticism. If 'socialist' feminists, in general, have largely subordinated the emancipation of women to the emancipation of the proletariat, the emphasis laid by women's liberation movements on self-organization and self-emancipation has often been inspired by this philosophy of *praxis*, in which changes of circumstances confront the transformation of consciences. While the Marxist analysis of the oppression of women has been the subject of systematic criticism, the Marxist method has often provided the theoretical and political tools for such criticism. Because the dominant and dominated groups in the concept of class do not exist independently of the relationship of domination that produces them, this theoretical framework has allowed men and women to be regarded, as Christine Delphy remarks, as two antagonistic groups that are socially constructed in a hierarchical and interdependent fashion (Delphy 1998:28).

The Feminist-Marxist approach is based, therefore, on exploitation and oppression. It is the absence of women from the relationships of production and their economic dependence, which is the cause of their exploitation. To that must be added the patriarchate, or the supremacy of men over women as groups. The Feminist-Marxist approaches accept that the two levels of oppression lie next to each other and interact together. From the economic point of view, the gender approach shows up the complex interaction among the social, economic, political and ideological aspects, rather than finding the determining factor in every case in the economic elements. Hence its interest.

The Gender Approach: A Tool of Scientific Analysis

One can talk of a science when there is a clearly identified object, with methods and tools. The economy, considered as an 'exact' science should be quantitative rather than normative, objective and with a higher status. It is true that it promotes itself with an ambitious, modernist and masculine image. Every discussion panel on television, for example, has to include an economist; every government advisory committee, whatever subject it is concerned with, has to include an economist, and every newspaper or periodical of general interest has in every issue one or two interviews with an economist. In short, the most striking factor in the promotion of economics as an 'exact' and masculine science, hostile to any feminine angle, lies in its character as a fortress protecting the neoclassical paradigm.[7] Economic theory, in its dominant form, is synonymous with liberal market ideology.

The gender approach, for its part, fixes an objective for the relations between men and women, a theoretical framework based on the theory of roles and needs, which has its instruments of measurement. The concept of gender brings an important epistemological contribution to the progress of scientific knowledge. The contribution of gender analysis is made at two main levels:

1. At the level of the demonstration of constructed character, as distinct from the natural character of the categories of men and women

2. At the level of the taking into account of political and conflictual relationships, that is to say of power relationships.

The scientific value of the analytical tool of gender is above all its relevance to any situation of inequality, whether this is connected with sex, race or age. Gender analysis enables renewed and integrated knowledge to be produced, which is capable of contributing to the elimination of the androcentric perspective, one that is always dominant in the humanities, and to the definition of new relationships between men and women.

Gender: A Concept and a New Approach to the Economy

The concept of gender is based on the fact that differences, roles and positions between men and women derive from a social and cultural construct that has a foundation which is basically inegalitarian. As a consequence of this, an approach to socialization based on the balance of relations between men and women should lead to the construction of a society that is more just and more equitable. The gender approach is based on the principles of equity, equality and social justice. In the economic field, it enables women to be taken out of their isolation and away from the relationships which they encounter that are always defined by men. If the great campaigns of feminism have today become legitimate, it is far from certain that the 'liberation of women' describes a movement that is over (perhaps happily so, since if you talk of an animal that is 'over', it means one that is of no more use.) Feminists seek to establish a concept of society, of citizenship and of politics, in the sense of participation in the life of the city, which is no longer based on the predominance of anyone (men in this case). In other words, it involves rethinking humanity, the relationships that we have with the other.

In this way, the feeling is becoming increasingly widespread that the problems of effectively promoting women require solutions that involve the responsibility and the future of all humanity as a whole. It is accepted, both in the countries of the north and in those of the south, that there can be no sustainable development[8] without the involvement of women or without taking into account the role, the position and the contribution of women to the process of creating added value and wealth. An approach to the gender concept places us in a position to make a realistic analysis not only of personnel processes, but also of global social and economic processes. It is in this way that we can observe the emergence of feminist economics.

Several theories underlie the movements of action or of reflection concerning women. In the field of development, for example, the different conceptual frameworks are translated into programmes for women. There are two main currents of thought that call for our attention. These are IWD (Integration of Women in Development), which has been influenced by liberal ways of approach, and GAD (Gender and Development), which is characterized by socio-Marxist ways of approach.

Gender in Strategies for Women's Self-insertion

The Integration of Women in Development and Liberal Thought

The integration of women in development appeared at the beginning of the 1970s, when it replaced the assistance programmes of the 1950s – 1970s, whose results had been far from satisfactory. Its objective was to eliminate discrimination and to improve the feminine condition, that is to say, it concentrated on practical needs. This approach was derived from liberal thinking and fitted into the perspectives of traditional theories of modernization. It held that inequalities between the sexes would fade away by themselves, when women became full economic partners. It was used in the framework of policies for economic growth and increased effectiveness, with the purpose of enabling poor women to increase their productivity by income-generating projects and of ensuring that development would be more effective and profitable, thanks to the economic contribution by women.

The practical needs of women, however, tend to be immediate and short term ones. They are specific to particular women, or they are linked to daily requirements: food, housing, income, children's health, etc. These problems are readily identifiable by women and can be met in precise ways. Because of their disadvantaged social status, the uplift of women had to be carried out by changing their social conditions. The meeting of practical needs could improve women's living conditions, but did not in general change their traditional roles and relationships.

The welfare that was achieved in this way did not call into question the subordination of women. It sought to help the most vulnerable groups, in which women found themselves, by giving priority to production. It created a damaging dependence. And so, while relativising the biological determinants of inequalities between the sexes, the logic of IWD was based on a certain social determinism. It called for a more egalitarian situation between men and women, by means of reforms to improve the social, economic and legal conditions of women. Nevertheless, it excluded any break with the established order from its strategy. In general, the IWD approach regarded women as beneficiaries and not as actors of development, and thus reinforced their passivity and dependence. Such an approach was not one of an alternative, and did not criticise the structures of oppression that led to sexist ideologies and of inegalitarian laws and customs. Hence the change of perspective through GAD.

The Gender and Development Approach and Marxist Thought

In the 1980s, there was some questioning relating to the IWD projects, which although they improved women's social conditions, did not change their basic social position. It was in this context, that the gender perspective began to emerge as an alternative. It had a wider vision. The theoretical base came from Marxist feminism, and laid emphasis on the productive sector at the expense of the reproductive aspects of women's work and life. This approach established a link between the relationships of production and reproduction and took all the angles of women's life into account. Unlike other theoretical frameworks, its object was not women as such, but rather the social realities that shaped the perspectives and attributed the responsibilities and the specific expectations of women or of men. It introduced the perspective of the sex-specific analysis, which enabled the differences and the constraints that affect women and men in their relationships with production to be taken into account. The gender analysis did not have woman as its object as such, but rather the social realities that shaped the perspectives and attributed the responsibilities and the specific expectations of women or of men.

It should be noted that in giving more weight to the oppression of classes than to any other form of oppression, the GAD approach is at fault through reductionism. It seems to subordinate the liberation of women to the suppression of the class war. A comparative table[9] helps us to understand the different approaches.

Table 2: The Different Approaches in Gender and Development

Integration of Women in Development (IWD)	Gender and Development (GAD)
1. The approach An approach that regards women as being the problem	A development approach
2. The focus of interest Women	Relation between men and women
3. The problem The exclusion of women (who represent half the potential resources of production) from the development process	The unequal relations of power (rich and poor, men and women) which prevent equitable development as well as the full participation by women
4. The objective A more efficient and effective form of development	Equitable and sustainable development, where men and women take decisions
5. The solution Integrate women into existing form of development	Increase the power of the least advantaged and of women. Transform unequal relationships
6. Strategies Projects for women Women's shares Integrated projects Increase women's productivity Increase the capacity of women to carry out the tasks traditionally linked with their role	Identify/consider the practical needs that have been decided by women and men, with a view to improving their condition At the same time, handle the strategic interests of women Confront the strategic interests of the poor by means of development based on gender.

None of this experience allows us, as far as I can see, to create an alternative strategy that could open the way to an ethically sustainable development. Economic reforms, whether carried out at the micro, meso or macro level, are stamped with masculine prejudices, which perpetuate the relative disadvantages of women. The feminist economy restores the visibility of the already existing links between gender and economics. It depends more on a specific theme, which is the role of women. It demonstrates that interdependence between gender and economics derives from the triangle:

1. Human relations,

2. Ways of considering gender, and

3. Economic realities.

This triangle may be obscured in everyday economic life, but women still have to live out its reality throughout their lives. From the point of view of gender, the daily round, for example, is important. The daily round is everyday life. The daily round is the struggle to stay alive, to survive for another day, to look for work, to prepare food, to wash the children and to wash the clothes, to exchange expressions of love, to find an immediate meaning for life. The daily round is the domestic world, the world of short term relationships, more direct relationships, which can sometimes affect bigger relationships. The daily round for women is introduced into universal science, to remind it of what is concrete and what is needed for life and for survival. The daily round is the routine and the habits of everyday life. The daily round consists of our personal histories, our feelings in the face of events that happen, our reactions to the different questions that arise from the news of what is happening around us.

Conclusion

Our research on women has shown how influential the concepts and definitions can be that we use about perceptions of social relations. The history of mankind seems to turn on questions of human freedom and of the control of production and of reproduction. These issues manifest themselves in struggles for power between nations, races and social classes; but the domination of women by men remains a constant factor, whether it concerns society, race or nation. Men have made use of their power, either in the form of violence or of a social contract, in order to control the work of other men. This has led them to use this power in order to impose limits on women. Even if the difference between the sexes is a natural one, the situation imposed on women is not a natural one. It is cultural and ideological. The Universalist philosophers 'calmly' opened a breach in the coherence of their system by excluding women, even though they were human beings, from their own definition of humanity.

Consideration of the relations between men and women has passed through some critical periods, each one of which corresponds with the pre-eminence of a particular theoretical model. Starting from a one-dimensional model, rooted in the biological dimension, researchers worked out 'two-dimensional' or 'multi-dimensional' models, to take account of the increasingly complex category of gender and its components. The re-appropriation of the feminine identity passes through a sort of injunction to otherness, to face the risk of a blurring of the difference between the sexes – or of their neutralization under the sign of the masculine. Rousseau seems to allow them to think at the same time of both femininity and equality. However, if no one else has better described the conditions of equality, it should not be forgotten that he did not include women in this. No one else did more than he did to make sexual difference the necessary condition for love, and no one laid more emphasis on the mission of maternal education. No one else vaunted femininity more, but he still enclosed it in the sweet kingdom of the woman in her home. In seeking for what 'is woman', might one not risk losing the famous 'remainder', in Rousseau's arbitrary vagueness?

If one has to indicate schematically the ground we have covered, one could say that the metaphysic of sex, on which the inferiority of women was based, has been progressively replaced by an apology for the feminine, which now concerns both sexes. This change can be discerned in a whole range of different fields - in philosophy, in social and political theory, in logic or in feminism. In most fields, it helps to develop a critical outlook towards the whole, to whatever is limited, to logocentrism, to mastery, for the benefit of what is 'not everything', of the infinite, of dispersal, of the limitless. Certainly, it is not possible to challenge the order of everything – the phallic order, the metaphysical order – but this order is 'not everything'. One can see here a loss in the value of 'modernity', in terms of mastery of the Subject, which can be compared to a loss in the value of 'virility'. We most now begin with individuals and their nature, in order to think and resolve the problems of social institutions. It is in this change that we may find some possible conditions for a better economy.

The wandering star of the major international financial institutions now turns around the economic, in a permanent search for profit. There is an imbalance between the social and the economic. The current model is devoted to the promotion of tools and means and not to people. Is there not some risk of our losing what remains of what is most precious to us, which is our own identity and our diversified socio-cultural values?

Autonomy is in the process of emerging in the political order. Decisive combats in the fields of life and of culture are now being fought in its name. Autonomy also has an economic dimension, which now needs pursuing. The concept of autonomy is indeed a decisive instrument for the criticism of economic ideology, for which the equal implies the commensurable, the human.

Notes

1. Theories about gender were developed towards the end of the 20th century. They are to be found in many works published by Francophone feminists, but above all by Anglo-Saxon feminists, particularly by North American ones. We quote here from the works of the Belgian philosopher, Françoise Collin, particularly 'Praxis de la différence – Notes sur le tragique du sujet', in Cahiers du GRIF, No. 46, Spring 1992, Paris, Cité d'Angoulême 75001. See also Julia Kristeva, *Histoires d'amour*, Paris, Denöel, 1983 and Luce Irigaray, *Ce sexe qui n'en est pas un*, Paris, Editions de Minuit, 1977.
2. Mathieu Nicole, Identité sexuelle/sexuée/de sexe: trois modes de conceptualization du rapport entre sexe et genre dans l'anatomie politique. Catégorizations et idéologies du sexe, Paris, Côté-Femmes, 1991; 'Etudes féministes et anthropologiques', in *Dictionnaire de l'Ethnologie et de l'Anthropologie*, Paris, PUF, 1992; Bissiliat Jeanne, *Relations de genre, Genre et développement*, Paris, Orstom, 1992 ; CEDEAC and 'Relais Femmes, Qu'est-ce que le Féminisme?' Montreal, 1997.
3. One talks of the gender approach to define the scientific method that takes into account the social relations of sex in the analysis and transformation of social realities.
4. Understood in the sense of decomposition or rotting.
5. J. J. Rousseau, *Emile ou de l'Education*, 1966, Livre V, Flammarion. p. 465
6. It is known that, for the physiocrats, the sovereign was regarded as the owner of all the land in the kingdom. This was what justified the fact that he could levy tax.
7. The neoclassical economists carry forward the classical ideas: the market economy, free competition, little or no state intervention, economic liberalism, the neutrality of the currency, etc. In addition, equilibrium is general, that is to say simultaneous in every market. Their reasoning at the microeconomic level is based on the behaviour of agents who meet each other in the market. These agents are assumed to be rational and seeking to maximise their utility or their profit. Markets are supposed to be in a state of pure and perfect competition. Overall, the neoclassical theory is a theory of relative prices and of the allocation of resources that are regarded, by definition, as scarce.
8. Sustainable development appears as a new form of human development, which concerns the global environment and the fundamental ecological balances that control both land and sea areas of the world. The ultimate objective is to be able respond to present needs without compromising the ability of future generations to respond to their needs. In short, it is a form of development that responds to the needs of the present without compromising the ability of future generations to respond to theirs.
9. Taken from: Another type of development. A practical guide to relations between men and women in development. CCCI, CI Match, AQOCI Ottawa, 1991.

Bibliography

Alternatives Sud, 2001, *Et si l'Afrique refusait le marché?*, Cahiers Trimestriels, Vol. VIII 3.
Aristotle, 1961, *Of the Generation of Animals, French Translation*, Paris, Les Belles Lettres, *Politics I*.
Badinter, E., 1986, *L'Un est l'Autre: des relations entre hommes et femmes* (Colt, Points, 29), Paris: Odile Jacob.
Bassiliat, J., 1992, *Relations de Genre et développement*, Paris: Orsillon.

Collin, F., 1992, *Différence et différend* in Duby, G., Perrot, M., eds., *Histoire des femmes*, T. 5, Paris: Plon.

Collin, F., 1992, *Praxis de la Différence: notes sur le tragique du sujet*, Paris: Les Cahiers du GRIF, No.46.

Collin, F., 1999, *L'homme est-il superflu, Hannah Arendt*, Paris: Odile Jacob.

Collin, F., 1984, *D'amour et de raison*, Paris, Cité d'Angoulême : Les Cahiers du GRIF.

Collin, F., Pissier E., Varikas E., 2000, *Les femmes, de Platon à Derrida. Une anthologie critique*, Paris: Plon.

Delphy, C., 2001, *L'ennemi principal 2. Penser le genre*, coll. Nouvelles questions féministes, ed. Syllepse.

Encyclopaedia Universalis, 1968, Femme, Vol. 6, Paris.

Gebara, Y., 1999, *Le mal au féminin. Réflexions théologiques à partir du féminisme*, Paris: L'Harmattan.

Heritier, F., 1996, *Masculin/Féminin: la pensée de la différence*, Paris: Odile Jacob.

Hobbes, T., 1996, *Leviathan, Dalloz*, French translation by F. Tricaud, 1999, *Of the Citizen*, Paris: Le livre de Poche.

Irigaray, L., 1989, *Le Temps de la Différence. Pour une révolution pacifique*, Paris: Le Livre de poche, Biblio Essais.

Irigaray, L., 1974, *Speculum, de l'autre femme*, Paris: L'Édition de Minuit.

Irigaray, L., 1977, *Ce sexe qui n'en est pas un*, Paris: L'Édition de Minuit.

Jacquet, I., 1995, *Développement au masculin/Féminin: Le Genre, outil d'un nouveau concept*, Paris: L'Harmattan.

Mill, J.S., 1992, *Of the Subjection of Women, (French translation)* Paris: Avatar.

Plato, Complete Works, *The Republic*.

Proudhon P.J., 1990, *De la justice dans la Révolution et dans l'Eglise*, Paris: Fayard, Vol. VI.

Rosanvallon, P., 1979, *Le libéralisme économique. Histoire de l'idée de marché*, Point Seuil.

Rousseau, J. J., 1996 [2000], *Emile ou de l'Education*, Paris: Flammarion.

Smith, A., 1966 [2001], *Researches into the Nature and Causes of the Wealth of Nations*.

Verschuur, C. and Bisilliat J., 2000, Le genre: un outil nécessaire. *Cahiers genre et développement No.1*.

Verschuur, C. and Bisilliat J., 2002, *Genre et économie: un premier éclairage, No. 2*.

Verschuur, C. and Bisilliat J., 2000, *Rapport de genre et mondialization des marchés*, CETRI: L'Harmattan.

3

'Celebrating' the Female Body in Global Trade: Fashion, Media and Music in Kenya

Edward Waswa Kisiang'ani

Introduction

As we settle our intellectual nerves into the cockpit of the 21st century, there is probably no terminology which attracts so much scholarly attention as globalization. The term may mean many things to many people. Nevertheless, whichever way one looks at it, globalization signifies certain fundamental principles. For example, the rule of multinational corporations and the dwindling powers of national-states could be one factor of globalization. Besides, globalization could also imply a new type of centralized power controlled by the West (Martin 1999). It is an experience in which the world is dominated by powerful nations. Such domination could be financial, social, cultural, political and even technological. Fundamentally, the Internet is the icon of globalization because it not only promotes the continuous domination of world affairs by the rich nations but also creates new frontiers which perpetuate that domination.

The impact of globalization on Africa is without doubt profound. Like many African countries which continue to experience the pressures of global forces, Kenya is still struggling to come to terms with the new developments. The focal point of this study is to interrogate Kenya's experience with contemporary forms of globalization. Specifically, the study undertakes to highlight how the female body has been constructed in order to fit in and enhance the force of global trade within the country. To accomplish our objective, we have deliberately focused on the diverse but complex representations of the female body in the fields of fashion, media and music.

Contextualizing the Problem

Our urge to undertake the present research was fuelled by the absence of serious scientific inquiry into the various ways the female body has been constructed and utilized in Kenya's public life. Most of the works on female gender have so far tended to focus on the role of women in such areas as family planning (Ayayo 1991), the environment (Khasiani 1992) as well as politics (Association of African Women for Research and Development 1998). Yet the tendency to overlook the female body as an analytical category has also meant that there is very little understanding of the female gender in Kenya.

Within the perspective of globalization, the female body has undergone varied and sophisticated constructions all over the world. For example, in the South-eastern Asian nation of Thailand, the female body has been effectively constructed and utilized to facilitate the lucrative enterprise of prostitution and tourism (Truong 1990). Here, the organized sex trade affects women at national and international levels. In general, pornography has become an attractive source of money in our world. Catherine Itzin (1992) has made profound efforts to address this question. Raising moral issues, Itzin has attacked the multimillion pound international pornography industry. Further, the author has meticulously explained how the woman's body, in pornographic literature, has been manipulated in order to make millions of pounds in a male-dominated world. Can we, therefore, say that pornography is a significant element in the fashion, media and music industries of Kenya? Closer home, Mbilinyi and Omari (1996) draw examples from Tanzania to demonstrate that, over the years, the female gender has been put in a position of being the docile recipient of the male gender's emotional and physical releases. How, we may ask, have fashion, media and music enhanced the docility of the female gender in Kenya?

In its formal disposition, colonial imperialism tended to alienate its subjects towards Western culture. Evidently, colonialism was itself a form of globalization that psychologically forced the native to adopt Western lifestyles. In *Black Skin White Masks* (Fanon 1970), revolutionary thinker Frantz Fanon offers an anguished and eloquent description of the psychological effects of colonialism on the colonized people, arguing that those who 'recognize themselves in it' (colonialism) will have made the right step forward (Fanon 1970:12). The attainment of political independence in Kenya ushered in a new type of Western hegemony. In its post-independence dispensation, the colonial project transformed itself into some form of mysterious, faceless and anonymous power. At the level of the female gender, this power has manifested itself through the diverse ways the female body has been constructed and utilized so as to promote global commerce. Thus in 'recognizing herself' in global culture, the Kenyan woman has continuously experienced varying constructions of her body along lines defined by the Western

global forces. Frantz Fanon calls this 'psychic alienation'. Our argument in this
paper is that the psychic alienation which has developed from globalization has
also caused the economic growth of multinational concerns. Other works which
do not directly deal with the Kenyan situation but which, nevertheless, emphasize
the marginalization of women through the exploitation of their bodies include
Hester (1992), Archer and Lloyd (1995) and Jackson (1996). This study has benefited
from these and many other works in related fields in an effort to fill the dearth in
the literature and politics of the female body in Kenya.

Generally, this study revolves around two fundamental premises. It is, first,
our contention that through the avenues of fashion, media and music, the female
body has been constructed and utilized to promote global trade in Kenya. Second,
the construction and subsequent utilization of the female body in global trade in
Kenya has signified the exploitation and inferiorization of the female gender.

However, in order to capture the intricate issues which characterize the study
of the female body in the context of global trade, this inquiry has employed a
composite methodological approach in its data collection. Both primary and
secondary data have been harnessed for the investigation. Primary data has been
derived from scheduled interviews that deliberately targeted men and women
from specific social groups. For example, we have targeted research university
students and members of the Kenyan public who are socially active to the extent
that they are variously involved in music, fashion and media activities. Rather than
engage in a structured questionnaire, the study has employed the free-discussion
approach with respondents so as to harness an engrossing explanation on how
the female body in Kenya has been appropriated within the global dimension of
trade. More primary data has also been procured from original music tapes and
cassettes. Furthermore, primary information has been obtained by watching original
film shows, videotapes and television commercials as well as through attending
fashion shows, local music performances and cultural displays.

Secondary data, on the other hand, was collected from a wide range of
documents available in local libraries as well as on the Internet. Overall, data
obtained has been examined through the prism of content and document review
analyses. In addition, the final product has been 'panel-beaten' through the theoretical
workshop on of the Foucauldian project about power and the human body.

Theorizing about the Body and Globalization

The task of theorizing about the human body remains one of the most critical
challenges of contemporary scholarship. Separated from the spirit, the body
becomes a useless mass of fat, flesh and bones. However fused with the soul, the
human body becomes a crucial site for cultural, intellectual and scientific
contestations. Such contestations have the inherent capacity to open up new frontiers

of knowledge for us which may, in turn, provide explanations about some important aspects of human existence.

In theorizing about the human body, I hung on the shoulders of distinguished French thinker, Michel Foucault. Like Friederich Nietzsche and Martin Heidegger before him, Foucault undertook to criticize the project of Enlightenment and Modernity. Thus, in a striking critique of modern society, Foucault has argued that the rise of parliamentary institutions and of new conceptions of political liberty was accompanied by a darker counter-movement marked by the emergence of a new and unprecedented discipline directed at the body (Bartky 1990:63). Consequently, more is required of the body now than mere political allegiance or the appropriation of the products of its labour. Indeed, the new discipline invades the body and seeks to regulate its very forces and operations, the economy and efficiency of its movements. However, in regulating the body's operations, the new discipline tends to endanger human freedom too (Flyn 1989:196). Foucualt's critique of the disciplinary practices which the modernist project imposes on the human body has an emancipatory agenda. Arguing that life is full of possibilities, Foucault reasons that as part of the experience of freeing itself from the oppressive tendencies of modernity, humanity will one day develop a different economy of bodies and pleasures that provides for greater possibilities and greater freedom (Foucault 1980:159).

Most of the disciplinary practices Foucault describes are tied to peculiarly modern forms of the school, the army, the hospital, the prison and the manufactory; the aim of these disciplines is to increase the utility of the body and to augment its forces. As he observes:

> What was then formed was a polity of coercions that act upon a calculated manipulation of its elements, its gestures, its behaviour. The human body was entering a machinery of power that explores it, breaks it down and rearranges it. A 'political anatomy' which was also a mechanics of power was being born; it defined how one may have a hold over others' bodies, not only so that they may do what one wishes, but so that they may operate as one wishes, with techniques, the speed and efficiency that one determines. Thus discipline produces subjected and practiced bodies, 'docile bodies' (Foucault 1979:138).

However, the production of 'docile bodies' necessarily requires that an uninterrupted coercion be directed to the very processes of the bodily activity, not just their result. This micro-physics of power fragments and partitions the body's time, its space, and its movements (Foucault 1979:28). In a school situation, then, a student is enclosed within a classroom and assigned to a desk he cannot leave except with permission to do so. The student must sit upright, feet upon the floor, head erect. He may not slouch or fidget; his animate body is brought into fixed correlation with the inanimate desk. Thus, a school becomes an instrument which curtails the movement and freedom of the human body.

The modern army, on the hand, operates in similar ways as the school. In the army, every soldier is trained to master certain drills and movements with a sense of urgency and perfection. Foucault summarizes the disciplinary practices the body of a soldier goes through. He says thus:

> Bring the weapon forward. In three stages. Raise the rifle with the right hand, bringing it close to the body so as to hold it close to the body so as to hold it perpendicular with the right knee, the end of the barrel at the eye level grasping it with the tight hand, the arm held close to the body at waist height. At the second stage bring the rifle in front of you with the left hand, the barrel in the middle between the two eyes, vertical, the right hand grasping it at the small of the butt, the arm outstretched, the trigger guard resting on the first finger, the left hand at the height of the notch, the thumb lying along the barrel against the moulding. At the third stage.... (Foucault 1979:153)

These 'body-object' articulations of the soldier and his weapons, the student and his desk, affect a coercive link with the apparatus of production. In regimes of power, the body's time is rigidly controlled as its space. The factory whistle and the school bell mark a division of time into discrete and segmented units that are the various activities of the day. However to achieve control of the body in schools and factories, relentless surveillance has to be maintained.

Jeremy Bentham's design for the panopticon, a model prison, captures for Foucault the essence of the disciplinary society. At the peripheral of the panopticon, a circular structure; at the centre, a tower with wide windows that open on the inner side of the ring. The structure on the peripheral is divided into cells each with two divisions, one facing the windows of the tower, the other facing the outside, allowing an effect of back-lighting to make any figure visible within the cell. All that is needed, then, is to place a supervisor in a central tower and to shut up in each cell a madman, a patient, a condemned man, a worker or a schoolboy (Foucault 1979:200). Each inmate is alone, shut off from effective communication with his fellows, but constantly visible from the tower. The effect of this is to induce in the inmate a state of conscious and permanent visibility that assures the automatic functioning of power; each inmate becomes a jailer to himself (Foucault 1979:201). This state of conscious and permanent visibility is a sign that tight disciplinary control has got hold on the mind as well. This condition is what Frantz Fanon once referred to as psychic alienation. In the perpetual self-surveillance of the inmate lies the genesis of the celebrated 'individualism' and heightened self-consciousness which are hallmarks of modern times. For Foucault, the structure and effects of the panopticon resonate throughout society. That is why it is not surprising that prisons resemble factories, schools, barracks, hospitals, which all resemble prisons (Foucault 1979:228).

However, let us pause one moment and go back to the issue of globalization. If globalization entails a type of centralized power controlled by the West, if it is the rule of Western multinationals, if it is the dictatorship of the Western-controlled information super-highway called the Internet then, indeed, globalization has similar characteristics as those of Foucault's school, hospital and prison. Thus, globalization is a type of panopticon which has put Africans on the continent under constant surveillance so that they do not possibly break the rules of Western financial, cultural, political, technological and cultural institutions. Furthermore, the Western panopticon has ensured that even without the direct supervision of Euro-Americans, the daily activities of the African people reflect the automatic functioning of Western power in Africa. Ultimately, then, the power of contemporary globalization has progressively gained access to individuals themselves, to their bodies their gestures and all their daily actions (Dews 1984:17). While punishing and imprisoning their bodies, this power seeks to transform the minds of those individuals who might be tempted to resist it. However the exercise of global power is done through specific institutions and avenues - schools, trade, music, beauty, fashion and media - yet the same power is also faceless, centralized, pervasive and anonymous. Here, the image of the panopticon returns: knowing that he may be observed from the global 'tower' at any time, the African 'inmate' takes over the job of policing him/herself. Hence, the Western gaze which is inscribed in almost every structure and institution of the African social life becomes internalized by the inmate. In this way, globalization produces in Africa what Foucault would call 'self-policing subjects ' (Foucault 1979:77). As a result, then, globalization induces in an African a 'state of conscious and permanent visibility' as reflected in the changing constructions of the female body in music, fashion and media.

Foucault's account in *Discipline and Punish* of the disciplinary practices that produce the 'docile bodies' of modernity is a genuine enterprise incorporating a rich theoretical explanation of the ways in which instrumental reason takes hold of the body with a mass of historical detail. Obviously, Foucault's observations are general theoretical guidelines about the human body (both male and female). Yet, in presenting these generalizations, Foucault also commits a serious act of omission. Throughout, he treats the body as if it were one, as if the bodily experiences of men and women did not differ and as if men and women bore the same relationship to the characteristic institutions of modern life. Where, we may ask, is Foucault's account of the disciplinary practices which engender the 'docile bodies' of women, bodies more docile than the bodies of men? As Sundra Bartky has correctly observed, 'women like men are subject to many of the disciplinary practices Foucault describes but he is blind to those disciplines that produce a modality of embodiment that is peculiarly feminine' (Bartky 1990:65). To overlook the forms of subjection that engender the feminine body is to perpetuate the silence and powerlessness of those upon whom these disciplines have been imposed. In this essay, we make an effort to address this hiatus by interrogating the female body in Kenya within the context of global trade. However, before we do this, let us make one fundamental clarification.

We are born male or female, but not masculine or feminine. True, male or female are natural categories but masculinity and femininity are social constructions. Femininity is an artifice, an achievement, 'a mode of enacting and re-enacting received gender norms which surface as so many styles of the flesh' (Butler 1990). In what follows, I shall examine those disciplinary practices that produce the body, which in gesture and appearance is recognizably feminine. Furthermore, I will examine these feminine disciplinary practices in the context of global trade and from the basic standpoints of fashion, music and media.

Fashion, Trade and the Female Body in Kenya

Without any clothing material on it, without makeup and without jewellery, the female body remains a natural category. However, the disciplinary practice which has provided clothes for human beings operates on the philosophy that the body is an ornamental surface. As globalization expands its space in Kenya, the ornamentation of the human body has also assumed complex dimensions. Fashion is a crucial medium through which ornamented bodies are produced. At present, both the young and elderly people of Kenya are variously affected by the overwhelming culture of fashion. Across the streets of Kenya's major towns, one can easily notice from the manner of dress how several people are trying to catch up with current trends in fashion and, especially so, trends consistent with contemporary Western cultural dispensations. This tendency is much more pronounced in women than in men.

Evidently, however, Kenya's fashion domain does not end at clothing. In addition to particular shoes, underwear, brassieres, necklaces, earrings, bangles, bracelets and dresses, the female body has to have something more. In the university where I teach, there is an annual ritual called the Culture Week.[1] In the cultural performances of this annual event, it has been observed that beauty and fashion shows are the most popular items of the extravaganza. I asked one female student to explain to me what a fashion show entailed. She said:

> It means good trendy shoes; it means a good necklace, if any. It means a matching and a not-so-common good dress. It means fitting earrings and bangles. It also means being sensitive about colours. Hey! You have got to know you are woman. But that is not all, a beauty and fashion show should give the public appropriate female bodies to wear the things I have mentioned.[2]

I was rather surprised by the way in which the above student was committed to detail so as to make her explanations clear to me. Her revelations, however, gave me motivation to interview ten more female students about this sensitive subject of beauty and fashion. Of the ten, two had participated in previous beauty contests in the university. In addition, two girls out of the ten had not only taken part in the previous beauty contests in the university but also competed in the preliminary contests for the Miss World beauty shows in their respective provinces of origin in the country. Four of the girls had never enlisted as models in the fashion and beauty shows anywhere but they said they liked attending beauty shows as part of the audience. The remaining two girls said they had never attended any beauty or fashion shows anywhere. I asked each of these ladies the following questions: What does beauty mean to you? Do you think that you are beautiful? What is the purpose of beauty and fashion shows?

On the first question, all the ten women had similar views about beauty. They concurred that beauty includes good clothes and accessories for a woman. However, good clothes and accessories, they said, should be won by a beautiful body. On the second question, the first six girls felt they were beautiful but of the last four, two thought they were ugly because nobody had ever told them that they were beautiful, while the other two felt that it did not matter to them whether they were beautiful or ugly.

Asked about what beauty and fashion shows were meant for, the first six girls felt they had been exploited especially by men because, they said, after parading their beautiful and well fashioned bodies, they ended up with nothing while multinational companies undertook to use such shows to market their goods, including drinks, sleek motor vehicles, cigarettes and beauty products. For these girls, therefore, beauty shows were avenues for commercial firms to make money. The last four girls intimated that although the idea of beauty and fashion was not bad at all, they thought that girls who attended the shows as models were socially reckless people trying hard to capture the attention of men! To be sure about the views I received from the university girls, I also undertook, though with a few gender modifications, to pose similar questions to some ten randomly-selected young undergraduate men. The modified questions were: What does beauty mean to you; Are you handsome? What is the purpose of beauty and fashion shows?

With regard to the first question, all the ten men, like the women, had the view that beauty involved dress and body. However, they argued that the issue of beauty and fashion was not so important for men as it was for women. Every man, ugly or handsome, they said, would always want a beautiful and attractive woman. Nevertheless, for each of these young men, their, beautiful and attractive woman varied from a slender tall girl, a light complexion lady, a long dark-haired woman to a modestly built lady with generous lips, eyes and fairly big cheekbones. Of the ten men, seven wanted their beautiful women to always wear makeup while three thought that makeup not only spoiled the natural beauty of women but it also concealed a woman's ugliness. The answers to question two were quite revealing. Six of the men thought they did not know whether they were handsome or ugly, two felt they were handsome, one thought he was average and one felt the question of being ugly or handsome was not important to men.

On the purposes of beauty and fashion shows, the answers were equally interesting. Seven of the above young men thought that these shows were good because they promoted tourism and increased the sales of such industrial goods as whiskies, beauty products, foods, drugs, clothes and electronics. However, two of the ten boys thought that beauty and fashion shows were un-African and were merely meant to exploit already spoiled girls. One boy felt that whether these beauty shows and contests took place or not did not matter to him. This was the same young man who had argued that being ugly or handsome did not really matter for men.

After talking to university students, I also interviewed some lecturers in the university as well as other private citizens. We received various views from both men and women, who expressed diverse views about beauty, women and fashion. Surprisingly, however, all the interviews I carried out from a cross-section of the Kenyan populace seemed to point at certain recurring variables about beauty and women. These variables include clothes, height, skin colour, length of hair, hairstyles, size of the body, size of the breasts, and even age. However, with specific regard to beauty shows and contests, these respondents lamented the rising tendency to appropriate the female body in order to market goods and services in Kenya. What then is the lesson which we can learn from these interviews?

As globalization shrinks the world into a village, and as the Internet dissolves distances and spaces, a new cultural dispensation has been developing with regard to beauty and fashion. Styles of the female figure, the dress and the ornamentation of the body have throughout history varied from culture to culture. However, in a highly globalized world like ours, dictated by neo-liberal tendencies, these diversities are also collapsing into some all-embracing, universal style. The currently fashionable body is taut, small breasted, narrow-hipped and of a sliminess bordering on emaciation (Bartky 1990:66). However, since ordinary women normally have quite different body dimensions, they must of course diet.

In the Foucauldian perspective, dieting disciplines the body's hunger; appetite must be monitored at all times and governed by an iron will. Nevertheless, dieting too could involve not just avoiding some foods but also taking some slimming pills and low fat foods.[3] Slimming pills and low fat foods abound in Kenya's leading supermarkets and women buy these products in the hope of achieving an ideal shape. The multinational food chains such as Steers, Unilever and Coca Cola are often ready to take advantage of these demands by the female body so as to sell their products and make profits that run into millions of dollars.

Fundamentally, since the innocent need for the organism for food will not be denied, the body becomes one's enemy. It actually becomes an alien bent on thwarting the disciplinary project. The disciplinary project is meant to bring out an 'ideal body' to fit in certain designer dresses. Among North American women, rates of bulimia and anorexia nervosa are rising by the day (Garner *et al.* 1980). In one study carried out on American college women, it was found that 61 per cent of this category of women had eating disorders (Rockett and McMinn 1990). Although studies are inconclusive in other parts of the world about women's eating habits, it can safely be argued that as globalization consumes the entire world, more and more cases of bulimia and anorexia nervosa will be reported in many Third World countries. Anorexia nervosa which has now become a big threat to the lives of millions of women in the world today is to women of the 21st century what hysteria was a few centuries ago. This is because dieting is one discipline imposed upon a body subject to the 'tyranny of slenderness'. It is also a discipline imposed upon a body subject to the tyranny of 'profitable trade' in multinational goods including clothes, drugs and diet foods. Out of the ten young women I interviewed in my university, six were on some sort of diet. Foucault coined the term 'bio-power' to describe this experience through which the body is subjected to certain tyrannies. 'Bio-power', Foucault argues, is a form of power exercised on the body and it carries specifically anatomical and biological aspects. It is exercised over members of the population so that their sexuality and individuality are constituted in certain ways that are connected with national policy, including the machinery of production (Foucault 1980:139). In this way, populations can be adjusted with economic processes. Consequently, what begins as 'bio-power' is transformed into a powerful 'busno-power' which thrives on the various manipulations of the body (Marshall 1995:2)

The second discipline – another form of bio-power – which is supposed to produce beautiful and right-sized bodies is exercise (Chernin 1981). Since men as well as women exercise, it is not always easy, in the case of women, to distinguish what is done for the sake of physical fitness from what is done in obedience to the requirements of femininity. However, with the widespread obsession with weight reduction, one suspects that many women are working out in the health clubs or at the gym with a different aim in mind and in quite a different spirit than the men. A variety of instrument machines are being used in several club houses and gyms in Kenya. Used by both men and women, they include Nautilus machines, rowing machines, motorized exercycles, portable hip and leg cycles, belt massagers, trampolines, tread mills as well as arm and leg pulleys. Depending on the financial status of the owners of these physical fitness centres, a club house or gym could have a few, several or all of the above apparatus. Some of these machines cost thousands of shillings and are beyond the affordability of ordinary people in Kenya. Like men, majority of women register in these clubs paying weekly, monthly and annual subscriptions. In one such ordinary gym ran by Kenyatta University, Nairobi, subscribers pay up to 100 dollars a year which is a lot of money in Kenya. The more advanced gym in the same university would cost twice as much for members of the teaching staff over the same period. Outside the university, the cost of working out in the gyms and club houses is even three to four times higher than the highly subsidized rates at the campus.

Inside these gyms, one notices separate rooms for women focused on their own programmes. Women have to work towards an 'ideal woman's' body.[4] The 'ideal body' for a woman must be slender, with little fat and firm muscle. The body should be disciplined to accept a size twelve or fourteen dress – an ideal body size of many Western female film stars and models ranging from the Hollywood sex goddess Marilyn Monroe of the 1940s, Jane Fonda of the 1970s and 1980s to Janet Jackson of the 1990s. At the peak of exercising in those gyms, women behave as if some Monroe, Jackson or Fonda were watching them from an invisible tower. Some of the manuals for operating these expensive physical fitness machines show pictures of very slender women working on them. As they struggle to catch up with the dictatorship of the 'ideal sizes' of the body, Kenyan women are now being driven crazy by commercial images of women models exercising on machines. The main beneficiary in the entire process of disciplining the body, through exercising, are the multinational firms selling machines and clothes but the woman's body is the loser because it has to subject itself to impossible disciplines that combine strict diet with exercise.

It then seems to me that disciplining the woman's body to an appropriate size implies also that the woman's body is her own enemy. However, against the backdrop of a bruising battle between the woman and her own body, business people make a kill by marketing and selling their products on the 'battle field'. Inside some gyms and club houses, one also finds diet foods such as club soda and diet coke, as well as wines and spirits, sold at exorbitant prices, almost twice above the ordinary price in the streets. An 'ideal female body' comes at a cost. Evidently, it is from the gyms and club houses that women in Kenya move on to model in fashion houses and to participate in beauty shows.

Yet, for the man in the gym, the emphasis could vary from cutting down body fat and weight to enhancing their muscles as a sign of masculinity. Indeed, the most important difference between men and women in the Kenyan gyms and clubhouses is that men have choices to make on how they want their bodies to look like but women do not. For instance, men have a choice to build muscles, to increase some weight, to reduce weight, to maintain an average body weight with average muscles, but women have only one thing to do: cut weight and reduce body size if they really want to be feminine, attractive and beautiful. Is this not oppressive?

In the gyms, there are classes of exercises meant for women alone. These are designed not to trim or reduce the body's size overall, but to resculpture its various parts on the current model. As M.J. Saffon, an international beauty expert, would say, his twelve basic facial exercises can erase frown lines, smooth the forehead, raise hollow checks, banish crow's feet and tighten the muscles under the chin (Saffon 1981). Body sizes given by the Western world have become the universal norm as well as the only option for the Kenyan woman. From the universal West, the female body in Kenya must be disciplined to go through many exercises: exercises to build the breasts and exercises to banish cellulite. There is also 'spot-reducing', an umbrella term that covers dozens of punishing exercises designed to reduce problem areas like thick ankles or 'saddlebag' thighs.[5] However, the very idea of spot-reducing is both scientifically unsound and cruel for it raises expectations in women that can never be realized. This is because the pattern in which fat is deposited is known to be genetically determined.

From the foregoing, we note that it is not only her natural appetite or unreconstructed contours that pose a danger to women. The very expressions of her face can subvert the disciplinary project of bodily perfection. Clearly, in the war against her own body, the multinational and local business firms undertake to market their goods, clothes, foodstuffs and even beauty products. Figure consultants and gym instructors have come to assume the role of military 'commanders' of women cadres fighting against their own bodies. In doing their job, both the figure consultants and gym instructors also market, sometimes unconsciously, intellectual goods in the form of ideas from the West on how to achieve ideal bodies. These 'commanders' are often paid handsomely, anything between 100 and 700 dollars, monthly, in order to psyche women against their own bodies.[6] Without doubt, multinational companies have this tendency to utilize the battleground, in which women are fighting against their bodies, to market various goods and services that do not immediately benefit the woman in the gym. The disciplinary practices which therefore go into the project of beauty and fashion also push the woman's body into Foucault's prison and Bentham's panopticon. We are arguing that it is in the prison and panopticon of globalization that the female body is appropriated and constructed as a site for trade transactions involving local and multinational companies in Kenya.

The Female Body and the Media in Kenya

Media embraces radio, television, newspapers and magazines. Because radio transmission does not show the body of a woman, our study concentrated on television, newspapers and magazines. Television exhibits women's bodies in motion while magazines present still pictures of female bodies.

Mass circulation of women's magazines run articles on dieting in virtually every issue. They also expose images of women with 'ideal sizes and beauty'.

Across the streets of Kenya's major cities which I visited – Nairobi, Eldoret and Kisumu – international sex and fashion publications such as *Vogue, Elle, She, Instyle* and *Claire* among others were commonplace. These magazines are sold at between five to forty-seven dollars and are popular with both men and women.[7] Inside the magazines are not just 'right-sized' women's bodies but advertisements of the accessories, foods, clothes and perfumes that would go into creating a desirable body. For example, in several of these magazines I went through, there were advertisements of ornamented female bodies and of perfumes such as Chanel, Christian Dior, Dune, Cleopatra, Allure and Revlon, among others. Alongside the perfumes were costly chains, bracelets, bangles, earrings, lipstick varieties and whole cocktails of makeup for women. A woman really needs to be very rich to fit in the lifestyle constructed in these magazines (see *Vogue, Elle, She* and *Cosmopolitan*). All these accessories, perfumes and guidelines on diet are crucial ingredients of the curriculum which goes into the disciplining of a female body.[8] Expensive though these ingredients are, a lot of women try very hard to purchase them, thereby enriching multinational firms. The most interesting aspect of our study was that of the ten women we interviewed about female images in the media, eight of them reported that they had tried to follow guidelines from magazines but failed to achieve their objectives of being right-sized and attractive.[9] However, when asked whether they would abandon those guidelines and stop reading the magazines, six out of the eight women said they would never stop reading the magazines and they would never abandon the task of trying even harder!

In addition, in an effort to domesticate the Western images of the female sexuality, a number of locally prepared magazines have also hit the Kenyan market. Although they advertise very few commercials, the local sex magazines are extremely popular. The list of these publications is long but it includes such titles as *The Whole Apple, True Sensation, Playgirl, Secret Emotions, Romance, Passions, Secret Desire, Life Seen* and *Love Dust*. Each of these publications costs about seventy Kenya shillings, which is approximately a dollar. The chief storyline in these magazines is sex and the female body. Both on their covers and in the inside pages, the magazines carry explicit pictures of women. They also carry features on how a woman's body could be appropriated to sexually satisfy herself and her man. Indeed, the publications are sex manuals of sorts, discussing the sensitive parts of female bodies and how men can put those parts to good use. Furthermore, some of the publications glorify infidelity, lesbianism, incest and even homosexuality. Wondering why these magazines were selling products exposing women's bodies and carrying story lines that glamorized infidelity, lesbianism, homosexuality and incest, I undertook to interview three workers (two women and one man) from the Love Dust company and three from Emotions (one woman and two men).

They accepted to be interviewed on condition that I did not reveal their identity and I gave them my word for that.

Asked why they chose to use pictures nude women in their publications, the six workers from the two companies said their companies were just doing what the West did, namely, commercializing the female body. Second, they also reasoned that the women who posed nude were being paid handsomely.[10] Unfortunately, these workers did not say how much the women who posed nude were being paid. On infidelity, homosexuality and lesbianism, all the six workers surprisingly referred us to popular American soap operas, then showing on Kenya's television screen, The Bold and Beautiful, and Miami Sands. The two programmes depict images of female bodies that are partially nude; their storylines are about fashion, intrigue, infidelity and incest. It was at this point that I discovered how deeply Western values had become entrenched in Kenya's public life.

However, the most interesting outcome of my encounter with the workers at Emotions was that once they began to trust me, they showed me American and European sex videotapes involving the female body. For example, I learned that the company had purchased original videos of Playmates, Street Punk, Sluts of All Nations and Outside Exhibitions. Each of the videos contained between two to six hours of hot sex including anal. They also highlighted several styles that went into the diverse field of lovemaking. These videos had price tags of 12 to 15 dollars. On the shelves, I too found several sex magazines showing women and men in explicit sexual acts. The magazines included The Best of Big and Black, Players, Big Girls and Swank among others.[11] From the foregoing experience, I came to realize two things. First, it was evident that the storylines that I had seen in local sex magazines had appropriated the spirit, content and philosophy of Western sex videotapes, films, and magazines. Secondly, because of that, I learned that, indeed, sex and the female body especially as constructed by the West had become global products. Through videotapes and magazines, the West has continued to sell its ideas about sex and about the female body to countries such as Kenya in exchange for dollars.

We should probably pause for another moment and go back to Foucault. The disciplinary practices which inform the female bodies in magazines (whether local or international) and videotapes are numerous. Visually, female bodies are trained to pose in inviting and alluring ways. They expose their breasts, their genitals and often, they give the impression of sexually starved creatures. For some, their bodies are usually adorned with good hair, good hairstyles, earrings, bangles, chains, lipstick, and nail polish of various colours. These are the disciplinary constructions the female body goes through so that a sex videotape, a sex magazine, or a sexy figure is produced and sold. It is all about money but to get this money, you have to lead women to declare war on their own bodies! By declaring this war on themselves, women undertake to vigorously reinvent and reconstruct their own bodies so as to fit into the commercial demands of global culture, disseminated from the West.

The discussion on the female body and its significance in global trade in Kenya will not be complete without examining the role of television media. Due to recent political developments in Kenya, many aspects of public life have undergone enormous liberalization. Before the onset of the multi-party political dispensation in the early 1990s, Kenya had only one state-owned television station, the Kenya Broadcasting Corporation (KBC). In the dissemination of information and the delivery of programmes, the station used to operate under strict censorship rules provided by the political establishment. Today, however, several television stations have emerged and are operating competitively besides the national broadcasting service. The stations include the Family T.V, The Kenya Television Network (KTN), the Stellavision Television (STV) the Nation as well as the Citizen television (Daily Nation, October 3, 2002).

Apart from airing their own programmes, these stations (including the KBC), have acquired franchises to broadcast selected programmes from such international and Western-controlled media houses as the Voice of America (VOA), the Cable News Network (CNN) the British Broadcasting Corporation (BBC), Sky News and the German-based DW Television (DW TV). The purpose of television media everywhere in the world is to inform, entertain and provide international space for business. Our research showed that the complex network of local and international television systems thrives, for a greater part, on the appropriation of the female body. Indeed, through the Kenyan television media, two fundamental messages seem to emerge. The first message is sex, and the second is business.

Let us begin with sex. Increasingly, sex is becoming a staple in Kenya's television diet. Because of the institutionalized heterosexuality, a woman must make herself 'object and prey' for a man. In local programmes shown on the KBC such as Penzi Hatari (dangerous love affair), Doa (blemish) and even Vituko (shocking acts), story lines are varied but their major theme is love in its heterosexual disposition. The programmes, usually aired in the evenings, present several women who have clearly undergone the disciplinary project of femininity, ready and willing to be 'consumed' by men. Alongside local programmes, there are also foreign television shows that are now frequent on the KTN, STV, Nation and even KBC stations. For example, one of the leading foreign television shows on the KBC is The Bold and Beautiful, an American soap opera that has run on average for three days a week since 1994 and whose story is sex and fashion. The programme glorifies money, infidelity, incest and intrigue while at the same time presenting nude women's bodies. Here, women are also displayed as sex objects to be used by one powerful man, Ridge Forrester. It is an environment where men exchange women at will. However, the women who are exchanged here are also models and others are highly learned beauties. Yet, when it comes to them dealing with men, these women are all reduced to a common denominator. They are merely sexualized female bodies, manufactured from the disciplinary industry of femininity, ready to succumb to the desires of men. The women of The Bold and Beautiful adore makeup, fitness, and fashionable dressing. Similar programmes to The Bold and Beautiful include Miami Sands and La Mujer Mi de Vida, showing on the Nation television channel and featuring alluring female bodies, as well as The Young and the Restless, another American soap opera, and the romantic British drama Days of our Lives now showing on STV.

In all the above programmes, one notices the manifest disciplinary project of the female body. Notably, however, the extensive measures of bodily transformation are beyond the realization abilities of an average woman in Kenya. Many women in the country are without time and resources to provide themselves with even the minimum of what the disciplinary project of femininity requires: make up, diet, fashionable clothes and the ability to maintain a right-sized and permanently youthful body. More painful to note is the fact that the disciplinary practices of the female body are in themselves a signification of shame. They imply just how much women feel ashamed of their natural bodies. However, as they struggle to meet prevailing standards of body acceptability, poor women have also to bear the burdens of both psychological and economic humiliation.

The commercial benefits of these television programmes in Kenya are enormous. Just before the shows commence, a number of commercials are often aired, advertising several local and international products. For example, in the recent past, The Bold and Beautiful as well as Miami Sands have been preceded, interlaced and even post-marked by the advertisement of the Russian popular whisky, Smirnoff. In this commercial advertisement, one man who is happily surrounded by gorgeous and partially nude women dancing around him boasts that when he takes Smirnoff, he imagines a beautiful environment surrounded by 'gorgeous babes'. Here 'beautiful', 'right-sized', partially nude and highly ornamented and fit female bodies are paraded where Smirnoff is being advertised for sale! Clearly, we have a socially constructed female body promoting the sale of a multinational product. Indeed, even the partially nude women in this particular advertisement have designer bras and thin-string attires ordered straight from Western European and American fashion houses.

Other products advertised against the backdrop of 'a disciplined female body' include beauty products from the firm Procter and Gamble of the United States ranging from menstrual pads to soaps and cosmetics.[12] Local firms with franchises to manufacture and sell classified foods, body creams, toiletries and perfumes also advertise their products at the time 'female bodies' programmes are on air. Our purpose here, however, is not to enumerate all the products advertised during the airing of such programmes but to acknowledge that female bodies have been used on television in Kenya as sites and catalysts for the sale of manufactured goods. In this way, local and international firms acknowledge that their sales increase whenever they advertise their products on television and, especially so, when the advertisements appear before the presentation of sexy television programmes.[13]

We have already signified that in the regime of institutionalized heterosexuality, a woman has to make herself 'object and prey' for a man. It is for him that her eyes are limpid pools and her cheeks baby smooth (Beauvoir 1968:642). In contemporary patriarchal culture, a panoptical male connoisseur resides within the consciousness of most women. They stand perpetually before his gaze and under his judgment. Woman, in this case, lives her body as seen by another, by an anonymous patriarchal other. Talking of patriarchy again, one might note that most of the multinational firms are patriarchal in form. They have the 'toughness' and the muscular ruthlessness towards business; they are masculine; they are macho. This is probably the reason they parade female bodies to sell their products. It gives them a chance to demonstrate male domination.

Music and the Female Body

Increasingly, music has become a multi-million global business enterprise all over the world. The Kenyan people have also maintained enormous interest in local and international music despite the serious economic problems facing their country. Generally, there are two fundamental music avenues upon which one can analyse the construction of the female body in Kenya. These are the local and the international passageways.

The local music scene embosoms several dimensions. We have for example the official schools and colleges' music festivals, the ordinary entertainers who have taken music as a career, as well as the church choirs. However, at the international level, the Kenyan public has been continually exposed to the music of renowned artistes from both the rest of the African continent and the rest of the world. Comparatively, American and Western European music seems to be more popular than any other variant which has ever penetrated the local scene. In our research, we found out that seven out of ten university and college students would prefer to listen and dance to Western music than to any other music from other parts of the world. Probably, the reason for this imbalance lies in the fact that compared to the rest of the world, the West has had more resources to aggressively market their music and thus globalize the world from a Euro-American perspective.

Our chief concern in this research, however, was not the various categories of music played in Kenya. Our aim was to investigate how the female body was constructed at various musical levels. Furthermore, we undertook to investigate the relevance of such construction to global trade. In the national schools and colleges music festival held in Nairobi during the month of August 2002, we picked out three recurring features that seemed crucial to this study. First was the way female bodies were adorned and constructed. Second was the way that the body was utilized in song and dance and third, the way some commercial firms undertook to market their goods at the various music avenues.

With regard to the construction of the female body, in the festivals the girls tended to sport different forms of ornamentation including the donning of beads around their necks and waistlines, the dyeing of hair, the use of several matching colours to decorate finger nails as well as parts of their stomachs and the deliberate exposure of certain parts of their bodies such as the back and areas around their stomachs and waists. Generally, the girl tied pieces of clothes to conceal the breasts (or was it to announce the spot where their breasts resided?) Indeed, we watched a variety of dancing groups working hard to win trophies. The songs were of different themes including those on marriage, drugs, alcoholism, diseases and leadership. However, throughout the songs, we observed that were the men were to be blamed because the women always seemed helpless, for instance, when it came to bad marriages. This too applied to diseases, bad leadership and drugs. Indirectly, by blaming men for all the ills of society, the dancers also signified that men, not women, were the chief controllers of human life. There was no presentation which gave a woman a dominating role, yet the songs came from the body of a woman. When it came to dancing, two features were generally noted. One, most of the girls smiled as they danced even in instances where it required that they frown or show moods of sadness. As they danced, secondly, there was an emphasis on belly dancing which was cheered by the audience! One man we talked to, Charles Omondi, explained that belly dancing had received cheers from the audience because it represented the sexual virility of a woman.[14]

As if to celebrate the objectification of the female body as a sex machine meant to add pleasure to a man's life, and as if to approve of the demeaning messages about women in the music hall, the multinational beverage firm Coca Cola had a busy time selling various brands of its drinks at prices that were about 40 per cent above the normal price in the shops.[15] Various brands of soaps and foodstuffs manufactured by the East African Industries, a subsidiary of the London-based Unilever Company, were also being sold at inflated prices. It thus dawned on us that the dominating tendencies of globalization had now invaded the female body and was using the disciplined body – disciplined by specific dancing styles, disciplined by ornamentation, dress and smile — to market multinational products without even considering whether or not the music festivals were 'inferiorizing' or 'superiorizing' the woman gender. Ornamental female bodies, dancing in provocative ways, are also commonplace in Kenyan night clubs as well as in places where commercial music entertainers go to sing. Such avenues of entertainment sold whiskies, soft drinks and cigarettes to celebrate the derogation of the female body.

The music of international artistes, we realized, was everywhere on television, video tapes as well as on cassette tapes.[16] Over the past ten years, Kenya has played host to several international music artistes and groups like Kool and the Gang, Shaggy, Kofi Olomide, Le General Defao, Aurlus Mabele of the Loketo beat, Brenda Fassie, Kanda Bongoman of the Kwasa Kwasa beat as well as Tshala Muana of the famed muswati belly-dancing style. There are many African, especially Congolese, musicians who have not yet visited Kenya but whose music is very popular in the country. Through television and internet connections, the music of prominent Euro-American musicians such as Dolly Parton, Celine Dion, Christina Aguilera, Janet Jackson, Rod Steward, Bryan Adams, Robert Kelly, Whitney Houston and Michael Bolton, among others, has penetrated both the public and private spheres of the Kenyan people.

In investigating the diverse constructions of the female body through music, we sampled a number of music videos. They include Janet Jackson's Rhythm 1814, Love Cannot Do Without You and It Is On You. We also examined Shaggy's It Was Not Me; Dolly Parton's Just Because I Am a Woman, and Bryan Adam's Everything I Do I Do It For You. From the rest of Africa, we picked up videotapes from Kanda Bongoman's Yesu Kristo, and Inde Moni, Aurlus Mabele's Embargo, Kofi Olomine's Andrada, and Loi, Defao's Anrie and Nadine, Brenda Fassies' Vuli Ndlela and Mimeza as well as Zaiko Langa Langa's Poison.

The videotapes from African musicians produced music which had some very critical commonalities. Whether one is talking about Defao, Koffi Olominde or Aurlus Mabele, one should appreciate that most of the Congolese musicians produced hard-hitting tunes which also elicited rigorous dancing. In every case, women's bodies were ornamented and they were deliberately dressed to produce sex appeal. Often, women dancers got introduced into the dancing floor once the songs climaxed into pitched beats. To these beats, the girls danced their hearts out, gyrating, wriggling and shaking their waists, throwing kisses and inviting the male audience to move closer to their 'electronic' waists. They also smiled and danced to rehearsed steps and body movements. The environmental settings of each song were, however, different. In some cases, songs were set in high-class houses or compounds showing expensive tastes: curtains, sleek vehicles, couches and swimming pools. The girls danced in designer costumes, thin-string vests, bras, very short trousers and no shoes. The hair was dyed with golden glosses. Their fingernails were long and coated with distinctive colours; lipsticks and general makeup were important features of the dancers' overall outlook. In general, as one finishes watching Loi or Andrada, one also notices that the spectre goes beyond mere entertainment. It is international business.

To produce music and sell it well, you need a disciplined and practised female body. Consequently, you will sell the music but other global firms will also benefit through the marketing of their goods. As a result, a single music video becomes a complicated diversity. Music videotapes of the above artistes could sell for 15 to 25 dollars, but the ultimate value of the tape should surely include the expanded commercial space of the audience. During the viewing of the tape, the consumers too have opportunities to see not just the music but also the designer chains, motor vehicles, earrings and clothes. Furthermore, the videotapes help to market different designs of Western houses and compounds; designs of curtains and cutlery, furniture, beds and all that goes into interior decorations and furnishing. More importantly, powerful music companies such as Virgin Records, Sony Records, Epic, Polygram Polydor and Motown, among others, get their share of profits in the entire enterprise because they are profoundly responsible for the successful careers, worldwide, of most of the big names in the music industry. All these things are achieved at a high cost to the female body, a body which has been constructed and produced by certain disciplinary practices.

Although in such video shows the man's body undergoes similar disciplinary processes, in almost all of these productions several themes are often collapsed into the subject matter of love. Notably, a male singer is presented adoring a woman's body, her movements and her general appeal. It ends up with some form of heterosexual love in which the man will finally use the female body to satisfy his desires. One can easily see that the narrow identification of a woman with sexuality and the body does little to raise her status. In the case of these video tapes of the African musicians, it is Kofi Olomide, Defao and Kanda Bongoman who are the real heroes of the public audience.

In a recent African music concert held in one of Nairobi's leading restaurants, I asked ten randomly selected women and men attending the show to name some of the women who routinely dance in Koffi Olomide's, Defao's and Arlus Mabele's videos. The respondents admitted that they loved the music of these Congolese artistes and that they liked the way the women danced but they did not remember the women's names. Yet, all the respondents knew Olominde, Defao and Mabele! It was at this point that I came to grips with the reality that, in fact, the music videos we have discussed above were avenues to 'celebrate' the 'triviality' of the woman's mind. By adoring their bodies, men forget the women's names and thus underline their insignificance. By privileging the 'disciplined' body over the woman herself, we actually celebrate the loss of the female identity. Yet this loss of identity, as well as the general trivialization of the woman's mind, all combine to establish an important site upon which global goods are marketed.[17] True, even the most adored female bodies complain routinely of their situation in ways that reveal an implicit understanding that there is something demeaning in the kind of attention they receive (Bartky 1990:173). Marilyn Monroe, Elizabeth Taylor, Farrah Fawcett, Whitney Houston, Virginia Marsden, Oprah Winfrey, Jane Fonda and many others have all wanted passionately to become actresses – artistes and not just sex objects to be exploited.

While the African woman in African music videos is possibly size 14 and 16, a few like Brenda Fassie of South Africa could be size 12. In the Euro-American world, most women music artistes, including the dancers, struggle to cut their body size to twelve. An example is Janet Jackson and Dolly Parton.[18] They work hard in gyms but a number of them fail to get to size 12 and remain at size 14. It all depends on how far one can go with the disciplining project of diet and exercise. In our research, we looked at one track Love Cannot Do Without You from Janet Jackson's videotape, Rhythm 1814. In this production, the small-sized Janet Jackson sings as she adores the gigantic body of a man she loves, telling him that she could not do without him. The man never answers back but merely dramatizes his power of muscle and protection to Janet Jackson. The issue, however, which concerned us so much in this videotape, was the dwarfing of Janet Jackson by such a gigantic man. In the other American music videos we watched, whether they were those of Celine Dion, Whitney Houston, or even Michael Bolton, among others, the woman had to be physically dwarfed by the man both in body size and in weight.

The lessons we gathered from these videotapes were quite instructive. Femininity had become something in which virtually every woman is required to participate. Further, the precise nurture of the criteria by which women are judged, not only the inescapability of judgement itself, reflects gross imbalances in the social power of sexes that do not mark the relationship of artists and their audiences. An aesthetic femininity, for example, that mandates fragility (as in Janet Jackson's case above) and lack of muscular strength produces female bodies that can offer little resistance to physical or even commercial abuse. It is of course true that the current fitness movement has permitted women to develop more muscular strength and endurance than was previously allowed; indeed, images of women have begun to appear in the mass media that seem to eroticise this new masculinity. Nevertheless in Kenya, as in America, a woman may by no means develop more muscular strength than her partner. The bride who would tenderly carry her groom across the threshold is a figure of comedy not romance!

However, against the backdrop of this 'weak' and 'disciplined' female body, the videos have backgrounds of opulence graced by designer houses, vehicles and compounds. In addition, inside the houses are tables serving food from Mcdonald's.[19] More importantly, the dresses worn by the female body are designer outfits complete with accessories. Some are tight-fitting, emphasizing the protruding breasts and buttocks while others can barely cover the body of the female dancer and singer. The males, whether in the audience or on the stage, wear oversize trousers and T-shirts as a sign of domination, authority and control. There is a difference between a female body and male one. These designs are now all over Kenya. College girls imitate the fashion styles of the 'disciplined' female bodies of American music icons but the boys have to dress like American basketball celebrities such as Michael Jordan or like music composers and performers such as Shaggy and Robert Kelly. These young Kenyan men have disciplined their bodies in this manner in order to perpetuate their domination of woman. In this study, we argue that behind the inferiorization of the female body through the prism of music, multinational companies undertake to sell oversize T-shirts, big Nike-type shoes, and oversize trousers for men.[20] Designer firms too sell tight-fitting wares to women. In Kenya, both men and women who cannot afford new outfits from America buy used ones. The idea is that against the backdrop of multinational profits, music has been appropriated to 'inferiorize' the female body.

At the beginning of this chapter, we intimated that globalization signifies a new type of centralized power controlled by the West. To a larger extent, this power is often administered through financial, social, technical, cultural, political and commercial domains. However, because the same power is ubiquitous and faceless, it affects Westerners in very peculiar and drastic ways. From the above discussion, it is undeniable that bodies of Western women have been exploited not just by men but also by Western multinational companies. As has been demonstrated through fashion, media and music, Kenyan women have been victims of similar forms of domination and exploitation not just by men but also by the Western multinational firms.

However, a number of observations would be in order in this regard. First, unlike the past forms of globalization, the current variants of globalization are mainly driven by the capitalist principals of profit-making. Thus, regardless of whether or not one is looking at Euro-America, Africa or Asia, one has to appreciate the fact that although women's bodies were dominated and controlled by men during the pre-modern era, such control and domination were not ruthlessly commercialized in ways that would match present practices.

Which brings us to another fundamental observation. In this era when female bodies are highly commercialized, the West often has the last laugh at the bank. Through the Western-controlled multinational corporations, as well as scientific/technological programs, the powerful nations of the West have been able to take home most of the huge profits which emanate from the intricate exploitation of women's bodies all over the world. Clearly, when a Western European woman's body is exploited through the avenues of fashion, media and music, she knows that such exploitation is being done within her culture and by people from her own economic environment, where her social identity is not distorted. Secondly, she also knows that profits made from such exploitation will never leave European countries but will be used to improve the quality of life in her own society.

However, the same cannot be said about an African woman living in Kenya. Like many African countries, Kenya exists in a fairly depressing and unequal relationship with the West. Living in the perpetual condition of 'otherness', Africans have been unable to dismantle forms of knowledge and economic practices that have condemned them to the demeaning status of supporting the development of Western economies in the midst of the continent's abject poverty. Evidently, African economies are controlled and dominated by the Western multinational companies such as Unilever and Coca Cola. These same companies are at the centre of practices which facilitate the exploitation and domination of the female body in Kenya. Hence, much of the profit which accrues out of the exploitation of the Kenyan female body (and indeed the African woman's body across the continent) finds its way back into the Western economies while the quality of life in Africa keeps deteriorating by the day. Furthermore, much of the construction of the female body in Kenya and in many parts of Africa follows the cultural principles of the West. As a result, what the African woman witnesses is not just her exploitation and domination but also her loss of cultural identity. These issues are cardinal in understanding the differences which separate the exploitation of the female body in Africa and the exploitation of the female body in Europe and America.

Conclusion

It was the objective of this paper to interrogate the female body within the context of global trade in Kenya. Globalization, we argued, may mean many things to many people: the rule of multinational corporations, the dwindling powers of nation-states, the emergence of a new type of centralized power controlled by the West and the dictatorship of the Western-controlled information superhighway called the Internet.

Focusing on the female body, we have demonstrated how Kenya is confronted by the challenges posed by global forces. Specifically, and with particular reference to the domains of fashion and beauty, the platform of media and the arena of music, this study has explored the various ways in which the female body has been reproduced and reconstructed so as to provide a major boost to global trade.

Borrowing heavily from the ideas of French theoretician Michel Foucault, our study has illustrated that modern society has established certain institutions which have become disciplining agents of the human body. Including schools, armies, prisons, media and fashion houses, such institutions have created rules which seek to regulate the economy, operations and efficiency of the body and its movements. However once the rules have been internalized by recipients, those enslaving institutions do not need to be always physically present to oversee the body's disciplinary practices.

The institutions have the perpetual effect of creating, in the human mind, a state of conscious and permanent visibility that assures the automatic functioning of power to the extent that the affected human being becomes his or her own body's jailer. We signified that, like schools and hospitals or the panopticon, globalization has similar effects on the human body. Global forces fiercely convey cultural goods that dictate the ideal body size, its beauty, its fashion, its makeup, its movements and its use to the extent that the owner of the body begins reproducing these disciplinary practices on him or herself as if he or she were being watched by someone from the global tower. In the end, the power exerted against the body is everywhere around and about but also anonymous.

Applied to the male body, we have shown that global power tends to 'superiorize' the man's body but when exerted on the female body it tends to inferiorize it. The study has established that it is against the backdrop of the 'superiorization' of the male body, on the one hand, and the inferiorization of the female body, on the other, through media, music and fashion that multinational corporations tend to market and sell their numerous products including magazines, perfumes, music tapes, cigarettes, foodstuffs, body creams, soaps, drinks and designer clothes. We have in conclusion sustained the argument that the marketing and sale of these products in Kenya is one fundamental way in which globalization celebrates the 'inferiorization' of the female body that has undergone the disciplinary practices of Foucault.

Notes

1. The author is a lecturer in the Department of History, Archaeology and Political Studies at Kenyatta University, Nairobi.
2. Interview with Loise Wanjiku, a third year Education student at Kenyatta University.
3. On the Kenyan market, for example, there are several variants of the slimming drug, Reductamin. Developed in America and now licensed for use in the European Union and the rest of the world, Reductamin combines all the three weight loss methods in one diet pill. First the pill reduces one's appetite and second, it makes one feel full even if one has no food in one's stomach. Third, the pill speeds up one's metabolism so that one's body actually burns up more calories, with accelerated speed, than is normally the case.
4. Interview with Jasmine Kweyu, an attendant at the Kenyatta University gym.
5. Interview with Abdul Mukasa, a physical trainer at Chipukizi Clubhouse, Nairobi.
6. Interview with James Mugo, a junior instructor at the gym and swimming pool owned by the Sirikwa Hotel in the town of Eldoret.

7. The cover price of the November 2001 issue of Elle is £3.50 which is about US $5. However, the October 2002 issue of Vanity Fair costs $47, while the Instyle issue of the same month costs $42.50.

8. In the March 2002 issue of Marie Claire, one comes across various advertisements for Revlon lipstick, Revlon perfumes and designer women's shoes manufactured by the famous Italian company, Salvatore Ferragami. Diamond chains and woollen outfits for women are advertised in the Elle issue of November 2001. In the She issue of March 2002 a body lotion from the Paris-based company Clarins Paris is also advertised. All these products are expensive, costing up to $600, but they are part and parcel of the ingredients which go into the disciplining processes of the female body.

9. This interview targeted women working in three beauty and fashion houses in Nairobi, Judith Mumo, Elizabeth Kimulu and Grace Indusa.

10. Interview with employees of Love Dust and Emotions who use the pseudonyms of Sly, Maggie Tass, Stephane, Gibby and Rust.

11. In the Best of Big Black, for example, emphasis was put on naked women bodies bearing big breasts. In Players, however, the focus was on nude female bodies with a lot of makeup and body accessories. The magazine too shows explicit pictures of women's bodies absorbing the sexual releases of men. Again Big Girls and Swank are all about big breasts.

12. In Kenya the popular brand name for the Procter and Gamble menstrual pads for women is Always.

13. Interview with Jackson Muchiri, a sales representative with Kenya Wine Agencies which also markets the various brands of Smirnoff Whiskey. A 700ml Smirnoff whiskey bottle costs about $12.

14. Charles Omondi, a music teacher from Sirikaru secondary school.

15. The normal price of the 300ml bottle of Coca Cola drink is twenty shillings. During the festivals, the same bottle went for twenty five and thirty shillings.

16. A non-pirated cassette tape carrying the music of international artistes costs between two and three dollars. However, an original videotape would go for $10 at the lowest and $25 at the highest

17. Once a woman loses her proper identity through these disciplinary practices, she becomes a worthless object represented only by her body parts and the movements those body parts make.

18. Some musicians such as Dolly Parton wear wigs to create the false impression that they have very attractive, sexy hair. Several female musicians including Parton have also undergone breast implants to maintain upright, youthful but big breasts.

19. McDonald's is one of America's leading food chains. It is also one of the leading food chains in the world.

20. A good Nike-type T-shirt costs $10 to $15 in Kenya. However, a modest Nike-type pair of shoes could cost up to $25. Women's outfits are even more expensive.

Bibliography

Books and Articles

Association of African Women for Research and Development, 1998, 'The Kenya Chapter', Women's Political Leadership, Nairobi: AAWORD.

Archer J. and B. Lloyd, 1995, *Sex and Gender*, Cambridge: Cambridge University Press.

Ayayo A. and B.C. Ocholla, 1991, *The Spirit of the Nation*, Nairobi: Shirikon Publishers.

Beauvoir de, S., 1968, *The Second Sex*, New York: Bantam Books.

Bartky, S.L., 1990, *Femininity and Domination: Studies in Phenomenology of Oppression*, New York: Routledge.

Butler, J., 1990, *Gender Trouble: Feminism and the Subversion of Identity*, London: Routledge.

Cheah, Phen, 1996, 'Mattering' in Diacritics 26.1.

Chernin, Kim, 1981, *The Obsession: Reflections on the Tyranny of Slenderness*, New York: Harper and Row.

Dews, P., 1984, 'Power and Subjectivity in Foucault', in New Left Review No 144, Mach – April.

Fanon, F., 1970, Black Skin, White Masks, London: Paladin.

Flyn, T.R.., 1989, 'Symposium Papers: Foucault and the Politics of Postmodernity', Vol. 23, Issue 2.

Foucault, M., 1979, *Discipline and Punish*, New York: Vintage Books.

Foucault, M., 1980, *The History of Sexuality*, Vol. I, New York: Pantheon.

Garner, D.M., P.E. Garfinkel *et al*, 1980, 'Cultural Expectations of Thinness in Women', Psychology Report, 47, pp. 483-491.

Hester, M., 1992, *Lewd Women and Wicked Witches, A Study of the Dynamics of Male Domination*, London: Routledge.

Itzin, C., 1992, 'Pornography: Women, Violence and Civil Liberties', New York: O.U.P

Jackson, S., 1996, *Feminism and Sexuality*, Edinburgh: Edinburgh University Press.

Khasiani, S.A., 1992, 'Groundwork: African Women as Environmental Managers', Nairobi: African Centre for Technology Studies.

Marshall, J.D., 1995, 'Foucault and Neo-Liberalism: Bio power and Busno-power' in Philosophy of Education.

Martin, Mary C., Gentry J.W., 1997, ' Stuck in the Model Trap: Effects of Beautiful Models in Ads on Female Pre-Adolescents and Adolescents', in Journal of Advertising 262, pp. 19-33.

Martin, R., 1999, 'Globalization? The Dependencies of a Question', Social Text 17.3.

Mbilinyi, D. and Omari, C., 1996, *Gender Relations and Women's Images in Media*, Dar-es-Salaam: Dar-es-Salaam University Press.

Saffon, M.J., 1981, 'The 15-Minute-A-Day Natural Face Lift', New York: Warner Books.

Truong, Thanh-Dam, 1990, *Sex, Money and Morality: Prostitution and Tourism in South-East Asia*, London: Zed Book Limited.

Rockett, G. and K. McMinn, 1990, 'You can never be too Rich or too Thin: How advertisement influences Body Image', in Journal of College Student Development, 31 pp. 278.

Silvestre, B. in Peterson, B., 1986, 'Some correlates of the thin standard of Bodily Attractiveness for women', in International Journal of Eating Disorders 5, 5, pp. 895-905.

Magazines

Big Girls, London, March 2002

The Big and Black, London, issue I/II, June 2000

Cosmopolitan, Cape Town, March 2002

Cosmopolitan, London, November 2002

Daily Nation, Nairobi, October 3 2002

Elle, London, August 2002
GQ, Pretoria, October 2001
GQ, Pretoria, London, August 2002
Honey, New York, March 2002
Instyle, New York, January 2002
Life, Nairobi, April 2002
Marie Claire, Johannesburg, September 2001.
Marie Claire, New York, January 2002
She, London, June 2002
Swank, July 2000
Players, Los Angeles, July 2000
Vogue, London, September 2002

Music Videotapes
Adams, Bryan, Everything I Do I Do It For You. (brian.adam.com)
Bongoman, Kanda, Inde Moni, Yesu Kristo (www.kenyaweb.com, buildafrica.org)
Bolton Michael, Soul Provider. (www.getmusic.com, www.mbolton.com)
Dion Celine, All Because Of You (www.Celine.net, members.aol.com)
Defao, Le Generale, Anrie, Nadine. (www.africasounds.com, defaoin.htm)
Fassie, Brenda, Vuli Ndlela (www.afromix.org, brenda_fassie
Houston, Whitney, How Will I Know, I Wonna Dance With Somebody (whitney-houston.com, Justwhitney.com)
Jackson, Janet, Rhythm, 1814, Love Cannot Do Without You (Janet_Jackson.com)
Mabele, Arlus, Embargo (www.marchafalk.iwebland.com., my_cd.html)
Nkolo Mboka Poison (www.thepothole.com)
Olomide, Koffi, Andrada, Loi (Koff.html, kenyapage.com)
Parton, Dolly, Just Because I'm a Woman (dolly.html)

Soap Operas
Miami Sands (www.geocities.com., miamisands.html)
La Mujer de mi vida (Javico.tripod; www.zinema.com; www.todacine.com)
The Young And The Restless (www.cbs. com, daytime/yr).

Oral Respondents
(a) Eleven female university students, ten male university students, fifteen university lecturers (eight female, seven male), eighteen private citizens, six employees of Love Dust and Emotion magazines, ten young male and female music lovers at the Florida 2000 club music extravaganza in Nairobi.
(b) (i)   Charles Omondi
    (ii) Jasmine Kweyu
    (iii) Loise Wanjiku
    (iv) Abdul Mukasa
    (v)   James Mugo
    (vi) Jackson Muchiri

4

The Impact of Globalization on Women Peasants and Traders in Nigeria's Delta Region (1986 – 2002)

Iwebunor Okwechime

Introduction

This study is an attempt to demonstrate how the dynamics of globalization have heightened the contradictions generated by the oil industry over the last 47 years in the oil-rich Niger Delta, and the impact of these on female peasants and traders between 1986 and 2002. In the Niger Delta women are the backbone of the communities and they also constitute over 50 per cent of the population. Although most of them have limited education, they are generally enterprising. Not surprisingly, the women folk play a significant role in the communities in the Niger Delta through farming, fishing and trading in agricultural and other goods. However, each of these is becoming increasingly difficult, given the effects of globalization on the oil industry, to which the Niger Delta communities have played host over the last four-odd decades.

Globalization places an especially heavy burden on female peasants and traders in the Niger Delta. The globalization of the oil industry has led to, among other things, the intensification of oil exploration and the further integration of the region into the market-driven global capitalist system. The consequence of this is well reflected in the increased environmental and social degradation, as well as wide-spread economic disempowerment among the female peasants and traders of the Niger Delta oil communities. Due to increased oil exploitation activities by the oil companies, huge tracts of arable land were annexed for oil industry-related activities, such as pipelines, flow stations, access roads and campsites for oil workers, among others. Furthermore, increased oil exploitation and production activities heightened the environmental devastation of land, water and air which were polluted by spills, blow outs, seepages and gas flares. All this resulted in diminished productivity, thereby threatening the viability of the local economy in which women play a vital role. "Since farms are failing, palm trees are not bearing fruit, and fish are depleted", said Grace Ekanem, a women's group leader, "women are not only unable to feed their families, but cannot earn money to send their children to school or to afford medical treatment" (cited in Esparza and Wilson, 1999:10).

It was against this background that the women mobilized themselves against the forces of globalization – the oil companies and the Nigerian state – demanding, among other things, community development and the provision of economic empowerment programmes, as well as employment for their children and an end to environmental degradation. Through their demonstrations, protests and sit-outs, the women have drawn the attention of the Nigerian state and human rights organizations to their plight. They have also largely succeeded in making the oil companies sign a series of Memorandum of Understanding (MoU) with them. At this point several questions are pertinent. How did poor, mostly illiterate, peasant women and traders unite and mobilize themselves against the forces of global capitalism? How did they overcome or transcend the constraints imposed by the patriarchal nature of their society? And what are the factors responsible for the relative success of these women-led protests over those of their male counterparts? These and other questions will be investigated in this study.

The context of the issues that provide the background for our investigation or our framework of analysis is based on a political ecology perspective. It recognizes, at a contextual and an analytical level, how state policies, interstate relations and global capitalism impinge on issues such as access to, ownership of and control over nature (natural resources such as crude oil, forests and water). In the specific case of the Niger Delta, this approach brings into clear relief the destructive impact of corporate globalization on the economic livelihoods of unwaged rural women. Also, within this framework, we are able to understand how the rural people of the oil belt, especially the women folk, bear the brunt of external policy constraints that originate from an institutional domain that they have no control over and little knowledge of (Redclift and Sage 1994).

The year 1986 is remarkable, not only for the purposes of our analysis, but for the Nigerian state as well. It was the very year the military government of Nigeria under the former dictator, General Ibrahim Babangida, officially adopted the Bretton Woods Institutions' imposed Structural Adjustment Programme (SAP), despite the overwhelming groundswell of public opinion against the adoption of the programme. 1986 is also a landmark year in the sense that it flagged off, at least officially, the process of deregulation and trade liberalization, essential components of the adjustment programme. In addition to all this, the year 1986 has a milestone significance in the contemporary political history of women's struggle in Nigeria, especially that of women in the Niger Delta.

In August 1986, a crowd of about 10,000 women from Ekpan in Uvwie Local Government near the oil city of Warri mobilized themselves and laid siege on the premises and production facilities of the Nigerian National Petroleum Corporation (NNPC). Chanting and dancing in their accustomed manner, the women called on the NNPC and the oil companies operating in their community to provide social amenities for them, as well as jobs for their qualified sons and daughters. Prior to the Ekpan women's uprising, the Ogharefe women had in 1984 successfully organized a mass resistance protest against a subsidiary of the American oil multinational corporation, Pan Ocean. Following the example of the Ogharefe women, the Ughelli women (also in the Western Niger Delta) organized a fierce anti-tax protest against the government. The anti-tax revolt came in the wake of the government's policy to levy taxes on women (see Turner and Oshare 1993). The taxation was necessitated by the parlous state of the national economy following the oil boom of the early 1980s and the consequent imposition by General Babangida's government of IMF loan 'conditions'. In the eyes of these women and their counterparts across the nation, the IMF and its adjustment policies were largely to blame for the hardship they were now going through. To be sure, higher taxes, as Turner and Oshare (1993) have noted, constituted a key element in IMF adjustment packages. Thus, it was these anti-tax protests that supplied 'the immediate atmosphere of popular, woman-centred mobilization within which the Ekpan women were moved to act' (Turner and Oshare 1993).

It is good to note that the protests against the imposition of structural adjustment conditions were not restricted to the oil-producing areas alone. True, similar protests and revolts were recorded in other parts of the country. However, those that occurred in the oil belt were unique in several respects. For example, in other parts of the country, mobilizations against the adjustment programme were characterized by 'instances of urban protest actions and anti-IMF riots' (Egwu 2001:49). In the Niger Delta, such protests not only originated from the countryside, but more importantly women (mostly peasants and traders) took the initiative. Explaining the reason for this is not difficult.

Women play a vital role in the local economy, as they constitute the bulk of the farmers, fisher folks and traders. However, the adjustment programme threw up new contradictions whilst deepening old ones in the oil-producing communities. For example, the process of land alienation pursued by the state in the late 1970s under the rubric of the Land Use Act was reinforced by the SAP. According to Egwu (1998), in the wake of the economic crisis and SAP, land alienation and land grabbing became pronounced in the countryside. By accelerating this process, he argued, structural adjustment impacted heavily on the 'agrarian and land' question.

Nowhere was this 'agrarian and land question' more fiercely contested than in the oil-producing areas of the Niger Delta (see Turner and Oshare 1993, Turner *et al.* 2001; Obi 2000 and 2001; Human Rights Watch 1999). In the process of opening up the economy to private foreign investments, as dictated by the Bretton Woods institutions, huge tracts of cultivable land were parcelled out to oil companies for oil exploration and production activities. Additionally, the attendant oil industry pollution devastated the available arable land and water, the main sources of income for these rural women, the majority of whom were breadwinners for their families. Land hunger which consequently became endemic in the region often resulted in inter-communal clashes. Reflecting on the impact of this development on women, Grace Ekanem, a women's group leader in Akwa Ibom State, noted that women were not only unable to feed their families, but could not earn enough to send their children to school, or to afford medical treatment. 'Women are now redundant,' she concluded (cited in Esparza and Wilson 1999:10). In other words, the women of Nigeria's oil belt have been economically disempowered, marginalized and excluded.

Apart from land hunger which the alienation of land by the Nigerian state engendered through the instrumentality of the Land Use Act, oil company operations have further exacerbated the crisis of land shortage in the oil-producing areas. Oil pollution resulting from gas flares and oil spills have rendered the soil virtually infertile. In the words of a young female farmer (cited in Ekine 2001:28):

> Since 1982 the soil has changed and crops do not grow well. It is not because of overuse because we know how to use our lands and our crops are rotated. It is because of the flares. The soil is now too hard - before a small child can turn the soil but now it's too hard. The yield of crops is very poor and there is lack of fish in this area. We have no help from Shell.

They have brought pollution and no development.

The foregoing serves as the general context out of which the argument pursued in this study flows. In the next section, an attempt is made at a conceptualization of economic globalization, and highlighting the centrality of the multinational corporations as well as the role of the IMF/World Bank-initiated adjustment policies in the process. The aim, it should be stated, is to underscore the critical interface between globalization, multinational corporations and structural adjustment.

Economic Globalization: A Conceptual Overview

Globalization has become the latest fad in the extant literature on the political economy of capitalist development. As a phenomenon promoted and sustained by neo-liberal economic perspectives, globalization generates differential impacts on states. These differential pressures can be ascribed to the role and position of these various states within the global capitalist system. In the words of one observer, globalization 'does not generate a single, uniform set of pressures on all states but affects them in different ways' (Jessop 2003:32).

As a concept globalization is a complex and contested notion (Aina 1997; Hoogvelt 1997; Scholte 1997; Obi 2000; Embong 2000; Rugumamu 2001). This, as Bob Jessop (2003:32) makes us understand, is because 'globalization is not a single causal mechanism with a universal, unitary logic but is a multi-centric, multi-scalar, multi-temporal, multi-form and multi-causal' process. Accordingly, he suggests that globalization is better seen as a hyper-complex, continuously-evolving product of many processes. Similarly, James Mittelman (2000:4) sees globalization not as a single unified process, but a syndrome of processes and activities consisting mainly of a set of ideas and a policy around the global division of labour and power.

What is worth noting is that globalization is not a new phenomenon. As such, it has been described as imperialism, a dynamic phenomenon, which changes in accordance with the law of capitalist expansion. Viewed from this perspective, globalization becomes the latest stage in the dynamic process of capitalist development which began with the slave trade, then with the 'legitimate trade', followed by colonialism and neo-colonialism (Nnoli 2000). Like Nnoli, Obi (2001) has argued that globalization is the historical outcome of a global capitalist project of an integrated world market. Yash Tandon (2000) corroborates the above assertions by noting that globalization is the final conquest of capitalism over the rest of the world. Bade Onimode (2000) has traced this 'conquest of capital over the rest of the world' to around 1870. Historicizing the phenomenon further, Aina notes that:

> The important point in terms of dating globalization is that we are looking at a post-Second World War phenomenon whose intensity and definite shape has clearly emerged from around the 1970s (Aina 1997:24).

This period, according to Amin, is largely characterized by an economic crisis which was precipitated by the long phase of structural transformation that resulted in the deepening of the globalization process (Amin 1992, cited in Aina 1997). It is important, however, to emphasize the salient contrasts between the current phase of globalization and the earlier one. When compared with the current phase, for example, the earlier phase of globalization occurred to a smaller extent - in terms of breadth and scope – and at a far slower space. As Ibrahim (2002), citing Arjun Appadurai (2001) pointed out, globalization in the contemporary world is characterized by objects in motion, including ideas and ideologies, people and goods, images and messages, technologies and techniques. It is a process anchored on flows, structures and organization.

Furthermore, the dominant actors or players in the earlier phase of globalization were imperial nation-states that were engaged in international economic competition. Conversely, in the contemporary phase, the critical players are the multinational corporations, transnational banks and multilateral institutions, notably the World Bank, the International Monetary Fund (IMF), the European Union (EU), the Organization for Economic Corporation and Development (OECD) and the powerful G7 countries. As in the earlier phases, international trade, international investment and international finance still constitute the major aspects of globalization.

It should however be emphasized that, in the current era of globalization, the sheer scope and volume of trade, investment and finance by far exceed those of the earlier phases. This, as Ohiorhenuan (1998) has observed, is because globalization in the contemporary era is located firmly in the context of a new market fetishism. What this demonstrates, in other words, is the centrality of the market in the globalization process. Market in this context refers to the market for finance and capital in cahoots with the multinational corporations – the major agent and conduit for the globalization of production. As Ohiorhenuan (1998:9) has said:

> The growth of FDI underscores the enormous role of Transitional Corporations (TNCs) in economic activity world-wide. The value of goods and services produced by foreign affiliates was estimated at $17,000 billion in 1995. Not surprisingly, production by TNCs is becoming the dominant mode of servicing foreign markets. With the dramatic fall in transport and communication costs over the last 40 years, firms are finding it efficient to locate different stages of production in different parts of the world. Foreign trade is becoming more and more intra-industry and intra-firm, especially for advanced economies. The TNC has also become the quintessential vehicle for knowledge and technology transfer. Significantly, the global assets of TNCs were estimated at over $8,000 billion in 1994, compared to global gross domestic investment of $5,681 billion.

Central to the process of globalization are the breath-taking improvements in communication and transportation. The technological breakthroughs in these areas have obliterated economic barriers of distance and, in consequence, facilitated the globalization process. The liberalization in the 1980s of African economies should be contextualized within the globalization process. A major consequence of this liberalization was that the predominantly raw material-based economies of African states were left at the mercy of the international markets. The Nigerian case is instructive. Liberalization led to the relaxation or even non-enforcement of existing rules and regulations guiding oil company operations in the Niger Delta and the making of policies that tended, in the main, to attract more foreign investment in the industry by introducing a new set of incentives to private foreign investors. Meanwhile, the environment from which the Niger Delta communities derive their sustenance was not protected. Consequently, the ecologically-fragile environment came under severe pressure as oil companies intensified their exploration and exploitation activities. This development generated firm opposition from the indigenes, especially the women who dominated the peasant and trading class. It could thus be said, as Kwanashie (1999:20) has argued, that globalization has 'created capacities for new and efficient responses to age-old problems'. The critical question is: are these capacities delivered fairly? It is in this context that globalization has been said to produce winners and losers.

For its proponents, globalization marks the dawn of universal equality, prosperity, peace and freedom (Scholte 1999). Through globalization, it is argued, efficient production processes are now possible as are cheaper products and a wider variety of services. Among the numerous claims of the proponents of globalization is the assertion that it engenders financial discipline in the economy and tackles the problems of unemployment, welfare, poverty, environment and crime, all within a global framework (Aina 1997; Onimode 2000; Rugumamu 2001).

The critics, for their part, regard the argument of the proponents of globalization as essentially Eurocentric (Aina 1997; Hoogvelt 1997; Korten 1996). Further, exploitation and marginalization, they argue, are the likely benefits that Nigerian-type countries stand to gain from globalization. 'To him that hath shall be given, from him that hath not shall be taken away', is how one critic described the distributive justice embedded in the globalization process (see Rugumamu 2001:15).

In the African context, this Biblical verse from St Matthew's Gospel certainly has the ring of truth. Since the 1980s, socio-economic conditions in Africa have considerably deteriorated, as the political economy of states become increasingly characterized by armed conflicts, debt crisis, dictatorships, famine, drought and dependency. It was under these inauspicious circumstances that African states were advised to liberalize their economies and adopt adjustment conditions to revamp their ailing economies. In this regard, critics have pointed out that not only do SAP and globalization derive from the same sources, but they are also interrelated and mutually reinforcing. Commenting on the relationship of SAP with globalization, Dembele (1999:74) has observed that 'globalization is the ultimate triumph of the neo-classical resurgence and in Africa it is the new face of adjustment'.

Furthermore, critics have exercised concerns over the failure of the proponents of globalization to highlight issues such as polarization, poverty, inequality, domination, social injustice, exploitation, coercion and conflict in their analyses. In the words of one analyst:

Instead, what we have are sugary notions of interdependence, global flows, exchanges…… Even when capitalism and capitalist restructuring are mentioned, one reads only of a benign, creative process producing new technologies and expanding opportunities. But there is little or nothing about monopolies, disruptions and dislocations of the labour and other markets, the emergence of a regulatory chaos and possible anomie and how these are being exploited for gains. Neither do we read of the pains of adjustment in the less industrialized nations, the spreading immiseration, social exclusion and alienation of an increasing number of people (Aina 1997:11-12)

This 'end of history' which was euphorically and triumphantly proclaimed by Francis Fukuyama (1992) is ill-advised because it cannot bring about a more egalitarian world. Rather, the neo-liberal doctrine which globalization represents will simply widen the existing gulf between the rich nations of the North and poor countries of the South. As Smith and Baylis have noted:

… Globalization allows the efficient exploitation of less well-off nations, and all in the name of openness. The technologies accompanying globalization are technologies that automatically benefit the richest countries in the world, and allow their interests to override local ones. So not only is globalization imperialist, it is also exploitative. The foregoing brings into sharp focus the dynamics of globalization, the place of the oil multinationals and the role of SAP in the process (Smith and Baylis 1998:10).

The last two issues will be discussed briefly in the following paragraphs.

The Place of Multinational Corporations

Multinational corporations, according to Miller (1995), are dominant actors in the world division of labour. Consequently, they play a central economic and political role in the countries in which they operate. They are pivotal to the drive towards global economic integration. In other words, the multinational corporations, it is argued, are the main conduits through which globalization takes place. As purveyors of capital and technology, multinationals wield considerable influence and power in the world economy, especially within Nigerian-type economies. A cursory look at the sheer volume of global capital flows, along with global investment flows and sales, shows that multinational corporations are a critical factor in the globalization process.

Indeed, it is on record that about 500 multinational corporations control 70 per cent of world trade, 80 per cent of foreign investment and 30 per cent of world GDP (Miller 1995). In the highly complex and competitive world of business, oil companies are arguably among the world's most profitable and powerful business enterprises. The incomes of individual oil companies far exceed that of many Nigerian-type countries. For example, in 1990, the Royal Dutch/ Shell Group posted a gross income of $132 billion. This was estimated to be 'more than the combined GNPs of Tanzania, Ethiopia, Nepal, Bangladesh, Zaire, Uganda, Nigeria, Kenya and Pakistan – countries that represent almost one-tenth of the world's population' (Miller 1995:35).

Furthermore, the United Nation's 1997 World Investment Report (The Economist 1997) shows that the multinationals raked in some $7 trillion in sales through their foreign affiliates. According to the Report, this amount is greater than the world's total export. With reference to global investment, the Report observed that at the end of 1996, the total stock of foreign direct investment, namely plant, equipment and property owned by businesses outside their home countries, stood at over $3 trillion. The key role which multinationals play in disseminating technology around the globe is amply reflected in the Report. As the Report indicates, 70 per cent of all international royalties on technology involve payments between parent firms and foreign affiliates.

From the above, it can be gleaned that the MNCs, including the oil companies, are the main forces behind global flows of capital, goods and services. It is not surprising, therefore, that their critics portray them as bullies, using their heft to exploit workers and natural resources with no regard for the economic well-being of any country or community. Conversely, advocates of multinationals view them as the ultimate triumph for global capitalism, offering advanced technology to underdeveloped countries and low-cost product to the developed ones.

As was stated before, there are, besides the MNCs, other important active forces behind globalization. Beyond these MNCs and the various multilateral channels, however, it must be emphasised that 'policies too have a major role to play by fostering and maintaining open trade and payments arrangements' (Kwanashie 1999:24). From this assertion, it can be inferentially deduced that states are also to a reasonable extent, agents of globalization. Through policies that seek to guarantee stability and protection to global capital, (African) states help to facilitate the rapid advance of globalisation.

As Nyamnjoh (2003:6) has rightly noted, 'what neo-liberalism wants of African governments are national and regional policies in tune with the profitability expectations of global capital, policies that minimize countervailing traditions, customs, world views and expectations of continuity'. The main concern of the MNCs with regard to the role of the African states in facilitating the globalization process is for these states to ensure that local labour and national interests are kept subservient to the interests and powers of big business.

The Role of the Structural Adjustment Programme (SAP)

The Structural Adjustment Programme (SAP), in its form and content, falls within the rubric of economic globalization. It has its roots in neo-liberal thinking and belief in the (efficient) role of the market forces. The Structural Adjustment Programme (SAP) came against the backdrop of the debt crisis in the early 1980s (Kiely 1998). The early 1970s witnessed the collapse of the Bretton Woods system of fixed exchange rates, following the devaluation of the US dollar against the price of gold. Consequently, a new system was to emerge which allowed for the operation of a system of floating exchange rates in the global economy. This period, 1973-74, was characterized, incidentally, by the dramatic rise in the price of crude oil. The exponential rise in the price of oil translated into huge revenues for the oil-producing countries, most of whom deposited these 'windfall profits' (Kiely 1998:3) in Western banks. The banks, in turn, loaned this money to some developing countries, notably those from Latin America, at relatively low rates of interest.

In the early 1980s, the international financial system came under severe pressure, as many Western Banks had lent far too much capital to some loan-seeking countries of the Third World. Saddled with increasing interest payments on their debts, these countries became unable to meet their debt obligations. In 1982, Mexico became the first in the long list of countries that were to declare a moratorium on their debt obligations.

A major outcome of the debt crisis was that the IMF and the World Bank, backed by governments committed to neo-liberal reforms, began to advocate policies that more or less reflected the neo-liberal paradigm (Kiely 1998). Beyond advocating policies, Hoogvelt (1997) argues that they were also commissioned and dispatched to the frontiers of the global economy to exact payments from and supervise the credits to the Third World. According to her, the IMF and the World Bank have been able in this capacity 'to profoundly affect the organization of production and trade in the periphery to the benefit of the core of the world capitalist system' (Hoogvelt 1997:166). This was largely achieved through the instrumentality of the Structural Adjustment Programme (SAP). As Hoogvelt again notes:

> Structural adjustment is the generic term used to describe a package of measures which the IMF, the World Bank and individual western aid donors have persuaded many developing countries to adopt during 1980s, in return for a new wave of loans (Hoogvelt 1997:167).

SAP was the neo-liberal solution to what was largely perceived as the inefficient 'orthodox' state-led development, including the Import-Substitution Industrialization (ISI) programme. It was the belief of the neo-liberal reformers that a sustainable strategy for Nigerian-type countries is the promotion of the private sector and the liberalization of their economies. The aim of SAP, as Leftwich has noted, 'was to shatter the dominant post-war, state-led development paradigm and overcome the problems of developmental stagnation by promoting open and free competitive market economies, supervised by minimal states' (Leftwich 1993:607). According to Hoogvelt (Hoogvelt 1997:168), the main conditions of IMF/World Bank proposals include 'currency devaluation, deregulation of prices and wages, reduction of public spending on social programmes and state bureaucracies, removal of food and other subsidies on basic necessities, trade liberalization, privatization of parastatal enterprises, and expansion of the export sector'.

In Nigeria, the adoption of SAP by the Babangida regime in June 1986 was largely occasioned by the national economic crisis. The crisis in question was, for a large part, a function of the oil price shocks that occurred in 1982, and again in 1986, when crude oil prices fell below $15 per barrel (Doyle 2002:163). Summarizing the general economic situation surrounding the adoption of SAP by the Nigerian ruling class, Ake notes that:

> Between 1973 and 1978, during Nigeria's first oil boom, oil revenue grew quickly, to more than 90 per cent of Nigeria's export revenue. This increase was matched by increased public expenditure, which quadrupled between 1973 and 1975. By 1976, expenditure already exceeded revenue. During the second oil boom between 1973 and 1985, the surge in oil revenue elicited such profligacy that real income began to decline rapidly, as much as 60 per cent between 1980 and 1983 when Nigeria recorded a negative growth rate of 6.7 per cent and a budget deficit rising to 13 per cent of GDP. Austerity measures instituted in 1982 and 1984 failed and the crisis deepened, especially with the sharp fall in oil prices in 1986, the worsening of the terms of trade, debt service obligations and a sharp fall in imports and exports (Ake 2001:83).

The implementation of SAP was meant to place further pressure on the oil industry and, in consequence, the Niger Delta, the main site of oil exploration and production. For instance, it was expected that oil revenues would underwrite the whole adjustment programme as well as the political transition programme that was being supervised by the military government. In accordance with IMF conditionality rules and the reality of dwindling oil prices, state policy became a matter of direct disengagement from the oil industry, and the encouragement of private foreign and local investments in the industry.

In a bid to increase oil revenues under the SAP project, a Memorandum Of Understanding (MoU) was signed between the government and the oil companies. Given the additional incentives that were included in the new MoU, the oil multinationals intensified oil exploration and production operation in the Niger Delta. Consequently, the fragile Niger Delta environment came under severe environmental degradation leading to further impoverishment of the people, as they became increasingly unable to engage in their traditional occupations of fishing, farming and trading. These were the general conditions under which the women of the oil-producing communities took up arms in defence of their environment. The state's response smacked of a classic rent collector: heavily armed troops were deployed to the restive communities, wher e women and young girls were beaten, abducted and raped (Manby 1999; Okonta and Douglas 2001).

The preceding amply demonstrates the role of SAP in the globalization of the Niger Delta environment. It also illustrates how adjustment, under the rubric of globalization, has detrimentally affected the peasants, especially the women of the Niger Delta oil communities. This is more so because 'structural adjustment has helped to tie the physical economic resources of the African region more tightly into serving the global system, while at the same time oiling the financial machinery by which wealth can be transported out of Africa and into the global system' (Hoogvelt 1997:171).

Globalization in the Context of the Niger Delta

The Niger Delta is the main site where oil exploration and production activities are carried out in Nigeria. Commercial production and export of oil began in 1956 following Shell-BP's discovery at Oloibiri, in present-day Bayelsa State. Given Shell's success, other oil multinationals such as Mobil (now Exxon-Mobil), Gulf (now Chevron-Texaco), Elf (now Total-Fina-Elf) and Agip came to Nigeria and acquired licences which also enabled them to start oil exploration and production activities in Nigeria. The major attractions for Nigeria's oil both then as now, among other things, are its low sulphur content, the generous incentives which the government placed before the oil companies, the country's relatively lenient oil mining regulations, as well as the proximity, safety and security of the Niger Delta environment relative to the volatile Middle East region.

The late 1960s witnessed the emergence of crude oil as a significant revenue earner for the Government. This development, however, coincided with the decline in the earnings from cash crops, which were hitherto the Government's main revenue earners. From the early 1970s, oil became the most important source of earnings for the Nigerian economy, growing from an insignificant 0.1 per cent in 1959 to 87 per cent in 1976 (Owabukeruyele 2000).

Today, 'oil revenues currently provides for 80 per cent of government revenues, 95 per cent of export receipts, and 90 per cent of foreign exchange earnings' (Douglas *et al*. 2003). Indeed, according to Dr Rilwanu Lukman, the former Presidential Adviser on Petroleum and Energy Matters, Nigerian government's earnings of $300 billion between 1970 and 1990 derived from the oil and gas industry (Faloseyi 2003). These huge revenues have been earned at an enormous cost to the people of the Niger Delta and their environment. Over four decades of crude oil exploration and production have laid the Niger Delta environment to waste. As the Sierra Club has noted:

> The oil industry has had devastating effects. Our report in 1993 found 'badly maintained and leaking pipe lines, polluted water, fountains of emulsified oil pouring into villages' fields, blow outs, and air pollution'. Farms and fishes are spoiled, and the mangrove swamps, which provide people with building and other materials and are a vital part of the eco-system, are disappearing. At the same time the people get little benefit from the immense wealth being generated. While the Federal government gets 80 per cent of the royalties and mining rents, 20 per cent goes to each State government; but the local people see little even of that (Sierra Club, no date).

The Sierra Club has been cited here to demonstrate the basic fact that the oil industry, as it is currently configured and controlled by the forces of globalization (the oil companies and the G7, IMF and World Bank), has impacted negatively on the livelihoods and well-being of the citizens of the region, especially the female peasants. Indeed, the enormous wealth that the Nigerian state has derived from the Niger Delta has benefited only the local and national elites, along with their transnational counterparts, while the vast majority of the people have continued to wallow in abject poverty. As Natufe (2001:7) has argued, the Niger Delta is 'representative of the exploitative nature of domestic and foreign capital'. So long as the presence of oil deepens the exploitation of the Niger Delta environment by the oil companies, the lot of female peasants in the region will remain unenviable. In other words, the paradox of poverty amid plenty will continue to remain an inescapable fact in the lives of the inhabitants, the female inhabitants in particular. Indeed, it is against this background of environmental devastation, exploitation, neglect, poverty and repression that we can begin to appreciate the heroic struggles of the women of the Niger Delta against the forces of globalization, namely 'the Nigerian state and the oil corporations (who) have a joint interest in maintaining silence about their activities' (Turner *et al*, 2002:34).

Globalization in the context of the Niger Delta is a western agenda that economically incapacitates and disempowers the rural poor, especially women, by targeting and appropriating their natural resources (petroleum, land, water and forestry), thereby denying them access to and control over the management of their environment. As Shiva (2001) has noted, the tendency of globalization to plunder resources and displace people from productive employment and livelihoods is facilitated by the alliance of undemocratic regimes with powerful forces of globalization, which centralize control over decision-making and resources as well. The impact of globalization in the Niger Delta can be seen in the dynamics of the contradictions it has thrown up across the entire oil-producing communities.

As already stated, petroleum has been the backbone of the Nigerian economy since the 1970s. However, the early 1980s saw the onset of the crisis in the global oil industry, which drastically reduced the amount of revenue accruable to the Nigerian state for the maintenance of its vast social infrastructure, unwieldy bureaucratic structures and mounting debt burden, among other critical constraints. In the face of the worsening economic crisis, the Government came under severe pressure to adopt the IMF-instigated economic adjustment programme. Among the conditions was that the oil industry should be deregulated and opened up to a free flow of oil multinational investment. The apparent objective of this economic policy was to intensify oil exploration by oil companies, to enable the State to meet its social and economic responsibilities, as well as service its huge foreign debts.

By intensifying petroleum exploration and exploitation in the Delta, the oil companies brought further pressure on the available scarce resources such as land and water, which were either alienated for oil industry facilities or polluted by oil company activities. This created serious contradictions in terms of 'worsening inequities in relation to access to and power over resources' (Obi 2000:51), thereby generating mutual animosity and, sometimes, leading to open clashes between two or more communities. Commenting on the linkages between corporate globalization and environmental security, Cyril Obi has remarked that:

> Globalization is one of the greatest threats to global environmental security. This is largely due to the ways it produces resource-scarcities, degradation, and sharpens social contradictions (Obi 2000:51).

Such contradictions as are engendered by economic globalization lie in what James Mittelman (2000:923) has referred to as 'a dialectic of inclusion and exclusion'.

The preceding discussion has provided useful contextual insights into the consequences of the interface between globalization and the Niger Delta ecosystem. As has been shown, the implications bode ill for the long-term viability of local economies and survival of the people of the oil belt, especially the women, who constitute the most vulnerable group of the rural poor in the region. As will be made clear later, the dialectical character of globalization, which Mittelman referred to in his analysis, is well illustrated by the women's demand for social and environmental justice through effective grassroots women's movements across the oil-producing communities (see Turner and Oshare 1993; Turner *et al.* 2001).

Disempowerment, Marginalization and Exclusion Through Globalization: The Travails of the Niger Delta Women

> The environmental degradation of the Ogoni environment affects we women more than men. This is because we women do most of the peasant farming, that is the main work of the Ogoni people… (Deborah Robinson's Ogoni: *The Struggle Continues*, p.65).

This assertion mirrors the experiences of rural women in the oil-producing communities. It also explains why women are usually found at the forefront of the struggle against environmental injustice and social neglect perpetrated by the transnational oil corporations, the most powerful proponents of the globalization forces. The heavy burden which women now have to bear was underscored in a comprehensive report by a group of nine US activists, academics and journalists after a ten-day fact-finding visit to the Niger Delta communities in September 1999. Commenting on the impact of loss of land and resources by the communities to oil company activities, the Report notes that, 'The diminished productivity and viability of local economies due to the environmental and social degradation caused by oil exploitation has affected the lives of women in unique ways' (Esparza and Wilson 1999:10). Since the great majority of the women folk have been marginalized and disempowered and, as a consequence, unable to perform their traditional roles within their families, they have inevitably been forced to adopt alternative coping strategies. The harsh situation has forced many of them into prostitution as a means of survival (Esparza and Wilson 1999). To be sure, this trend has generated its own contradictions within the households as well as within the larger society of the oil-producing communities. In many cases, for example, younger wives have reportedly abandoned their matrimonial homes and eloped with other men working for the oil multinationals. And for a society that is predominantly patriarchal, social mores have been severely undermined.

It should be noted, however, that the marginalization, disempowerment and exclusion of women in the Niger Delta did not begin with the introduction of economic adjustment. However, insofar as it became a strong point for 'indigenous feminists' (Turner and Oshare 1993:330) to latch on to in their fight against environmental injustice in the 1990s, the mindless exploitation of nature (land, water and oil) by the forces of globalization alone can be held responsible. A 1993 World Bank Report on the impact of globalization on women lends credence to the experience of women in the Niger Delta (see Ake 2001:64) As a result of globalization, the report noted, the lot of women has steadily deteriorated: they must struggle, sometimes dangerously, to eke out an existence out of dwindling resources. Elaborating the reasons why Ogoni women have championed the struggle against increasing marginalization, disempowerment and repression in the Niger Delta oil communities, Diana Wiwa notes that:

> The constant acquisition of new territory for oil exploitation, and resultant pollution from the industry, has left the Ogoni women with no means to feed or support their families. Women have to go further away from home to find unpolluted water for their domestic chores. Their children have not received employment in the oil industry (a mere fifty Ogoni were employed until 1993, mainly as cleaners and drivers), making young men and women a continuing responsibility for their mothers long after they have been independent. These changes have brought a resultant rise of tension in the home. Testimonies of older women confirm that in the past there was less tension (Wiwa 1997:13).

What is underscored in this citation is that the women (and also children) are the most affected groups. They suffer most because, unlike the men, they cannot easily migrate to the urban centres, to start life afresh. It underlines too the reason why the women have championed the fight back from below against capital-driven globalization. It also highlights the emergence within the predominantly patriarchal culture of the Niger Delta, the reconfiguration of existing gender relations or what has been described as 'gendered class alliance'. This occurs 'when women organized autonomously against the exploitation of oil corporations and local male dealers' (Turner et al. 2001:21). Often, the alliance is reinforced when men forsake the male deal and join the ranks of the autonomously organized women to challenge capital and male dealers within their communities.

Following the example cited elsewhere of the Ogharefe and Ekpan women in 1984 and 1986, respectively, women from other parts of the region have confronted the oil companies when their farms and fish ponds have been polluted. The Ogoni, the Egi and Eket women have at different times in the 1990s confronted the oil companies and voiced the demands of their communities to the companies (see Saro-Wiwa 1995; Wiwa 1997). At times, the demonstrations and protests turned bloody, as happened in April 1993 when a crowd of Ogoni women demonstrated peacefully against Wilbros, an American pipeline contractor firm working for Shell in the village of Biara. As Ken Saro-Wiwa (1995:156) reports:

> The women held twigs as they had been advised to do to indicate that they were protesting peacefully. The soldiers emptied their live ammunition on them. Eleven people were wounded, among them Mrs Karalole Korgbara, a mother of five children who was shot in the left arm - it was subsequently amputated.

Furthermore, during the long-drawn-out (1993-1999) military occupation of Ogoni in Rivers State and the one year-long militarization (1998-1999) of Ijawland in Bayelsa State, women were the worst victims of state-sponsored repression (*Tempo*, August 3, 1995; Robinson 1996; Banjo 1998; Ekine 2001). For them, it was a double struggle in which they were raped and beaten; their husbands and sons were killed or jailed, and their daughters either raped or taken away. Also, during this period, the women were constantly harassed by soldiers who extorted money from them and even prevented them from going to the farm or market. In most cases, trading activities became impossible, since market squares were constant targets, where goods were looted and/or set ablaze, and valuable personal effects as well as money carted away from homes (Wiwa 1997:13).

Like their Ogoni, Umududja and Ijaw counterparts, the Egi women have had their own fair share of confrontation and repression at the hands of companies. In September 1998, the women took to the streets to protest against the activities of Elf, the giant French oil company. Their demands centred around the provision of basic social amenities such as water and electricity. During the protest, the women were quick to emphasize the stark contrast between their own residential areas and those of Elf workers, which were well supplied with basic amenities. The women also complained about the destruction of their farms and fish ponds by Elf and the consequent loss of their sources of income and food.

Two months later, in November 1998, the Egi women were out on the streets once again. Despite the formidable presence of over a hundred armed Mobile Policemen, the women marched intrepidly towards the Elf gas installation plant and occupied it. They re-stated their earlier demands for water, electricity and compensation for loss of livelihood. Beyond this, the women also demanded the immediate release of Egi youths who had been detained. As a result of their pressure, 'the youths were released, only to be charged in court' (Turner 2001:29). Barely one year later in August 1999, about five thousand women from the Egi women's movement again laid siege on Elf's facility, shutting it for one day. This time, they demanded, non-violently, for clean air and water, as well as Elf's investment in community development projects. According to Esparza and Wilson (1999), Elf's reaction was to deploy about forty local youths to whom it allegedly paid $2,000 each to aggressively break up the non-violent protest. Furthermore, Elf Oil Company is on record as having 'paid the youths another $75,000 to sign an agreement with the company, claiming that their youth group represented the entire Egi community' (Esparza and Wilson 1999:16). Elf's behaviour is indicative of oil companies' insensitivity towards host communities' plight and just demands, as well as attempts to divide and rule, rather than investing in genuine and productive community development projects within their host communities.

Today, the situation is much the same. The women of the Niger Delta remain as marginalized and economically disempowered as ever, waiting for the dividends of globalization! Apparently impatient to wait any longer for promises from companies that treat them as cows to be milked, the women are again up in arms against those oil companies.

In July 2002, a two-week long sit-out protest was organized by hundreds of Itsekiri women from Ugborodo and Ogidigben when they occupied the Chevron-Texaco's Excravos Tank Farm, demanding, like their counterparts in other oil communities, the provision of basic social amenities such as water and electricity. They complained about the loss of their traditional occupations as a result of Chevron-Texaco's activities, which have devastated their farmlands and polluted their fish ponds. The women also asked Chevron-Texaco to employ their children, so 'that we the mothers will survive' (Awowede 2002:44).

A few days later, following the resolution of the Escvavos Tank Farm occupation, hundreds of aggrieved peasant women from the Ijaw communities of Gbaramatu and Egbema laid siege to four oil flow stations belonging, again, to the Chevron-Texaco oil corporation. For almost two weeks, the women occupied the flow stations of Abiteye, Maraba/Otunana, Dibi and Olero creek. Like their counterparts from Ugborodo and Ogidigben, they charged Chevron-Texaco with neglect and environmental degradation. The Ijaw women, however, went one step than their Itsekiri counterparts. They demanded, among other things, that each protester be paid the sum of two million naira as recompense for the two-week long occupation, which they argued, had cost each of them her trading and/or farming. A twenty million naira micro-credit scheme was also demanded by the women for each of the ten-odd communities that made up Gbaramatu and Egbema (Awowede 2002). The Ijaw women later called off their siege, as did the women from the Itsekiri communities of Ugborodo and Ogidigben, following the signing of a Memorandum of Understanding (MoU) between them and Chevron-Texaco.

Of great importance in the women's anti-globalization struggle in Nigeria's Delta region is the direct, resolute and non-compromising attitude that these grassroots women have adopted in their demands for environmental remediation and recompense. Given that the Niger Delta oil communities are predominantly patriarchal in nature, it becomes easier to appreciate the daring courage exhibited by these women. Indeed, it is reasonable to suggest that these female peasants and traders decided to pick up the gauntlet in frustration as well as in defiance of their men folk who habitually engaged in 'male deals' with the oil companies at the expense of the communities (Turner and Oshare 1993). It is also fair to observe that the struggles of the Niger Delta women against the onslaught of economic globalization on their subsistence is a testament to the fact that even in patriarchal African societies such as those of the Nigeria's Delta region, there exist channels through which women can fight for their rights.

In the light of the above, it is clear that from the embattled Itsekiri communities of Ugborodo and Ogidigben, to the Ijaw communities of Gbaramatu and the Urhobo women of Ekpan, all in Delta State, to the Ilaje community in Ondo State, the women of the Niger Delta are waging renewed battles against 'anti-corporate, anti-war movement for globalization from below' (Turner and Brownhill 2001:805). The following statements by Queen Uwawa and Christiana Mene, respectively, are instructive:

> For 38 years Chevron has been taking oil from Escravos (with) nothing to show for it, no development. We used to catch fish and crayfish for food, but that is not possible. The fishes and crayfish have gone away. They left because Chevron has polluted rivers and creeks (Awowede 2002:44).

> We want Chevron to employ our children. If Chevron does that we, the mothers, will survive, we will see food to eat. Our farms are all gone due to Chevrons pollution of our water. We used to farm cassava, okro, pepper and others. Now all the places we have farmed are sinking. That is why we told Chevron that Escravos women and Chevron are at war (ibid).

The foregoing analysis has shown how globalization has blighted local subsistence production by destroying the physical environment of the people of Niger Delta. The analysis has also demonstrated that women, especially the farmers and traders, have been badly hit in the process. As a consequence, they have been in the vanguard of demonstrations and protests against the devastation of the environment on which they depend for their livelihoods and survival. This struggle has, of course, led to some transformations in gender relations within the communities of the oil-producing region. The emergence of gendered class alliances amid long-established patriarchal structures has enormously strengthened the gathering of the wind of globalization from below.

Implications

In the light of the above, what, we may ask, are the likely implications of all this for the women of Nigeria's Delta region? The implications are several and range from economic, socio-cultural to political. One of the significant economic implications is that the women are no longer able to perform their traditional roles as farmers, traders or even as mothers. Given the vital role women play in the local economy, to destroy their main sources of income is tantamount to destroying the entire communities. Nowhere is the reality of economic redundancy more keenly felt than among the fisherwomen and the fish merchants, as decade of pollution have virtually decimated the fish population in the creeks and rivers that crisscross the Delta region. Indeed, it was gathered that one of the victims of this economic displacement from Ughelli, Delta State, now spends much of her time in alternating visits among her children who live in different parts of the country.

As already pointed out, prostitution has become more rampant in the last ten to fifteen years. In this regard, Esparza and Wilson's (1999:10) report has commented that the number of fatherless children has increased during this period. Expatriate oil workers and their well paid Nigerian counterparts in the oil and oil servicing companies (who the locals preoperatively refer to as 'Abuja men' because their financial recklessness can only be compared to that of the politicians in Abuja, Nigeria's capital city) are said to be the major culprits. One unfortunate outcome of this trend, according to the people, is that many homes have been broken as a result. Joy Yowika (1999), an Ogoni woman activist, has described this as a violation of women's rights and has consequently embarked on a project of ensuring that the expatriate fathers are made to take responsibility of such children. According to her, the oil companies have been co-operative in this respect.

Globalization has also impacted the people's culture. Culturally, certain practices were preserved for women. For example, the 'fattening room' is a popular traditional practice among Ogoni women. A woman usually undergoes the 'fattening room' process after the birth of her first child and this usually lasts for one year. During the period, she receives instructions on local medicines and how to care for her child and look after the home. As a rule, she is attended to by elderly women as well as women from her own family. She is to rest and remain within the confines of the compound for the duration of the event. It is reported that given the pressures the young women have to contend with, the practice, when it takes place at all, rarely exceeds two months. Commenting on this fast-dying cultural heritage, Diana Wiwa has remarked that:

> loss of the fattening room and other traditions led the Ogoni women to make a conscious decision to organize against the oil industry on their land - a force they saw as being clearly responsible for cultural degradation in Ogoni (Wiwa 1997:13).

It would be misleading if our analysis thus far suggested that globalization is devoid of any positive aspects. To be sure, the realities of deepening marginalization, disempowerment and exclusion experienced by women in the Niger Delta over the past fifteen years stem largely from the processes of globalization. As it devastates their environment and displaces women from productive enterprises and livelihoods, globalization paradoxically creates the objective conditions which politically empower the women, in terms of uniting them against their common enemy - the powerful oil transnationals. This unity of purpose can be observed across the oil-producing communities, where some of the most effective and dynamic grassroots women's movements in Africa have emerged. Notable among these are the Federation of Ogoni Women's Associations (FOWA) and the Egi Women's Movement. These have been at the forefront of the movement for globalization from below, through their gendered class alliances and their international networking for co-ordinated action (Turner *et al* 2001; Turner and Brownhill, 2001). Through these mediums, the rural women of the Niger Delta have been able to participate in the global fight back against economic globalization.

Conclusion

An attempt has been made in this study to analyse the impact of globalization on unwaged women, namely peasant farmers and traders in Nigeria's Delta region. The pressures engendered by globalization in the oil-producing communities, it is argued, have given rise to new contradictions, whilst heightening old ones. This is evident in the ease with which globalization has undermined the active role the women used to play at home and in the local economy. Consequently, many rural women have become economically disempowered or even redundant, leading to a situation where many have either reconciled themselves to their fate or been forced to seek alternative coping strategies. However at the same time, globalization, as we have seen, has been instrumental in the modest successes these women have thus far been able to achieve in terms of grassroots mobilization, in terms of their effective actions against corrupt and collaborating male dealers in their communities and in terms of international networking, through the female elite in their society, against corporate globalization. This is not to suggest that there was nothing like local mobilization by women in the Niger Delta before the era of globalization. On the contrary, documented evidence exists of local women's mobilization in that region (see for instance Turner and Oshare 1993; Turner *et al.* 2001), before the onset of globalization in the 1980s.

However, the nature, scale and sophistication of the contemporary social movements have reduced the earlier ones to mere child's play. A lot of variables, to be sure, are at work here. And these include, among others, the contradictions thrown up by globalization itself. The milestone changes that have attended the global environment over the past decade and the crop of environmentally-conscious leadership that has emerged from among the women folk themselves are highly instructive. Indeed, the character of leadership provided by the likes of Diana Wiwa, Grace Ekanem, Joi Yowika, Annie Brisibe and Sokari Ekine, to name just a few, has accounted in no small measure for the cohesion, vision and resolve that have been exhibited by the women in their environmental rights campaigns. Beyond this, the leadership should intensify their grassroots mobilization by sensitizing the rural women on issues that have an impact on globalization, environmental justice and human rights. Also, the existing social movements should work and coordinate their activities with other international non-governmental organizations and anti-globalization movements around the world, as this will keep the local social movements abreast of how similar struggles are being waged by exploited and repressed rural people in the other parts of the world. This is the only way the women in Niger Delta can win the battle against global capital and their local collaborators.

Bibliography

Aina, T.A., 1997, *Globalization and Social Policy in Africa: Issues and Research Directions,* Working Paper series 6196, Dakar, Senegal: CODESRIA.

Ake, C., 2001, *Democracy and Development in Africa,* Ibadan: Spectrum Books.

Amin, S., 1992, *The Empire of Chaos,* New York: Monthly Review Press.

Appadurai, A., 2001, 'Grassroots Globalization and the Research Imagination' in Arjun Appadurai (ed.) *Globalization,* Durham: Duke University Press.

Awowede, O., 2002, 'The Case against Chevron', *Insider Weekly,* August 19.

Banjo, W.S., 1998, *The Politics of United Nations Fact-Finding Mission in Nigeria,* African Research Bureau Monograph Series Vol. 1. No 3.

CRP (Constitutional Rights Project), 1999, *Land, Oil and Human Nigeria's Delta Region,* Lagos: CRP.

Dembele, D.M., 1999, 'The Political Economy of Debt, Adjustment and Globalization in Africa', in Yassine Fall (ed.) *Africa: Gender, Globalization and Resistance,* A WORD Book series.

Douglas, O. *et al.,* 2003, 'Alienation and Militancy in the Niger Delta: An Alternative View', www.fpif.org/papers/nigeria2003_body.html

Doyle, J., 2002, *Riding the Dragon: Royal Dutch Shell and the Fossil Fire,* Boston: Environmental Health Fund.

Egwu, S., 1998, *Structural Adjustment, Agrarian Change and Rural Ethnicity in Nigeria,* Uppsala: Nordiska Africa Institute.

Egwu, S.G., 2001, *Ethnic and Religious Violence in Nigeria,* Abuja: AFRIGOV, p49.

Ekine, S., 2001, *Blood and Oil,* London: Centre for Democracy and Development.Embong, A.R., 2000, 'Globalization and Transnational Class Relations: Some Problems of Conceptualisation', *Third World Quarterly,* Volume 21 Number 6.

Esparza, E. and M. Wilson, 1999, *Oil for Nothing: Multinational Corporations, Environmental Destruction, Death and Impunity in the Niger Delta,* USA: In works press.

Eteng, I., 1998, 'The Nigerian State, Oil Exploration and Community Interests: Issues and Perspectives', in Funmi Adewunmi (ed.) *Oil Exploration and Exploitation, the State and Crisis in Nigeria's Oil-Bearing Enclave,* Lagos: Friedrich Ebert Foundation.

Faloseyi, M., 2003, 'Oil, Gas Fetch Nigeria $300bn in 20 years', *Punch,* Lagos, August 5.

Fregene, P., 1998, 'Oil Exploration and Production Activities: The Socio-Economic and Environmental Problems in Warri Division – Itsekiri Homeland' in Funmi Adewumi (ed.) *Oil Exploration and Exploitation, the State and Crisis in Nigeria's Oil-Bearing Enclave,* Lagos: Friedrich Ebert Foundation.

Fukuyama, F., 1992, *The End of History and the Last Man,* New York: Free Press.

Gbadegesin, A., 1997, 'The Impact of Oil Exploration Production Activities on the Environment: Implications For Peasant Agriculture', Seminar Paper on Oil and The Environment organised by Friedrich Ebert Foundation's in Port Harcourt.

Hoogvelt, A., 1997, *Globalization and the Post-colonial World: The New Political Economy of Development*, London: Macmillan Press Limited.

Ibrahim, J., 2002, 'Notes on Globalization and the Marginalization of Africa', Dakar, Senegal: CODESRIA *Bulletin,* Numbers 3 and 4.

Jessop, B., 2003, 'The Future of the State in an Era of Globalization', *International* Politics and Society 3.

Kiely, R.., 1998, 'The Crisis of Global Development' in Ray Kiely *et al.* (eds.) *Globalization and the Third World*, London: Routledge.

Korten, D.C., 1996, *When Corporations Rule the World*, London: Earth-Scan Publications.

Kwanashie, M., 1999, 'Concepts and Dimensions of Globalization' in *Globalization and Nigeria's Economic Development*, Ibadan: The Nigerian Economic Society.

Leftwich, A., 1993, 'Governance, democracy and Development in the Third', *Third World Quarterly*, 14 (3).

Manby, B., 1999, *The Price of Oil: Corporate Responsibility and Human Rights Violations in Nigeria's Oil Producing Communities*, USA: Human Watch.

Miller, A.L., 1995, *The Third World in Global Environmental Politics*, Colorado: Lynne Rienner Publisher, Inc.

Mittelman, J.H., 2000, 'Globalization: Captors and Captive', *Third World Quarterly*, 14 (3).

Mohan, G., 2000, 'The Environmental Aspects of Adjustment', in Giles Mohan *et al.* (eds.) *Structural Adjustment: Theory, Practice and Impacts*, London, New York: Routledge.

Natufe, I., 2001, 'Resistance Politics: An Essay on the Future of Nigeria', http://waado.org/Niger Delta/Essays/Politics Page.html

Nnoli, O. 2000, 'Globalization and Democracy in Africa', in Dani W. Nabudere (ed.) *Globalization and the Post-Colonia African State,* Harare: African Association of Political Science.

Nyamnjoh, F.B., 2003, 'Globalization, Boundaries and Livelihoods: Perspectives on Africa' *Philosophia Africana*, Vol. 6. No 2, August.

Obasek, P.J., 1999, 'Policies and Strategies for Dealing with the Problems of Globalization', in *Globalization and Nigeria's Economic Development*, Ibadan: The Nigerian Economic Society.

Obi, C.I., 2000, 'Globalised Images of Environmental Security in Africa', *Review of African Political Economy*, No. 83:47-62.

Obi, C.I., 2001, *The Changing Forms of Identity Politics in Nigeria under Economic Adjustment: The Case of the Minority Oil Moment*, Uppsala: Nordiska African Institute.

Ohiorhenuan, J.F.E., 1998, 'The South in an Era of Globalization', *Cooperation South*, Number Two.

Okonta, I. and O. Douglas, 2001, *Where Vultures Feast: 40 Years of Shell in the Niger Delta*, Ibadan: Kraft Books Limited.

Onimode, B., 2000, *Africa in the World of 21st Century*, Ibadan: Ibadan University Press.

Onosode, G.O., 2003, *Environmental Issues and Challenges of the Niger Delta; Perspectives from the Niger Delta Environmental Survey*, Lagos; Lilybank Property and Trust Limited.

Ovirire, B.G.O, 1998, 'Oil and the Environment: Our Blessings and Woes' in Funmi Adewumi (ed.) *Oil Exploration and Exploitation, the State and Crisis in Nigeria's Oil-Bearing Enclave.*

Owabukeruyele, W., 2000, 'Hydrocarbon exploitation, Environmental degradation and Poverty in the Delta Region of Nigeria', http://www.waado.org/Environment/Petrol Pollution/Env. Economics html

Redclift, M. and C. Sage, 1994, 'Introduction', in M. Redclift and C. Sage (eds.) *Strategies for Sustainable Development: Local Agendas for the Southern Hemisphere*, Chichester: John Wiley and Sons.

Robinson, D., 1996, *Ogoni: The Struggle Continues*, Switzerland: World Council of Churches.

Rugumanu, S. M., 2001, *Globalization and Africa's Future: Towards Structural Stability, Integration and Sustainable Development:* AAPS Occasional Paper Series Volume 5, Number 2 Books.

Saro-Wiwa, K., 1995, *A Month and Day: A Detention Diary*, Ibadan: Spectrum Books.

Scholte, J.A., 1999, 'Global Capitalism and the State', *International Affairs*, Volume 73. 3, 427-452.

Scholte, J.A., 1997, 'The Globalization of World Politics' in J. Baylis and S. Smith (eds.) *The Globalization of World Politics: and Introduction to International Relations*, Oxford: Oxford University Press.

Shiva, V., 2001, 'Globalization and Talibanization', *Outlook*, India October 30.

Sierra Club: Environmental Update, Human Rights and the Environmental, International Campaigns: Nigeria. Website: www.sierraclub.org/human- rights/nigeria/background/survival.asp

Smith, S. and J. Baylis, 1998, Introduction, in J. Baylis and S. Smith (eds.) *The Globalization of World Politics: An Introduction to International Relations*, Oxford: Oxford University Press.

Tandon, Y., 2000, 'Globalization and Africa's Options', in D.M. Nabudere (ed.) *Op. cit. Tempo*, August 3, 1995.

The Economist, December 4, 1997.

Turner, T. and M. Oshare, 1993, 'Women's Uprising against the Nigerian Oil Industry', *Canadian Journal of Development Studies*, Vol. XIV, No.3.

Turner, T. *et al.*, 'Fightback from the Commons: General Class Alliances and Petroleum Struggles in Nigeria's Oil belt: 1980-2002' *Cambridge Review of International Affairs*, Winter 2001/2, Vol. XIV, No. 3.

Turner, T. and Leigh S. Brownhill, 2001, 'Gender, Feminism and the Civil Commons: Women and the Anti-Corporate, Anti-War Movement for Globalization from Below', *Canadian Journal of Development Studies*, Vol. XXII.

Wiwa, D., 1997, 'The Role of Women in the Struggle for Environmental Justice in Ogoni', Delta, 3 October.

Yowika, Y. J., 1999, 'In Niger Delta, Women Suffer Most', *Survival*, No 001, August.

5

Globalization and the Question of Women Smugglers in East Africa: Observations of a Cross Kenya-Uganda Boundary (1980-2002)

Samwel Ong'wen Okuro

Defining Globalization and the Place of Africa in the Global Debate

To many people, globalization has meant a wide range of complex and contradictory processes and a phenomena characterizing contemporary history. It has become a powerful but malleable metaphor that accommodates widely divergent theoretical, empirical, and ideological paradigms, positions, and possibilities. For its triumphalist supporters, globalization is celebrated as inevitable and progressive, marking the end of history, while for its detractors it reinforces global economic inequalities, political disenfranchisement, and environmental degradation. Depending on how it is defined and perceived, globalization has its advocates, adversaries and those who are ambivalent (Zeleza 2002); it has several conflicting meanings, and in fact the debate about how to characterize globalization and its impact is so contentious that the only consensus is that there is no consensus.

For instance, there is a line of thinking that regards globalization as a compression of time and space. In other words, with new technologies that speed transactions and shrink distances, both time barriers and spatial differences are lessened. It is a part of the inherent unfolding modernity and a spur towards interconnectedness. We live in an increasingly interdependent, de-territorialized world, created by the emergence of new transnational information and computer technologies which tear asunder the spatial-temporal divides and distances of the past and they shrink the world, if not into a global village, then into neighbourhoods that are more familiar with each other. The motive is to diminish barriers to the flows of goods, services, information, capital, technology and people.

In his introductory remarks to the *Third World Quarterly Journal of Emerging Areas*, a special issue capturing globalization, James Mittelman admitted that, in the whole debate of space and time compression, one must look at the link between this compression and social relations, because globalization processes are not socially and politically neutral. Moreover, globalization is not yet a total phenomenon, as sizable pockets of the globe remain largely removed from it (Mittelman 2000:917-929). It is worth stressing, and I totally agree with Mittelman, that globalization is not a single, unified process, but instead a set of interactions that may best be approached from different observation points yet cognisant of the central theme that international connections have indeed grown in speed and with an intensity never witnessed before.

In summary, firstly, globalization may be seen as a complex historical process. The trajectories differ in various regions of the world, although all are directly or indirectly tied to the central institutions and growth mechanisms of the world economy. Second, globalization may be understood as a material process closely related to the accumulation of capital. It is caught up with the innovations in capitalism, especially the inner workings of competition, pressure that may be called hyper-competition. Third, globalization may be regarded as an ideology – the neo-liberal belief in free market and faith in the beneficial role of competition (Cox 1996 and Mittelman 1996). Hence, globalization is an extensive set of interactions, dialectically integrating and disintegrating economies, polities and societies around the world.[1] The globalization trend, it is assumed, offers many gains in productivity, technological advances, higher living standards, more jobs, broader access to consumer products at lower cost, widespread dissemination of information and knowledge, reduction in poverty in some parts of the world, and a release from traditional hierarchies in many countries. Yet, there is a dark side of globalization: the integration of markets threatens tightly-knit communities and sources of solidarity, dilutes local culture, and portends a loss of control, particularly in very poor countries, such that, whatever the position one adopts, the reality is that globalization creates both opportunities and constraints. In short there are winners and losers, the majority of the latter being confined exclusively to developing economies such as Kenya and Uganda.

As a student studying history and being an African for that matter, I must admit at this point that the forces driving globalization and globalization itself are not new in Africa and neither are its consequences. globalization is actually the fourth stage of outside penetration of the continent by forces, which have had negative social consequences on the African people's integral development. This penetration has taken place over five hundred years: the first was slavery, the second was colonialism, followed by neo-colonialism and now globalization. This process is tied to the expansion and dynamics of slavery and capitalism and their contradictions. Capitalism, as we know it today, was born as part of the global system. Indeed, resorting to the international system has been a constant practice in the history of capitalism.

David Held once argued:

> While the diffusion of European power mainly occurred through the medium of sea-going military and commercial endeavours, Europe became connected to a global system of trade and production relations. At the centre of the latter were new and expanding capitalistic economic mechanisms, which had their origins in the sixteenth century, or in what is sometimes called the long sixteenth century, running from about 1450 to 1640. Capitalism was from the beginning an international affair, capital never allowed its aspirations to be determined by national boundaries alone. Consequently, the emergence of capitalism ushered in a fundamental change in the world order: it made possible, for the first time, genuinely global interconnections among states and societies; it penetrated the distant corners of the world and brought far-reaching changes to the dynamics and nature of political rule (Held 1993:30).

And, like capitalist modernization, globalization proceeded unevenly as in the earlier phases. Seen in this way, the world has been globalizing for a long time, although the process only accelerated rapidly during the course of the twentieth century and onwards.

The process reached Africa under the auspices of the World Bank and other bilateral donors to African countries, who adopted a wide range of policy reforms of African economies after a decade of depression (Pheko 1999; Lim 1999; Riham el-Lakany 1999 and Horgan 2001). The forces crystallised under the Structural Adjustment Programmes (SAPs), which have been the key instruments through which countries are expected to harness the benefits of globalization by pursuing policies that were intended to open their economies to global competition, foreign investment and technology. It was hoped that through these policies, African economies would be tightly connected within the world capitalist system, and that capitalism would survive in Africa.

However, what quickly comes to mind in Africa when one talks about globalization is increasing liberalization, privatization and deregulation, to the extent that the last two to three decades have been spent opening up economies through liberalization of trade and deregulation. These policies have been formulated and advocated for by the Bretton Woods Institutions since the 1980s. The programme involves the disbursement of trenched support in the form of SAPs or Sector Adjustment Loans, typically on concessionary terms, which are conditional upon policy reform. In fact, trade reforms are absolutely central to SAPs because there are powerful economic arguments in favour of free trade particularly.

However, summaries of literature emanating from the social, political and economic impact of SAPs are disappointing. The process of Africa's integration into the world capitalist system has been disastrous. And since the end of the 1970s, conditions have considerably deteriorated in most economies and social sectors. Indeed, the conditions have become worse than they were in the 1960s. The number of Africans enduring absolute poverty increased by almost two-thirds in the first half of the 1980s, accounting for more than half of the total population. The number of African women living in poverty reached nearly 50 per cent in the 1980s. Up until today, as I will show, the situation has not improved; Africans, particularly the women, are yet to find a better story to tell about SAPs. Zeleza may have been right when he opined that:

> Clearly, Africa and globalization have a long and unhappy history together. Africa's purported marginalization from globalization hardly means that the continent is not integrated into the world, as such, but that it is integrated in a subordinate position. The degree of this subordination may have changed in recent decades, but its basic structure has not altered fundamentally since the emergence of modern world system. In a large sense, then, for African globalization represents an old problem in new context: hegemony of Northern processes, practices and perspectives (Zeleza 2002:7-8).

Globalization, Trade Liberalization and Women

As explained above, globalization is a very complex process supported by several policies, one of which is liberalization. globalization and liberalization are integrally interdependent and mutually reinforcing. While globalization is the substantive process of both economic and technological expansion, promoting the opening up and the integration of the entire world into and under one capitalist economic system, liberalization provides the policy lubricant and produces an appropriate regulatory/legal framework to ensure the smooth and speedy implementation of the process. Simplistically, trade liberalization is all about reduction of tariffs and trade barriers to permit more foreign competition and foreign investment in the economy. However, in the context of this paper, trade liberalization will connote the relaxation or elimination of tariffs and removal of duties and/or quotas on export; alterations in non-tariff barriers such as import quotas and quantitative restrictions; changes in licensing and direct allocation of foreign exchange and in specific regulations for products; and removal or relaxation of export subsidies.

Bienen (1990) provides a detailed analysis of the debates of trade liberalization in Africa. He argues that many African countries have used tariff and non-tariff barriers to further import-substitution strategies. For example, in the 1970s, Kenya placed increasing reliance on import control and quantitative restrictions to save foreign exchange and to encourage domestic manufacturing. This was administered in different ways. There were times when Kenya reduced quantitative restrictions, lowered and rationalized tariffs, and applied minimum tariff rates on goods previously exempted or that had very low tariffs. The idea was to reduce effective protection levels by reducing the spread between the highest and lowest tariffs. The Kenyan government's halting steps towards trade liberalization in the 1980s were typical. During this period, African governments backed off from trade reforms either because their competitive trade positions did not improve or they were losing foreign exchange. The Kenyan government moved from restrictive licensing by the Ministry of Commerce to restrictive foreign exchange allocation introduced by the Central Bank (Branson 1984).

The success of these initiatives depended on the condition of the private local manufacturing industry that a country had at stake in order to benefit from a protected market and here Kenya scored favourably. However, these policies tended to benefit powerful civil servants, politicians, the military and those living in the urban areas (due to food subsidies). The civilian and military employees of the State have always had direct economic interests in the maintenance of state-dominated trade and hence political considerations have become a major factor working against trade liberalization. That is why, on the whole, many African countries have undertaken stabilization policies, including devaluation of their currencies. Others have embarked on fundamental public sector reform programmes, but few have liberalized their trade extensively. However, as we move further into these globalized times, trade liberalization is increasingly regarded as a panacea to the problems of the developing countries. Underlying its prescriptions are the neoclassical economic assumptions that markets work and are generally completive and that market signals are good guides to efficient resource allocation.

In examining the impact of trade policy in Africa, Bienen (1990) contends that African governments must account for the extent to which factors of production are mobile. Also, they must assess their own strengths and weaknesses and the prospects for political instability that may arise not only from economic policies but also from ethnic tensions and institutional factors in their countries. This is so because trade liberalization policies lend themselves to incremental change in that tariffs can be removed product by product and also altered by degree. Equally, trade liberalization policies may also alter the power, status and income of institutionally-based groups as well as occupational ones. Moreover, these policies alter the relative welfare of different social groups which can conveniently be defined in terms of the owner of factors of production, different sectors (say, agricultural versus industrial or import verses export) and in terms of gender, particularly women verses men.

Using the concept of relative price changes, intersectoral factor mobility and ownership of factors of production, Bienen (1990) divides society into gainers and losers from liberalization policies, but while he expands his analysis on the losers and gainers to institutional and ethnic terms as well as economic ones, he pays no particular attention to the gender differential impact of these policies. He however succeeds in pointing out that the whole panoply of import controls has increased corruption in Africa. Those who have benefited most have been public sector officials with the power to control licenses, quotas, and access to foreign exchange, and with knowledge about future policy. Also benefiting have been business associates of public officials who have been awarded scarce goods. Again, those who received wages from the state and parastatal corporations and who received side payments from their operations benefited enormously from the system. In Kenya, allocation of imports was left to the discretion of officials and therefore corruption was inevitable. The removal of trade restrictions and import controls helped to end artificial scarcities and decreased the benefits that accrued to the middlemen involved in smuggling and other illegal actions by which profits were made.

As can be observed, the advocates and beneficiaries of trade liberalization are found among the ascending countries and technocrats, the dominant economic enterprises and commercial classes, while the adversaries are concentrated in the dominated countries among peasants, workers and all small businesses. Those ambivalent about liberalization consist of classes and enterprises that both won and lost from specific policies. The plain truth, to Zeleza, is that market liberalization by itself does not 'lift all the boats', and in some cases, it has caused severe damage (Zeleza 2002). Therefore, in selling it to Africa, the whole process promised an improvement in economic welfare through more rapid growth that is labour intensive and poverty reducing. In the words of Mkandawire, 'all good things flow from globalization' (Mkandawire 2001). However, the period over which trade liberalization is said to have accelerated has witnessed slower growth rates in almost all regions of the world except for Asia and the Pacific. In many regions, globalization has been responsible for the ever-increasing social, economic and even political upheavals. It has accounted for the situation in Africa which has been ever worsening since the 1990s when market liberalization was noticeable especially in trade, finance, and liberalization of politics. The dogma enunciated by large and powerful financial institutions was that the only way Africa could survive and solve its enormous economic and political problems is by becoming fully integrated into the world economy (Lumumba-Kasongo 2001).

The UNCTAD document on *Trade, Sustainable Development and Gender* (UNCTAD 1999) noted that the gender effect of globalization is complex and its effects are mixed. Overall, globalization to date has done little to minimise gender inequalities. While in some circumstances it may have decreased them (particularly in countries where it has led to an unprecedented employment of female labour) in other cases it has intensified them. Thus, overall, globalization, as a new form of intensified market-driven activity, has not yet managed to overturn gender-based discriminatory forces of economic development where they have traditionally been at work. The realities of feminzation of the labour force are quite complex and lead to certain ambiguities, as there are political, economic, cultural and even health impediments which have not only made many countries adopt this female-led export strategy but also made it difficult for women to claim economic betterment. Thus, as the borderless world takes on increasing significance, women are largely displaced, either as a result of technological improvements or just because of other cheap migrant workers (Beneria and Feldman 1992). Moreover, there is compelling evidence showing the deleterious health hazard – both physical and mental – when it comes to the condition of women workers within the Export Promotion Zones (EPZs) worldwide.

Hence a growing literature, particularly from developing nations, shows that globalization has become synonymous with negative issues rather than positive ones. Women thus have been the prime victims in this general economic and social chaos. The suppression of food subsidies, cutbacks on water supplies, the decline of food production, the dismantling of the public sector and the new race for access to ever-dwindling resources, as well as the rise in market value have all combined to exact a heavy toll on women. In the agricultural sector, the weakening of state assistance and the emphasis on export crops has restricted women's access to assets, inputs and credits. The decline in food production has affected female labour, increased Africans' food dependency and increased the risk of famines, starvation, diseases and hunger, leading to what has been globally referred to 'feminization of poverty'. Increased poverty, changing state-society relations, and a breakdown in public services has increased insecurity for women. The level of violence against women both in private and public domains has markedly increased in recent years, including domestic violence, murder, physical and psychological violence (Taniguchi and West 1997; Mkandawire 1989; Sen 1996; Oloka-Onyango and Deepika Udagama 2000; Gladwin 1991 and Gibbon 1993).

However, overall, the picture is not all that gloomy. The globalization process, particularly direct foreign investment, has benefited some women. This may be understood when one considers paid employment in the ever-expanding informal sector. Women in the manufacturing sector, particularly those in EPZs, stand to benefit together with women employed in the service trade and to a lesser extent agriculture, where non-traditional export crops may offer better employment prospects for women than traditional ones. Therefore, the process of economic liberalization has spawned huge growth in the informal sector and increased female participation therein. The sector has also provided better opportunities for women when it comes to combining paid work with household chores.

Despite the remarkable contribution, there is always a price to pay. Female workers in the export promotion zones find unionization and collective bargaining nearly impossible and therefore such labour forces are usually underpaid (Pheko 1999; Lim 1999; Riham el-Lakany 1999; Horgan 2001). Furthermore, feminization in the informal sector has had contradictory experiences for most women. On the one hand, becoming economically independent has led to many women having more choices about what to do with their lives. On the other hand, the double burden faced by all women because of their roles in the family means that the lives of women workers everywhere are fiendishly difficult as they try to reconcile work and family life.

Conceptualizing Border and Border Activities

Anthropologists, geographers, historians, political scientists and sociologists who have studied borders from the traditional point of view conceptualize borders as tools of separation and control, limiting people's movements within territories and marking the point where the authority of one state ends and that of another begins. To them, borders are primarily sources of political conflicts that undermine national peace and slow down the pace of international cooperation and integration. The border residents are seen as potential deviants who conduct subversive cross-border activities, including smuggling, prostitution and illegal immigration, which demonstrates the ambiguity of borderlanders' identities. Given the above, borders should be kept under close government supervision via police controls, customs and immigration regulations, barbed or electrified wires, watch towers and even military planes constantly flying over the borders (Hasting 1999). Some scholars in this camp also point out that border regions are typically rural and are socially, politically and economically marginalized (Kamazima 2000).

Following the above traditional view, many nation states developed policies and structures immediately after independence to tighten their borders. This they did in order to control, prevent and regulate economic, political and social interactions between borderlanders. Despite these regulations and given the economic and social status of the borderlanders, many of them have discerned avenues to solve common border problems for their survival. In doing so complex mechanisms of formal and informal cross-border activities have resulted in transforming borders into living realities that need to be carefully examined. As a coping strategy for the impact of trade liberalization and the implementation of Structural Adjustment Programmes (SAPs), the Nigeria-Benin borderlanders, for example, have turned the border into a busy area to be conceptualized as rural or as socially, economically and politically marginalized (Flynn 1997). The doctrine of mutual necessity has motivated borderlanders to conduct highly specialised cultural, economic and political interactions, which cannot be reduced to illegal, underground, or informal activities. As a result, the meaning of the borders has changed, so that border residents understand borders as symbolic representations of social groupings, defined by residence on both sides of the international border, where membership is determined by the length of stay as opposed to ethnicity, nationality, kinship or ancestral claims to land. Many borderlines operate under a set of rules and institutions (or the border regime), formal and informal, that aim at and succeed in regularizing neighbourhood behaviour, allowing cooperation across international boundaries but do not aim at integration that would lead to the formation of a transborder nation (Studdard 1986 and MacGaffey 1988).

Consequently, two types of economies have thrived along the borders – the informal economy and the formal economy. Indeed the former sector is frequently the fastest growing part of an economy during this era of globalization in Africa (Henriot 1999). Smuggling, which is the focus of this study, falls under the informal economy or sector. The International Labour Organisation (ILO) defined the informal sector as that sector of economic activities characterized by relative ease of entry, reliance on indigenous resources, family ownership, small scale of operation, labour intensity, reliance on skills acquired outside the formal educational system, and unregulated and competitive markets. The sector can conveniently be divided into two: the modern informal sector where goods and services produced are similar to those in the formal sector and in the hands of the well-to-do, while the other sector comprises the community of the poor, which accounts for about 90 per cent of the informal sector (Malunga 1998). Within the informal sector, we must also pay attention to the underground economy or the illegitimate economy that flourishes outside the law and includes theft, corruption, bribery, prostitution, drug trafficking and smuggling. This is particularly true considering international business deals; prostitution spreads with sex tourism in many countries; smuggling of stolen cars is a big business in many states in Africa; and drug trafficking is reaching horrendous proportions throughout the world.

Smuggling or the form of trade under investigation has been variously referred to as a second, hidden, parallel, underground or informal economy, all terms intended to convey the sense of economic activity which is not officially reported to state authorities and which is therefore not directly taxable. Even though such activities are or may not be necessarily illegal, they may involve a wide range of degrees of illegality. While small-scale enterprises of the urban poor in particular, which make up an important part of the informal sector, have been a subject of frequent studies (Musyoki and Orotho 1993), far less research has been done on various forms of exchange which are also part of the informal economy (Ellis and MacGaffey 1996). The present aim is to examine this trade as it is affected by trade liberalization and how it eventually affects women whose livelihood depend on it. In our case, smuggling involves the illegal transport of goods and persons in and out of a country to avoid taxation. It is that type of cross border trade that avoids imposed duties and restrictive trade laws and requirements. The evasion of tariffs and taxes on such commodities can realize sizable illicit profits. This has been realized in many parts of Africa and is particularly the case when it comes to the smuggling of timber in the Congo Basin Region and Cameroon where timber is felled and exported illegally.

A great variety of commodities are involved in underground economic exchange. One major category, both within and between African countries, is foodstuffs. Food crops moves between African countries and are exported to African communities in European cities. Canned and processed foods travel the same routes. Spices, fist, ivory, hides and skins are especially exported from East Africa, sometimes clandestinely. Cattle are moved in large numbers across African borders. Some export crops such as coffee, tea and *papaine* may be fraudulently smuggled as exports. Minerals are major commodities in clandestine exports, notably gold, diamonds and other gemstones, malachite and cobalt. The transit trade in drugs from Latin America and the Far East is increasing.

While some commodities move out of Africa, manufactured products are imported. These include pharmaceuticals, construction materials, vehicles, fuel, spare parts, soap, household goods and electrical appliances, electronic goods, office equipment, cigarettes and alcoholic drinks. These come increasingly from Asia, particularly via Dubai. Clothes, new and second hand, shoes, jewellery and other accessories are imported from Europe, as are beauty products from the Caribbean, the USA and Europe. Cloth, particularly wax prints, is imported from Europe and China and exported to other regions of Africa, and is the basis of an extremely lucrative trade, largely controlled by women. However, this study will focus not on goods of high value such as arms, ammunition and drugs, but on those goods that are easily tradable by the majority of women. It will also exclude those women smugglers enjoying state patronage and in cartels or associations.

The context of smuggling is diverse and continuously changing. For example, tax variations on particular basic consumer goods between neighbouring countries encourage smuggling to some extent. The more the governments in different countries increase taxes on tobacco, the greater the temptation for smugglers to sell contraband. At the same time, there are lax border controls, porous borders or just inadequate controls in neighbouring and regional transit points, and ample routes for smuggling drugs, weapons, explosives and other contraband goods. This has been encouraged by corruptible police and security forces, which make sub-Saharan Africa an inviting operating environment for international criminals. The convergence of growing economic disparity, continuing civil conflict and human rights violations as well as increased access to global communication and the transport network over the past two decade, have also all led to a significant increase of *human cargo* – the movement of undocumented or fraudulently documented foreign nationals to prosperous countries such as the United States of America. In this context, smuggling of goods and human cargo has risen as a result of the unbearable social and economic difficulties for many people, particularly the inability to acquire basic needs exacerbated by the whole process of globalization.

Within East Africa and particularly along the Kenya-Uganda border, informal cross-border trade or what has commonly been referred to as smuggling has continued since independence. Cross-border trade has in many instances become one of the major activities along the border. Available evidence indicates that cross-border trading activities, especially between Kenya and Uganda, involve substantial quantities of agricultural and industrial goods being carried out informally. Rent-seeking practices in public and bureaucratic procedures encourage large and small-scale traders to use illicit means and/or undesignated routes. A report on cross-border trade between Kenya and Uganda indicated that this trade has been made possible by seasonal variations in climate, in exchange rates, seasonal halting of importation of certain crops, imposition of prohibitive tariffs and various non-tariff barriers such as phytosanitary conditions or generally impediments to trade among others (Ackelle-Ogutu 1996). Sites such as Suwam, Busia, Lwakhakha and Chepkube are historically known for smuggling goods across the Kenya-Uganda border. In most instances, smuggling has been carried out by women, especially those who are uneducated, as a response to declining economic opportunities in the wage economy by moving into grey areas of 'illegal' trade. It promotes the economic empowerment of women as it has several economic advantages for the livelihood of those who practise it, particularly for women who smuggle primary commodities across the border in exchange for basic commodities.

Due to the weakness of the state in addressing the marginalized position of women, and its inability to control this 'unorthodox' form of trade, many women and their families have benefited socially and economically through smuggling. In this trade, some women have been able to make up the deficit in household budgets and to maintain a certain status in society. Thus, while this clandestine trade impoverishes the state, it brings considerable wealth to the people who have no other means of acquiring it, particularly women (Niger-Thomas 2000). In the above context, smuggling should be seen as one among a variety of techniques designed to exploit opportunities offered by the state and to gain access to the profits generated by operating between local and international sectors but outside state regulation.

Snapshots of Women Smugglers along the Kenya-Uganda Border: Preliminary Observations

In order to adequately comprehend the complex and rather contradictory experience of female smugglers during this period, a brief history of smuggling in this region will be important. Given the nature of smuggling as an economic activity, it is difficult to predict with certainty when it began in any part of Africa. However, the political and economic crisis which most Africans have long been experiencing has left almost everybody supplementing their derisory wages and salaries with underground economic activities. This makes engaging in smuggling a means of survival when the political and economic situations preclude other possibilities.

The political upheavals or conflicts in Uganda and particularly during President Idi Amin's regime encouraged some form of smuggling between Uganda and Kenya. Amin, on taking over power in 1971, gave most key shops belonging to departed Asians to his soldiers and other persons in his government. Inexperienced as they were in business, the overnight beneficiaries soon found their stock finished. They flocked to Nairobi to purchase goods at retail prices. Prices skyrocketed, upsetting the market and creating a shortage in many commodities. This encouraged a thriving black market or just smuggling of basic goods into Uganda. Similarly, Amin's government exported Ugandan coffee to Libya but denied farmers the proceeds, which he used instead to purchase military hardware. So the farmers started smuggling their coffee over Lake Victoria to Kenya (*The East African*, May 27, 2000). Many women participated in this trade either due to their presumed innocence by the law enforcement agencies, as a response to the declining economic opportunities in wage economy or just to avoid state control.

In Kenya, and with regards to coffee smuggling, the situation was a little different. It arose out of the inability by state agencies concerned with marketing coffee to pay farmers promptly and adequately since 1975. Sinceswdddddf then, large quantities of coffee have been smuggled into Uganda. Most of the farmers involved in this trade cite poor and delayed payment by their societies. An official at the Sasur Farmers Coffee Society in Mt Elgon, Mr Komon Cheprum, attributed the smuggling to delayed payment by the Kenya Planters Co-operative Union. He also said that farmers from the Sasur Factory alone were owed more than KShs 1 million as dues for coffee supplied during the 1998/1999 period, and therefore because they were pressed to pay school fees on time, they opted to get quick cash by selling the crop to Ugandan traders. This confirms the assertion by Bienen (1990) that small producers have been forced to export through state-organized commodity boards that have not only skimmed profits by paying lower than world market prices but have also short-changed farmers through many other practices. The response in many countries to state pricing and other monopoly practices has been, in the first instance, to smuggle where possible.

However, in the same year, the Executive Director of Western Province of Kenya Human Rights Watch, Job Bwanyo, acknowledged that some police officers at the border are involved in smuggling by setting up informal customs offices.

Further, research has confirmed that Kenya has comparative advantages in manufacturing and processing. Kenya's exports to Uganda are processed agricultural products (e.g. wheat flour) and manufactured goods such as hardware, textiles and beverages. Ugandan exports to Kenya are highly unprocessed agricultural commodities such as maize and beans and there is a substantial unrecorded cross-border trade between the two countries (Ackello-Ogutu 1996). This regional disparity, combined with seasonal climatic variations, flexible exchange rates, restrictive and prohibitive tariffs and non-tariff barriers, as well as the seasonal halting of importation of certain goods and the geographic positioning of Uganda in relation to Kenya seems to promote smuggling.

After the above lengthy theoretical exposition, in September 2002 I went to the border region for two weeks to survey and to listen to women themselves about what they think, not only about smuggling but also about trade liberalization. I wanted to establish the role of ordinary women in reconfiguring borders, cross-border trade and liberalization. My study started in Nairobi where a fellow who has researched in this area introduced me to some female and male smugglers at the Busia border. After having thoroughly explained what exactly I was doing, the women became friendly and were very willing to talk to me. The discussions were very informal and the numbers were very small. However, after some time, realized that this was a very large industry employing women from different social and economic backgrounds, some being in this business for more than twenty years. I had prepared a specific set of questions to ask, but eventually I realized that I had to keep on probing for detailed information. I endeavoured to write as much information as I could in my field notebook, although at some point mobile calls interrupted our discussions.

Most of these women do not permanently reside at the border. They travel long distances to Kisumu, Nairobi, Mombasa, Kampala, Mwanza and Dar es Salaam and even as far as the Democratic Republic of Congo. Some stay for some time at the border to ensure that their goods are safe. While here, they know when their consignments will arrive and so make necessary preparations to escape customs officers. These women argue that the customs officers are always aware of their activity and as such negotiations are always completed before the arrival of the consignment, normally in big trucks. This activity is not exclusively for women although it has several female petty smugglers. It is always normal for women to strike smuggling deals with men.

Asked why they prefer the activity, these women give several reasons, including hard economic times, to acquire property, to educate children, to get quick money, to survive and some women treat the trade just as any other form of employment.

For example, when asked why she particularly participates in the activity, Nyalengo explains, "Where do you work?" (she asked me and I responded) "…this is also where I work and earn a living." However, some women hold a different view. To them customs officers, at least a majority of them, are comfortable dealing with women smugglers since they are least suspected to be smugglers. It is, however, when thinking about the commodities that are being smuggled and their quantities that one is able to appreciate the different classes of women involved in this activity.

Some of the goods commonly smuggled include cigarettes, batteries, soap, bread, blankets, cosmetics, biro pens, soft drinks, cooking fats, petroleum products, contraband goods, alcohol (particularly wines and spirits) and other consumer goods. The quantities differ. Some women deal in small quantities while established and wealthy smugglers transact in large quantities which are always hauled in big trucks across eastern Africa. It is at this point that a special group of female smugglers emerge. These are women who act as agents. These agents depend on petty smugglers to supply them with smuggled goods. Since the agents have the ready money, they are very popular with petty female smugglers. The petty smugglers supply goods in small quantities and get instant pay. It is these agents that at times sell the smuggled goods to established smugglers. Agents are found along borders like Busia, Chepkube and Suwam. Some of them are well known to security people. I asked Nyalengo to comment on the efficacy and the relevance of customs police in combating smuggling and she responded, "The security officers are always too harsh and hard on us, since they know we make a lot of quick money within a short time. And depending on the goods smuggled, the customs police usually demand high bribes. However, despite the bribes, they are our friends. Who doesn't want money? We know many of them do business together".[2]

Smuggling as an economic activity thrives because of abnormal profits that accrue as a result. In the case of the Kenya-Uganda border, smuggling thrives because of two major reasons. First is the scarcity of goods such as cigarettes, bread, cooking fat and fresh drinks in Uganda. Since these goods can be found easily in Kenya and at a favourable price, there is the likelihood of making huge profits should one succeed in smuggling such goods into Uganda. From Uganda, smugglers are also able to smuggle goods such as alcohol, cosmetics, contraband goods and other consumer goods, which are cheap in Uganda and expensive in Kenya. These goods normally find a ready market in many parts of Kenya particularly among the poor. Second is the question of price distortions across the border. Smuggled goods, even after bribing customs officials, elicit high profits because they are acquired cheaply and sold at a much higher price.

Over Lake Victoria, petty smuggling is very common and involves very many consumer goods such as paraffin, batteries, cloth, bread, cooking fat, cosmetics, other valuable minerals and wild animal skins. Here, the demand for bribes is low and depends on when one is arrested as the value of the goods is at times too low to warrant a high bribe. By the end of the interview, one wonders if trade liberalization has succeeded in what it was supposed to do. Trade liberalization was and is still premised on the assumption that the removal of trade barriers/ restrictions and import controls would help to end artificial scarcities and decrease the benefits that accrue to the middlemen and women involved in smuggling and other illegal actions by which quick and big profits are made. However, this has not been realized between Kenya and Uganda; trade restrictions still persist and middlemen and women have not given up on smuggling.

Similarly, state officials have continued with their behaviour of unlawful accumulation, hence impoverishing the state. It is in this process that a group of women have decided to carve a niche for themselves. This they have achieved by using the weakness of the state law enforcement agencies and enriching themselves. Several women interviewed confessed having traded almost exclusively on smuggled goods including paraffin, petroleum products, cooking fat, soup, bread, sodas, cigarettes, blankets and electronic goods among others. Their success has depended on the availability of trade barriers (high taxes and pricing imposed on imported goods), vast borders, available and quick markets, non-availability of certain goods across the boundary and the easily corruptible customs officers at the borders.

During my stay in Busia, The East African Standard newspaper, Saturday, September 21, 2002, reported 'Shs 20 Million Cigarette Netted'. In this report, Haroun Wandalo acknowledged that:

> Customs officers at Busia Border impounded un-customed cigarettes worth KShs 20 million and arrested a suspect. Western Provincial Police Officer, Mr Francis Waithaka, said Busia OCPD had mobilized a squad of customs police who netted 412 cartons uncustomed haul after a tip off. Informed sources said that the cigarettes belonged to a local private company (*The East African Standard*, September 21, 2002).

The following month, *Daily Nation*, Thursday, October 31, 2002, reported 'KShs 6 Million Worth of Cigarettes Burnt'. The article quoted Mr Timona Namutila, a deputy commissioner of customs in charge of western region, saying, 'the authority was widening its scope in the fight against smuggling by escorting trucks ferrying the cigarettes right from the factories to the border'. He further acknowledged that trade in contraband goods was booming in border towns, but that the loopholes were being sealed. Apart from the cigarettes, the article also stated that the smuggled consignment had several cartons of smuggled Tiger brand batteries, which could not be destroyed and were kept at Kisumu Customs Stores.

Therefore, whatever the reasons put forward, smuggling thrives on most borders in Africa. It has several economic values for those who practise it, while at the same time it denies the state its much-needed revenue and also exposes it to unwarranted business practices threatening its very foundation in Africa. It was hoped that the implementation of trade liberalization in Africa would eliminate this trade; however, the evidence available indicates that goods and services have not moved as freely as envisaged. What seems to be the case is that the trade has adjusted itself appropriately as the governments in Kenya and Uganda have failed to take broad measures and procedures to liberalize their trade. The customs officers inspecting the formal borders continue to be involved in corrupt practices, taking millions of shillings from women traders to allow their goods across the boundary.

Conclusion and Recommendations

This study proposed to examine the extent to which globalization, particularly trade liberalization, has negatively or positively affected smuggling across the Kenya-Uganda border. Putting forward the case of women smugglers, the study has illustrated the assumed theoretical contradiction between trade liberalization and smuggling by arguing that, with the implementation of trade liberalization policies, smuggling as practised by women or men would be regulated or simply eliminated. However, preliminary observations show that this is yet to be realized. The concept of a borderless world is far from being a reality; borders are still traditionally managed, making them favourable sites for state officials to be actively involved in primitive accumulation. While this is detrimental to the state, in terms of revenue, a group of women have taken it upon themselves to gain from the situation.

While both petty and established women smugglers advance different reasons for their participation in the illegal activity, it seems that the unfavourable economic and social impacts of Structural Adjustment Programmes, together with the ravages of the HIV/AIDS pandemic, have pushed many people, particularly women, into illegal activities. However, smuggling in the case of Kenya-Uganda thrives because of the comparative industrial advantages that Kenya enjoys, particularly when it comes to manufactured goods. No wonder that it is the value and the types of goods smuggled that keep on changing and not the intensity of the trade.

Since this study remains theoretical, it would be intellectually stimulating if research is carried out on the extent to which this activity will affect the prospects for re-establishing the East Africa Community currently underway, particularly when it comes to a customs union. Further research should question the gender participation in this trade and even estimates of the profits accrued. As smuggling remains illegal, the question should be, how can it be eradicated without upsetting the border economies? What makes African economies favourable for the trade in contraband goods? What makes the state agencies weak in combating the illegal trade? What other economic avenues are open to women along the border points? These are some of the questions that further research should attempt to answer.

Notes

1. In fact, other observers such as Peter Henriot likened globalization ideology to that of neo-liberal capitalism with absolute values on the operations of the market and subordinating people's lives, the function of society, the policies of the government and the role of the state. To Henriot, neo-liberal policy supports economic growth as an end in itself, uses macro-economic indicators as the primary measurement of a healthy society, promotes an export-oriented strategy of economic development in the context of free trade and privatization, imposes austerity measures that hurt those who are already hurt the most, curtails social programmes that may be demanded for the common good but are referred to as 'too costly', disregards environmental concerns, restricts the regulatory, protective role of the state, and reinforces the concentration of wealth and power in the hands of a small and undemocratic elite.
2. Oral interview between 17-19 September, Nyalengo, Nyakirindo, Madam X and Madam Y.

Bibliography

Ackelle-Ogutu, C., 1996, 'Unrecorded Cross Border Trade between Kenya and Uganda', pro-ceedings of a workshop held at the Mayfair Hotel, Nairobi- Kenya, December 6, 1996.

Ackello-Ogutu, C. and Protase Eshessah, 1997, 'Unrecorded Cross Border Trade Between Kenya and Uganda, Implications for Food Security', Technical Paper No. 59. SD Publication Series, Washington: USAID Bureau for Africa.

Afshar, H. and Dannis, C., 1992, *Women and Adjustment Policies in the Third World*, London: Macmillan Academic Professionals.

Aina, T.A., 1996, 'Globalization and Social Policy in Africa: Issues and Research Directions', *Working Paper Series 6/96*; Dakar: CODESRIA.

Beneria, L. and Feldman, S., 1992, eds. *Unequal Burden: Economic Crisis, Persistent Poverty and Women's Work*, Colorado: West Press.

Bienen, H., 1990, *The Politics of Trade Liberalization in Africa in Economic Development and Cultural Change*, Volume 38, Number 4, July.

Branson, W., 1984, 'Stabilisation Programmes, Stagflation and Investment: The Case of Kenya', a paper presented at the National Bureau of Economic Research/World Bank Conference on SAPs and Real Exchange Rates, Washington DC, November 29 - December 1, 1984.

Bunwaree, S., 2002, 'EPZ, Gender and Globalization: An African Scenario', paper presented during the CODESRIA Gender Institute 2002.

Butegwa, F., 1998, 'Globalization and its Impact on Economic and Social Rights in Africa', a paper prepared for the AAS &HURIDOCS: Economics, Social and Cultural Rights Violation Project.

Castels, M. and Portes, A., 1989, 'The World Underneath: The Origins, Dynamics and Effects of Informal Economy', in Portes, Castels and L., Benton eds., *The Informal Economy: Studies in Advanced and Less Developed Countries,* Baltimore: John Hopkins University Press.

Cox, R.W., 1996, 'A Perspective on Globalization' in *Globalization: Critical Reflections,* (ed.), J. H., Mittelman, pp. 21- 30, Boulder: Lynne Rienner Publishers.

Dembele, D.M., 1998, 'Africa in the Twenty First Century' in *Bulletin* No.1, Dakar: CODESRIA.

De Sato, H., 1989, *The Other Path. The Invisible Revolution in the Third World*, London: Taaurus.

Donnan, H. and T. Wilson, 1999, *Borders: Frontiers of Identity, Nation and State*, Oxford: Berg.

Ellis, S. and J. MacGaffey, 1996, 'Report on Sub- Saharan Africa's Unrecorded International Trade: Some Methodological and Conceptual Problems', in *African Studies Review*, 39 (2), pp.19-42.

Flynn, D., 1997, 'We are the Borders: Identity, Exchange and the State Along the Benin-Nigeria Border', American Ethnologist 24(2) pp.311-330.

Gibbon, P., ed., 1993, 'Social Change and Economic Reform in Africa', Uppsala: Nordiska African Institute.

Gladwin, C.H., 1991, ed. *Structural Adjustment and African Women Farmers*, Florida: University of Florida Press.

Grown, C.A., 1999, 'Towards a Wider Perspective on Women's Employment', *World Development*, Volume 17, 7.

Hart, K., 1973, 'Informal Income Opportunities and Urban Employment in Ghana, *Journal of Modern African Studies*, Vol.2, No.1.

Hasting, D., 1999, *Borders: Frontiers of Identity, Nation and State*, New York.

Held, D., 1993, 'Anything But a Dog's Life' in *Theory and Society*, 22, pp. 293- 304.

Henriot, P., 1999, 'Globalization: Implication for Africa', Jesuit Centre for Theological Reflection, 1/12/1999.

Horgan, G., 2001, 'How Does Globalization Affect Women?' in Issue 92 of *International Socialism Journal*, published Autumn 2001.

Kamazima, W.R., 2000, 'Rethinking Cross-Border Cooperation, Regional Integration, and Globalization: Some Theoretical and Methodological Issues', paper presented at the Graduate Student Workshop, Sociology Department: University of Minnesota.

Kinyanjui, M.A., 1992, 'Medium and Small Scale Manufacturing Industries in Central Province of Kenya', unpublished Ph.D thesis, Nairobi University.

Lim, L.L., 1999, *More and Better Jobs for Women: An Action Guide*, Geneva: ILO.

Lumumba-Kasongo, T., 2001, 'Globalization, Capitalism, Liberal Democracy and the Search for New Development Paradigms in Africa' in occasional paper series, Volume 5, Number 1.

MacGaffey, J., 1988, 'Evading Male Control: Women in the Second Economy in Zaire' in Stichter and Parpart (eds.), *Patriarchy and Class*, Boulder: Wistview Press.

Malunga, J.S., 1998, Women Employees in the Informal Sector, Kampala, Uganda, OSSREA Gender Issues Research Series, Addis Ababa.

Mkandawire, T., 1989, 'Structural Adjustment and Agrarian Crisis in Africa: A Research Agenda', *Working Paper 2/89*, Dakar: CODESRIA.

Mkandawire, T., 2001, 'Globalization and Social Equity', *African Sociological Review*.

Mkandawire, T. and A.O. Olukoshi (eds.), 1995, *Between Liberalization and Oppression: The Politics of Structural Adjustment in Africa*, Dakar: CODESRIA.

Mittelman, J., 1996, 'How does Globalization Really Work?' in Mittelman, J. (ed.) 1996. Globalization: Critical Reflections, London: Lynne Rienner Publishers.

Mittelman, J., 2000, *Third World Quarterly Journal of Emerging Areas*, pp. 917-929.

Mustapha, R.A., 1992, 'Structural Adjustment and Multiple Modes of Livelihood in Nigeria', in Gibbon P, y Bagura and A Ofstad, eds, *Authoritarianism, Democracy and Adjustment: The Politics of Economic Liberalization in Africa*, Upssala: Scandinavian Institute of African Studies.

Musyoki, A. and Orodho A., 1993, 'Urban Women Workers in the Informal Sector and Economic Change in Kenya in the 1980s', in Gibbon P ed. in Gibbon P, Y. Bagura and A. Ofstad eds. *Authoritarianism, Democracy and Adjustment: The Politics of Economic Liberalization in Africa*, Upssala, Scandinavian Institute of African Studies.

Niger-Thomas, 2000, 'Women and the Art of Smuggling' in *African Studies Review*, Vol. 44, No. 2, pp. 43- 70.

Nyang'oro, J., 1989, *The State and Capitalist Development in Africa: Declining Political Economies*, New York: Praeger.

Oloka-Onyango, J. and Deepika Udagama, 2000, 'Preliminary Report Submitted in Accordance with Subcommission Resolution 1999/8'.

Pearson, R., 1992, 'Gender Issues in Industrialisation', in Hewitt, T. *et al.* eds. *Industrialisation and Development Process*, Oxford University Press with the Open University.

Pheko, M., 1999, 'Privatisation, Trade Liberalization and Women's Socio-economic Rights: Exploring Policy Alternatives', in Fall (ed.).

Prunier, G., 1993, 'Le Magendo: essai sur quelques aspects marginaux des échanges commerciaux en Afrique Orientale', *Politique Africaine*.

Riham el-Lakany, 1999, 'WTO Trades of Women's Rights for Bigger Profits' in *Women's Environment and Development Organization News and Views*, Volume 12 No. 2 and 3 November 1999.

Sen, A.K., 1996, 'Economic Interdependence and the World Food Summit', in Development 1996, No. 4, *Journal of the SID*.

Standing. G., 1999, 'Global Feminzation Through Flexible Labour: A Theme Revisited', in *World Development*, Vol. 27, No.3, pp. 583-602.

Studdard, E.R., 1986, 'Problem Solving Along the US-Mexico Border: A United States View', in Martinez Oscar J. (ed.), *A Cross Boundaries Transborder Interaction in Comparative Perspective*, Texas: Western Press.

Taniguchi, M. and West J., 1997, 'On the Threshold of Global Economy' in *OECD Observer*, No. 207 (August/September): 5-8, 1997.

UNCTAD, 1999, 'Trade, Sustainable Development and Gender', Expert Workshop Report, Geneva, 1999.

United Nations Economic Commission for Africa (ECA), 1989, *African Alternative Framework to Structural Adjustment Programmes for Socio-economic Recovery and Transformation*, E/ECA/ CM.15/6/Rev.3, New York: United Nations.

Wandalo, H., 2002, '2O Million Cigarettes Netted', *East Africa Standard*, Sept. 21, Nairobi.

Wamutila, T., 2002, 'Kshs. 6 Million Worth of Cigarettes Burnt', *Daily Nation*, Oct. 31.

World Bank, 1989, 'Women in Development: Issues for Economic and Sector Analysis', in WID Division Working Paper No. 269, Washington DC.

Zeleza, T., 2002. *Rethinking Africa's Globalization Vol. 1, The Developmental Challenges*, Trenton: African World Press.

6

Gender and Fair Trade in Cameroon

Gérard Tchouassi

Introduction

Trade is indispensable for the cohesion of any society since it involves the exchange of goods and services between natural persons and corporate bodies. However today, the producer and the consumer are not well informed of the manner in which international trade is conducted: the producer does not know the destination of his product and the consumer does not know the true origin of the product he consumes. Powerful intermediaries such as trademark owners, big industrial corporations, financial bodies as well as large-scale distributors and buyers impose their own rules, methods of production, prices and even their own choice of products on producers and consumers alike. A new and socially responsible international trade model is steadily becoming popular and is generating optimistic debate among community-based organizations, non-governmental organizations (NGOs), governments, local communities and even international organizations. Fair trade, an alternative to the current trade model, places the wellbeing of producers in the South, rather than the profits of intermediaries, at the centre of international trading transactions (Tadros and Malo 2002).

Trade creates relations among people, enterprises, multinational corporations, bodies and institutions; consequently, it has become a means to exercise power and earn profit through short-term speculation. This form of unfair trade promotes a 'dominant/dominated' type of relationship. It is not trade as such that is a problem; rather it is its use as a tool for economic domination. In this type of trade, profits are transferred downstream. Producers' profit margins are reduced under pressure from industrialists and distributors, a situation that impoverishes producers and excludes them from all economic benefits, disrupts the organization of their work and prevents them from satisfying their basic needs and those of their families. This type of trade is responsible for the worsening of the terms of trade. While the prices of raw materials are dropping steadily on the world market, the prices of finished products that the producers of these raw materials import from industrialized countries are increasing daily.

Under this system, producers process and manufacture products under inhuman conditions that are similar to slavery. This often has grave consequences for the economic, social and cultural environment. This can easily be observed in local, regional and international trade. Consequently, the aim of the social and mutual entrepreneurship[1] of women, through fair trade for sustainable development, is to enable producers and consumers to sustainably preserve their dignity and autonomy, improve their skills and better organise their activities.

Even though globalization (Touna 1998) is generating a lot of debate, small producers[2] and craftsmen in the South are still subject to intense pressure from harsh trade rules. The prices of raw materials from which workers and producers in the South earn a living are dropping steadily each year on the international market. Markets for food products are very unstable (sharp price fluctuations) and oligopolistic (four multinational companies control 90 per cent of the coffee market). For example, the price of coffee, which stood at •1.69 in March 1998, dropped to •0.55 euros in October 2001. The pressure exerted by intermediaries (multinationals, large-scale buyers, major industrial groups, large-scale distributors, etc.) on producers is increasing: prices as well as production, working and purchasing conditions are imposed on them. This pressure is even worse on small producers who do not have direct access to the world market.

Under such conditions, an isolated small farmer or craftsman in the South cannot sustainably earn a decent living from his work. Worse, he is routinely obliged to work under conditions that are close to slavery, to force his children to work along with him and to forsake his social, economic and cultural environment. To put an end to all these pressures, 'anti-globalization' and 'other world' movements have come together and formed associations as well as social and mutual solidarity undertakings to defend producers and consumers, and to promote fair trade and ethics so as to ensure sustainable development. Sustainable processes (the production of goods and services) and institutions (organizations, associations, communities, etc.) require that certain criteria such as fairness, ethics and gender equality be respected. These processes and institutions must not deplete resources that would eventually be needed by future generations. Capacity building should constantly be provided for the people in these institutions (education, technical training, etc.). Responsibilities and benefits must be shared equitably between men and women in families, communities and associations, etc.

Can one therefore consider fair trade as a means to enable women to participate in world or international trade? In this chapter, we shall start with a review of existing literature on gender and show how the principles and rationale of fair trade can help to improve the participation of the woman in international transactions or her access to world trade. Working from the hypothesis that it is mostly women who set up fair trade enterprises, we will analyse data collected from the field, using a socio-economic approach. In the first part, we shall examine the evolution of the various gender approaches and in the second, take a look at the rationale and principles of fair trade, highlighting the manner in which women can be granted access to international trade.

Conceptual Analysis of Gender

In the North as well as in the South, there can never be fair trade, and hence sustainable development,[3] if women are not involved or if their role, place, participation and contribution to trade and to the creation of added value and wealth are not taken into account. For this reason, feminist researchers and international organizations, etc. in different countries have developed various approaches. We shall examine concepts, approaches and recent trends in gender theories, moving from biological sex to gender, from concepts such as 'integrating women in development', 'women and development' to 'gender and development'.[4]

From the beginning of the twentieth century, debate on the relationship between sex and gender has reached a peak on several occasions, each of them corresponding to a period in which a particular theoretical model was predominant. Moving from a 'unidirectional' model based on biological factors, researchers developed 'bi' or 'multidimensional' models to explain the increasing complexity of the gender category and its components.[5]

In the 'one-dimensional' model, which predominated right up to the middle of the last century, the man and the woman, the male and the female were considered as belonging to the opposite poles of a continuum. Anything that lay in-between the two was not considered as a true human reality. This model was first founded on notions like 'biological essentialism' (according to which men and women are naturally different) and later, on the 'bipolar' nature of gender that clearly mapped out the respective roles and identities of the two sexes and provided severe sanctions against any person who failed to behave like an 'authentic' man or woman. This model was based on the consistency of the various constitutive elements of gender (personality traits, attitudes, value systems, most common behavioural patterns, etc.).

At the personal and social level, it was believed that there was a clear relationship between the person and what he was expected to be because of his biological sex. Indeed, it was considered that all men were masculine and naturally inclined towards virile activities such as politics, war or other public undertakings. Also, all women were expected to spontaneously prefer household activities, as confirmed by their ability to bear children, and private income generating activities. These societal attitudes were, in this case, entirely determined by the biological sex, because any behavioural or psychological departure from the established norm identified the sexes and established reciprocal expectations. Any departure from such expectations appeared as a break from of natural laws. This 'one-dimensional' model, which certainly dates back to the Stone Age and even beyond, still has a great influence on the organization of social and economic structures, even in industrial countries[6] which are considered to be very egalitarian societies.

The first 'bi-dimensional' theories, developed in academic institutions in the early 1970s in the wake of liberation movements, adopted the word 'gender' to signify that realities such as masculinity and feminity were independent from biological sex. In fact, at that time, the development policy with regard to women was dominated by the so-called 'social security' approach that was associated to the accelerated growth model. In that model, the role of the woman was mostly limited to reproduction, that is, to her function as mother or wife. Nobody was interested in her as a producer of added value or as a person capable of generating income. In the course of that decade, a major evolution took place under the combined influence of feminist movements in the United States, increased awareness of women's issues in developing countries, the works of Ester Boserup and, above all, the institution of the first United Nations Decade for Women.

The Integration of Women into Development concept was developed in the 1970s and 1980s by the economist, Ester Boserup (1983). This concept highlighted the fact that there was little or no information on, and evaluation of the contribution made by women to, development. It advocated the direct participation of these actors in the development process so as to render the process more efficient, more practical and more realistic. Gender integration is a strategy to attain gender equality. It evaluates the different effects that any planned action has on women and men and incorporates the concerns and experiences of the two sexes into the design, implementation, control and evaluation of projects and programmes so that men and women should benefit equally from them. This way, inequality would not be disrupted. Indeed, gender integration does not exclude the specific activities of women or positive actions (BIT 2000).

The Women and Development or the Role of Women in Development concept, developed in the early eighties, is based on the view that although women participate in the development process, they do so on a poorly defined and unequal basis. Consequently, women are marginalized; a situation that is certainly detrimental to a balanced, efficient, equitable and sustained development. Even that early, it was thought that efforts should be made to improve women's access to resources and involve them in policy-making. The new policies that resulted from this approach have since then had a powerful influence and promoted priorities such as equity, the fight against poverty and exclusion, efficiency and access to resources. According to the proponents of this approach, failure to recognize the role of the woman as producer leads to inefficiency in the use of resources. Promoting efficiency paved the way for a break from the social security policies that had been implemented before. This approach was also developed because of the need to 'sell' the basic equality component of the 'women and development' concept to development agencies and government bodies.

The 'gender and development' approach, developed in the 1980s to promote equality in the design and evaluation of sustainable development issues, helped to make reparation for omissions and discrimination against women. This new approach calls for the mainstreaming of the gender dimension into development polices so as to increase efficiency and improve the distribution of resources and enhance equity. The originality of this vision lies in the fact that 'women are concerned that their problems are perceived from the point of view of sex, the biological difference between them and men only, rather than from the point of view of gender, which are the social roles and relationships between men and women and the forces that disrupt and modify such relationships' (Tchamanbe 1999). The new approach therefore calls for an analysis of the relations between these two social actors so as to find ways to correct some of the errors of the 'women and development' concept, notably the lack of foresight in matters of power relations. During the implementation of structural adjustment policies, positive attempts, based on the need for efficiency, were made within the framework of gender and development to transpose gender analysis from the level of projects to that of macro-economic policies. In this respect, gender is often subjected to some neo-classical limitations such as market distortions, rigidity, lack of information,[7] etc.

In the two previous approaches, women were systematically assigned secondary and inferior roles while their needs were met without taking into account the general context. The 'gender and development' strategy seeks to reduce the gender gap by improving gender equality and equity. In addition, it recognizes that women are part and parcel of all development strategies. However, unless some design and methodology problems are resolved, the initial objective of integrating equality may not be attained. Thus, the 'gender and development' approach would only lead to the marginalized institutional niche, the only way out of which is through the 'women and development' approach. The issue at stake is certainly the operational viability and credibility of the gender and development concept itself. However, some international organizations are now increasingly aware of the need to integrate gender concerns and women into the development process. Indeed, for some years now, the United Nations

Development Programme (UNDP) has adopted two new indicators that show the disparity between the two sexes. These are the Gender Related Development Index (GDI) and the Women Participation Index (WPI).

The Human Development Index (HDI) measures average achievements in three basic areas: life expectancy, literacy rate and gross domestic product (GDP) per capita. The GDI is based on these criteria and distinguishes between the male and female. Thus, the life expectancy index (LEI) is adjusted to take into consideration the biological advantage that women enjoy in this area. Measuring the contribution by men and women to the GDP is more complex. Indeed, the measurements are based on their respective contributions to the production of income from labour. These contributions are measured using the difference between women's average wages and those of men and the percentages of women and men in the active population.[8]

In addition, the Women Participation Index (WPI) is made up of variables explicitly defined to measure the degree of control that men and women can have over their lives in politics and the economy. This falls in line with the notion of 'capability' proposed by Armatya Sen (1985). The Women Participation Index takes several criteria into consideration; these include: the contribution of women to per capita income; the participation of women in political life and policy making, based[9] on the percentage of men and women in parliament and finally the percentage of men and women who hold managerial positions and those involved in technical, liberal professions, etc.

The evolution in the perception of the role of women has helped to highlight the important role that women have played in recent decades in the production system (production of quality goods), especially in trade as an entrepreneurial activity (social and mutually beneficial activities) both in the North and in the South, irrespective of whether this role has been in the area of production, management, setting up of job-creating structures or simply contributing (formally and informally) to the growth of the production sector (Tchamanbe 1999).

In Cameroon, women participation, already very noticeable, is becoming even more active, although the trading activities they carry out are only income-generating ones that are limited to small units that manufacture quality products. This can-do spirit can be seen in the presence of women in almost all sectors (primary, secondary and tertiary) of economic and non-economic activity operating in a context of economic globalization[10] and emergence of social and mutually beneficial activities that respect the principles of fair trade.

Analysis of the Rationale and Principles of Fair Trade for Gender Equality in Trade

Developed some time ago by various associations in the world, the notion of fair trade is built around simple and elementary principles based on the need to enable small producers of the South to earn a decent living and manage their own development. A large number of products are being traded under the fair trade model. Two main groups of products are sold under fair conditions: handicraft products, art objects, clothes, jewellery, light furniture, etc. and consumer food products such as sugar, banana, cocoa and coffee. Although these two categories of products belong to very different markets, they follow the same basic principles of fair trade because they provide higher incomes to actors in the South and limit the number of intermediaries in the distribution process.

In Cameroon, mostly food products (coffee, cocoa, bananas, etc.) and handicraft articles (wooden sculptures, pottery, etc.), locally processed or manufactured by women or in the South, are sold under fair trade principles. These same principles can also be applied to industrial products. Fair trade is definitely a modern and effective solution to the imbalances observed in international trade and their consequences on the producers of raw materials such as agricultural and forestry products. One of the issues on the agenda of the World Trade Organization (WTO) Fifth Ministerial Conference in Cancun, Mexico in September 2003 was fair trade.

By establishing partnership relations between stakeholders, fair trade strengthens ethical, economic, social and cultural exchanges that lead to sustainable development. This trading system is based on a number of principles.

There is another way to trade, to conduct commerce, another way to produce and to consume. In recent years, fair trade has come to be regarded as a means to effectively reduce the gap between production costs and consumer prices and give women the place they deserve in international trade. Fair trade, which is aimed at establishing mutually beneficial trading relations (for producers and consumers) based on gender equality, has the following characteristics:

- It adequately rewards marginalized producers and craftsmen for their labour and enables them to satisfy basic needs: health, education, housing, social protection, etc.;
- Guarantees the respect for basic human rights (no exploitation of children, no slavery, etc.);
- Establishes sustainable relations between the various stakeholders and economic partners;
- Promotes protection of the environment and the ecological system;

- Provides quality products for consumers that meet production and 'traceability' standards. 'Quality products' must first of all meet production standards and comply with the labour rules laid down by the International Labour Organization (ILO). These rules include: prohibition of child or forced labour, respect for trade union freedoms, etc.

Therefore, what are the principles and fair trade objectives that can ensure gender equality?

To guarantee fair trade, a certain number of principles must be respected. Quality products should be bought directly from small producers, who should be organized into social and mutually beneficial enterprises such as cooperatives, common initiative groups, etc. The purchase price of products from the producer must be determined fairly and at a level higher than market prices. A system for the pre-financing of harvest should be put in place so that farmers should not be forced to turn to Shylocks for loans at cut-throat interest rates. Trading partnerships, in other words, contractual relations should be sustained and must be based on long-term partnership contracts. Also, small producers must undertake to supply only quality products and to meet production standards. The profits should be shared by the social and mutually beneficial enterprise on the basis of democratic principles. Such profits should mostly be used to finance local and sustainable development.

Fair trade has several objectives: improve the living conditions of small producers in the South who are hampered by lack of financial and material resources and lack of experience in production, distribution, marketing, etc., through creating markets for agricultural and handicraft products in the North; set up a network of consumers; sensitize public opinion on the unfair nature of international trade rules; and convince political and economic policy makers to contribute towards greater North-South solidarity so as to ensure a more sustainable and balanced trade.

Set up in 1997, the French platform for fair trade is the only national body that brings together stakeholders interested in promoting fair trade. This platform includes importers (*Solidar' Monde, Artisan du Monde*, etc.), importers and retailers (*Azimuts – Artisans Monde, Alter Eco, Boutic Ethic*, etc.), shops (*Artisan du Soleil, Artisans du Monde*, etc.), promotion associations (*Association de Solidarité aux Peuples d'Amérique, Echange dans l'Organization et la Promotion des Petits Entrepreneurs, Echoppe*), labelling associations (*Max Havelaar*),[11] solidarity and trading bodies involved in the organization and promotion of small entrepreneurs (*Comité Catholique de Lutte Contre la Faim, Ingénieurs Sans Frontières*, etc.).

In Cameroon, fair trade is a reality. Indeed, in the wooden handicrafts sub-sector, Cameroonian craftsmen and women, organized into associations (*Bois Décor Industrie, Harmony, Promoteur des Masques, Noire Afrique Promotion, Nodi Bois,*

Assiciation KKED, etc.), play an important role in wood processing. The quality approach adopted by these associations has three stages: supply, processing and distribution. The various types of wood (*bubinga, bété, iroko, sapelli,* etc.) used by craftsmen come mainly from Cameroonian community forests (belonging to cooperatives or common initiative groups, etc.) The other inputs are bought from formal market channels that respect ethics. During the processing of this wood, safety standards and international labour rules against child or forced labour are respected, and men and women receive equal wages for their work.

The distribution channel is instrumental in establishing a 'fair price' for the manufactured products. Such a price is dictated by real production costs and not by multinationals or major distribution chains. Distributors avoid speculation. Producers should receive a 'fair' price for their products, that is, a price that can provide the producers and craftsmen in the South with a vital minimum income. Fair trade organizations in the North must therefore provide craftsmen and small producers with a living wage that can allow them to satisfy their basic needs and those of their families in food, housing education and health (Tadros and Malo 2002).

To promote partnership[12] for gender equality and sustainable development, trade relations should be established between the owners of community forests who, together, produce timber (their aim being to preserve the environment, its resources, rare species and to encourage the local processing of wood and prevent the plundering of species, etc.), guilds (sculptors, carpenters, etc.,) involved in wood processing and associations or stores in the West that encourage fair trade.[13]

Conclusion

To ensure a social and mutually beneficial approach to fair trade, it would be necessary to first of all improve the lot of the marginalized producer in the South within the framework of sustainable development. It would thus be necessary to systematically reject all forms of slavery or forced labour, including child exploitation, especially exploitation of minors, and gender inequality. It would also be necessary for the various parties to sign contracts and establish guarantees, notably on prices that provide a fair return for the various economic stakeholders. This fair return must take into consideration the following: the needs of producers and of their families, especially education, health and social security needs; the quality of the products; payment of advances to help producer organizations that lack the working capital needed to buy raw materials, or the means to survive in the period between the order and the final payment, difficult periods or delays in supplies.

This entrepreneurial approach must also give priority to long-term trade relations with producers so as to ensure sustainable development. For producers, it is the long term and therefore the future that matters. Efforts must also be made to promote transparent relations among the various partners through the free circulation of information, at every stage, on working conditions, salaries, duration of relations, the production and distribution processes, prices, profit margins, etc. It would also be necessary to accept control to ensure that these principles are all respected throughout the process.

There are many ways in which the various stakeholders, particularly women, can be integrated into international trade and into the formal policy-making process, even though the legal framework may stand in the way (Tadros and Malo 2002). This desire to involve women and ensure gender equality calls for a certain transformation of the entrepreneurial model, which can be in the form of an association or a cooperative. Indeed, the social and mutual entrepreneurship of women who produce quality products is very original, especially with regard to fair trade, which guarantees fair participation in international trade. It can help to mobilize resources and products other than those of a capitalistic enterprise. Partnership contracts between enterprises of the North and of the South and well-defined terms of trade between the two that take into consideration the specificities of the social and mutually beneficial fair trade enterprises could make it possible to face the challenges of this new form of entrepreneurship and usher in a new manner of conducting commerce and exchanging goods that integrate the gender approach.

Fair trade has its limits. "It is not charity", says a Malian woman producing cotton under the label *Max Havelaar*. "We work hard and manufacture products of very high quality for which we receive a fair price." Who defines what a 'fair' price is, the producer or the distributor? In the figures mentioned above, is it not obvious that the millions of euros generated by fair trade never get back to the countries in the South that manufactured the products being sold? Another handicap is also the fact that producers who desire to have their own label have little or no room to manoeuvre, especially as they are compelled to respect definite specifications and production rules.

In addition, most quality products are intended for the export market. We are therefore faced with a 'vicious cycle' in which the choice of products manufactured in the South is determined by demand in the North. Fair trade envisages the possibility of processing some products locally and others elsewhere. Even though this creates jobs in the South, it creates even more highly paid jobs and generates greater wealth in the countries of the North, which refuse to reduce the many taxes they levy.

Notes

1. Social and mutual entrepreneurship is not a stable notion. It has undergone changes, evolved and grown more complex in time and space. Indeed, it is considered as a response to the changes taking place in the trading systems and in the dominant economic, social, ecological and technical systems. Social and mutual entrepreneurship structures in

Cameroon include cooperatives, common initiative groups, economic interest groups, mutual societies, farmer organizations, non-governmental organizations and associations that produce goods and services. These structures are all governed by the same basic principles and observe the same management rules that bind them together and make for their specificity: development of the human person, his primacy over capital, production, trade for the satisfaction of needs rather than for valorization of capital, democratic method of management, independence from public authorities and voluntary nature of membership.

2. These small producers are completely helpless in the face of the overwhelming influence of multinationals, which impose prices and working conditions on them. They are incapable of formulating long-term development strategies (diversification, investment, improvement of production techniques, etc.) As a result, development is stalled and the situation becomes even more precarious as the gap widens.

3. Sustainable development is considered as a new form of human development that takes into consideration the global environment and the fundamental ecological balance on land and in the seas. The ultimate objective of this type of development is to satisfy present needs without depriving future generations of the possibility of satisfying theirs.

4. In this section, we drew much inspiration from the works of Mark Lansky (2000 and 2001).

5. For a summary of the bibliographical reverences on this subject, see Korabik (1991).

6. The recent debate on night work by women shows that the question by John Stuart Mill on justice is still very topical today. According to him, the following question has been asked for more than 130 years: would it be consistent with justice to refuse women their fair share of honour and distinction, or to deny them the equal moral right of all human beings to choose their occupation … according to their own preferences, at their own risk?

7. For a more detailed analysis, consult the works of Paul Collier, Ingrid Palmer and other authors on this subject. Also see the works of Razavi and Miller (1995) and Razavi (1997).

8. In 1999, the GDI was measured in 103 countries by the UNDP. Two comparisons are generally used to measure inequalities between the sexes: the value of the GDI of a country compared to its HDI, and its GDI classification compared to its HDI classification. In other words, when the GDI is close to the HDI, there is less inequality between men and women. In all countries, the GDI is lower than the HDI. This means that for the countries concerned, there are inequalities between men and women. When the GDI classification is lower than that obtained in the HDI, it means that average progress made in human development is not distributed equitably between men and women. When the contrary happens, human development is more equitably distributed between the two sexes.

9. For more information see UNDP report (1999).

10. Globalization is a state in which the world economy is characterized by excessive liberalization and the domination of a few firms whose sole objective is to attain their goals, serve their interests and sustain their existence.

11. Max Havelaar is a prominent European label very popular in the Netherlands, Switzerland and France notably. This structure helps to develop fair trade in some 20 producing countries and guarantees six categories of products: coffee, honey, banana, cocoa, tea and sugar.
12. Partnerships are also established in the area of training. Craftsmen in the South are trained by their partners in the North to enable them meet production standards and improve product quality.
13. In a partnership that promotes fair trade, two French social and mutual enterprises are marketing products manufactured by Bois Décor Industrie Cameroun in European markets. Indeed, in 2000, Bois Décor Industrie signed a partnership contract with Ethnic. Org for the production of portfolios, pen cases, table mats made in glued laminated wood and in 2002 with Suds-sarl (EDEA label) for the manufacture of household furniture and decorations (tables, chairs, shelves, consoles, etc.).

Bibliography

Albert, O., 1998, 'Le double objectif du commerce équitable' and 'Des partenaires-producteurs au Sud', *Pour un commerce équitable: expériences et propositions pour un renouvellement des pratiques commerciales entre les pays du Nord et ceux du Sud*, Paris, Éditions Charles Léopold Mayer, pp.15-18 and 45-61.

ATOL, 1997, 'Les femmes entrepreneurs et les ONG d'appui en Afrique subsaharienne. Un éloge de la diversité et de la complexité' *Rapport final: Recherche-Action sur l'entrepreneuriat féminin en Afrique subsaharienne*, 125 pages.

BIT, 2000, *Genre! Partenaires et égaux*, Geneva, Bureau de l'Égalité entre Hommes et Femmes.

Blackden, C.M. and Bhanu C., 1999, *Inégalité des sexes, croissance et réduction de la pauvreté, Programme spécial d'assistance pour l'Afrique, Rapport sur la pauvreté en Afrique subsaharienne de 1998*, Washington, World Bank.

Boncler, J., 2002, 'L'économie solidaire: une nouvelle forme d'entrepreneuriat?', *Actes du 2ème Congrès de l'Académie de l'Entrepreneuriat, des 17 et 18 avril 2002*, Bordeaux, pp. 77-95.

Boserup E., 1983, *La femme face au développement économique*, Paris, PUF.

Brown, M.B. and Adam, S., 1999, 'Le commerce équitable dans les échanges Nord-Sud', in J. Defourny, Develterre, P. and B. Fonteneau (eds.), *L'économie sociale au Nord et au Sud*, Belgium, De Boeck University, 278 pages.

Korabik, K., 1999, 'Sex and Gender in the New Millennium', in G. N. Powell (ed.), *Handbook of Gender and Work*, Thousand Oaks: Sage, pp. 3-16.

Lansky, M., 2000, 'Du genre, des femmes et de tout le reste', Part I, *Revue Internationale du Travail*, Vol. 139, No. 4, pp. 539-566.

Lansky, M., 2001, 'Du genre, des femmes et de tout le reste', Part II, *Revue Internationale du Travail*, Vol. 140, No.1, pp. 95-131.

Lesdain, S.B., 1999, *Femmes camerounaises en région parisienne*, Paris: L'Harmattan.

Polanyi, K., 1985, *La grande transformation*, Paris: Gallimard.

Prades, J., 1985, *La création - destructrice*, Paris, L'Harmattan.

Razavi, S. and Miller, C., 1995, 'From WID to GAD: Conceptual Shifts in the Women and Development Discourse' [Working document UNSRID No.1, Fourth International United Nations Conference on Women, February, Geneva].

Razavi, S., 1997, 'Fitting Gender into Development Institutions', *World Development*, Oxford, Vol. 25, No.7, July, pp. 1111-1125.

Rispal, H., 2002, 'Entreprendre en économie solidaire', *Actes du 2ème Congrès de l'Académie de l'Entrepreneuriat, des 17 et 18 avril 2002, op. cit.*, pp.277-289.

Sen, A., 1985, *Commodities and Capabilities*, Amsterdam/New York, Oxford University Press.

Sen, A., 2000, *Repenser l'inégalité (Inequality reexamened*, 1992), Paris, Le Seuil.

Sen, A., 2000, *Un nouveau modèle économique: Développement, justice, liberté*, Paris, Editions Odile Jacob.

Tadros, C. and M.C. Malo, 2002, 'Commerce équitable, démocratie et solidarité: Equal Exchange, une coopérative exceptionnelle au Nord', Revue Nouvelles pratiques sociales, Volume 15, No.1, 17p.

Tchamanbe, D.L., 1999, 'La femme camerounaise face aux enjeux économiques du XXIème siècle' [Communication from seminar on 'Femmes, leadership et développement: un regard prospectif sur le 21ème siècle', organized by MINCOF, Yaoundé, May].

Tchamanbe, D.L. and Tchouassi, G., 2003, 'Femmes camerounaises : renforcement de leurs capacités entrepreneuriales par la formation', B. Ponson and M. Niculescu, (eds.), 'La formation à l'entrepreneuriat', *Actes des VIIèmes Journées Scientifiques du Réseau Entrepreneuriat de l'AUF*, Ile Maurice, 4-6 July 2001, pp. 167-176.

Tchouassi, G., 2000, 'Femmes entrepreneurs au Cameroun: une approche par les récits de vie', *Revue Congolaise de Gestion*, Double issue 02-03, January-December, pp. 63-77.

Tchouassi, G., 2000, 'Les comportements d'épargne des femmes au Cameroun: une analyse à partir de leurs récits de vie', *African Review of Money, Finance and Banking*, Supplementary issue of *Saving and Development*, pp. 117-133.

Tchouassi, G., 2002, 'Entreprendre au féminin au Cameroun : possibilités et limites', *Actes du 2ème Congrès de l'Académie de l'Entrepreneuriat, des 17 et 18 avril, op. cit.*, pp. 509-521.

Tchouassi, G., 2002, 'Epargne des femmes au Cameroun: épargne individuelle, épargne collective ou épargne solidaire' [Communication from the second inter-university meeting on the theme 'Sens et portée de l'économie solidaire', Lyon, 5-7 February].

Touna Mama, 1998, (ed.), *La Mondialisation et l'économie camerounaise*, Edition Saagraph-Friedrich-Ebert-Stiftung: Yaoundé.

UNPD, 1999, *Rapport mondial sur le développement humain*, Paris, Editions de Boeck et Larcier.

Internet sites consulted:
- www.andines.com
- www.artisans-du-soleil.com
- www.artisansdumonde.org
- www.bouticethic.com
- www.EDEA.fr
- www.equalexchange.com
- www.penserpouragir.org
- www.solidarmonde.fr

7

Trade and Information Systems: The Case of Wrap Sellers in Brazzaville (Congo)

Mathias Marie A. Ndinga

Introduction

Information and Communication Technologies (ICTs), which developed in advanced countries in the 1980s, now represent one of the main vectors of globalisation. These technologies (digitalisation, the Internet and mobile telephones) have led to a new era of interdependence among networks, which have transformed the worlds of creation, dissemination and the use of technology.

This represents a transformation of the conditions of production and exchange, brought about by the spread of information and communication technologies which developed progressively in Africa during the 1990s. The forms of ICT that are most used are mobile phones and, to a lesser extent, the Internet. The African continent had just 2 million mobile phone users in 1999, but this went up to 30 million in 2001. This was almost one and a half times the number of fixed line subscribers.

There were expected to be a hundred million (100,000,000) mobile phone subscribers in 2005 (Marot 2001). According to the same author, Africa is only at the beginning of a similar revolution with the Internet. There were estimated to be 4.4 million Internet users in Africa at the beginning of 2001 (mainly in South Africa and the Maghreb countries). They represented 0.5 per cent of total world users, as against 50 per cent in the developed world. The spread of Internet use may only reach 1 per cent in 2005. These figures show two different speeds for the spread, in Africa, of mobile phones and the Internet: fast for mobile phones and slow for the Internet. This is certainly true for the Republic of Congo (Brazzaville).

The mobile telephone network has developed vigorously in the Congo Republic, in response to the liberalisation of the market since 1997. Ninety five per cent of the 108,400 subscribers to the various telephone networks are mobile phone subscribers (Marchés Tropicaux 2001). There are three mobile phone operators in the Congo: Cyrus, Celtel and Libertis. In addition to these three providers, one should also note the National Office of Posts and Telecommunications (ONPT) for fixed line telephones. The Internet is still at its very early stages, with just a hundred Internet cafes (mainly in Brazzaville and Pointe Noire). Until very recently, the service provider was Congo Net, a subsidiary of ONPT, whose links had to pass through South Africa. Congo Net was joined in June 2001 by the Africa-wide company Africa Telecom and by Celtel Telecom.

The purpose of the present paper is to establish whether information and communications technologies (ICTs) have had the same effects in Brazzaville as elsewhere, and particularly whether they have tended to increase or reduce gender inequalities in the wrap (*pagne*) trade. The choice of this subject is appropriate, since the wrap trade attracts as many men as women as agents. As for the women, it has given rise to a group of women called 'The mothers of Lome' from the name of the town from where they obtain their supplies, as Congo no longer produces any wraps.

The problem which underlies this consideration of the effects of ICTs on the wrap trade in Brazzaville derives both from the context of globalisation, characterised by the development of ICTs, and also from the speeding up of changes in the relationships between men and women in African societies. This is why this investigation is based on the following questions: What is the determining factor over access to ICTs by the men and women who engage in this activity? What is the degree of use of ICTs by the wrap sellers in Brazzaville? What is it that distinguishes men from women over access to ICTs in carrying out this activity? What role do ICTs play in the wrap trade in Brazzaville?

Taking these concerns into account, the main object of the present research project is to analyse the role and incidence of ICTs in the wrap trade in Brazzaville. It is essential to undertake an analysis of the conditions of access and then go on to undertake a study of the ways of utilising ICTs in this activity, since these two conditions control the effects of ICTs on the wrap trade.

Our observation of the daily reality for men and women who engage in the wrap trade in Brazzaville leads us to argue that access to ICTs is unequal in at least two ways: vertical (men – women) and horizontal (men – men and women – women). There are also differences to be noted in its use. This discrimination is largely due to the lack of training and to the cost of equipment. I also argue that the ease of access to information that is provided through Information and Communication Technologies contributes to reducing costs and to improving the quality of services provided by both men and women.

The present chapter is based on the gender approach used in the analysis and methodology of collecting information from field studies. Questions concerning access to ICTs and the different ways in which it is used are then considered. Finally, an examination is conducted into the effects of ICTs.

The 'Gender' Approach, Observation of the Area to be Studied and Investigation Methods

It is necessary to explain the method of approach adopted in the present study, as well as the methodology of data collection on which the subsequent analysis is based. The gender approach, which is favoured in the present study, is the result of changes in the way in which women's problems are considered. The 'gender and development' approach has taken the place of the 'women in development' and 'women and development' approaches, which are open to criticism mainly because they imply that the basic problem is constituted by women, whereas it is much more a problem of the allocation of resources between men and women (Bisilliat 2000). It is because the earlier approaches have been questioned that the use of the 'gender and development' approach has gradually spread.

The 'gender and development' approach can be used to analyse social relationships, while taking into account their differences, their complementarities, their synergies and sometimes their conflicts. Gender enables us to take into account the relationships of unequal power in society between men and women and to accept that this is responsible for an inequitable division of resources, responsibilities and power between men and women.

An analysis differentiated by gender also enables us to take into account other categories of concern and other specific questions, since the categories men and women are not homogeneous: age groups, ethnic origins, dominant/dominated status, levels of wealth/poverty, religion, socio-professional categories, etc.

An analysis of the socio-economic and gender differences in the population involved in a development programme is a necessary preliminary to a full analysis of the problems that affect the quality of any development project. In the context of the present study, an analysis in terms of gender enables us to integrate our taking into account the dynamics of social change in a globalization situation, characterised by the development of ICTs, and also to follow up their further development, notably over reducing or increasing inequalities between men and women, in the wrap trade in particular.

Such an approach can be linked to the neoclassical market approach. One should note, of course, that the analysis of the market from the economic point of view has undergone significant changes since the seminal article by George Akerlof (1970) about the problems caused by the lack of information on the market. The latter is the subject of our investigation and has moved from a neoclassical analysis of a situation with complete information (the Walras approximation) to a situation of asymmetrical information marked by opposing choices and/or moral questions. Obtaining information can thus give an operator a dominant position over his competitor. It is in this context that information theories are used in the analysis of the market for wraps in Brazzaville.

I should add that I collected both primary and secondary data at different stages of my research. Taking into account the subject matter of the present study, namely the place and effects of ICTs on the wrap trade in Brazzaville, I used the following methodology, based on two models of investigation.

The documentary research consisted of using various data, starting with an analysis of the available documentation on ICTs in commerce in general and in the commerce of wraps in particular. I thus consulted research documents, articles and other documents related to the subject of the present research. This was done in various organizations, institutions and ministries, in particular the ministry concerned with women's questions.

Field research, carried out in a multidisciplinary and participative context, produced information about changes in the supply and sale of wraps, following globalisation, and notably about the development of ICTs. Preliminary observation of the environment in which the wrap trade is carried out enabled some information to be collected on the numbers involved, the groupings by associations or groupings by areas of the market and the number of points of communications.[1]

With respect to the numbers involved, it should be noted that not all the salespeople could be present in the market at the time when the researchers were making their enquiries. Information about the salespeople who were absent was obtained from those who were present. This concerned their sex and where they carried out their trading activities. Despite all our efforts, it is very likely that some isolated salespeople or some who were absent at the time of the enquiry were not taken into account. This omission should be very small, especially to the extent that a comparison of the figures obtained with those of the various market committees shows that in every case, the researchers managed to find two or three more salespeople.

The first action consisted of a survey of the area of study and enabled us to establish that men were in a minority in the sale of wraps in the various Brazzaville markets. They represented 10.71 per cent of the total number of salespeople counted. Taking the markets individually, there were no men selling cloths in the markets at Bourreau, Commission or Ouenzé. Their share of the market was greater in the markets at Moungali, Mikalou and Bouémba, reaching 20 per cent or more. This first survey suggested that the trade in wraps was almost exclusively in the hands of women at Brazzaville.

The numbers seen selling in the markets can be divided as follows: out of a total of 181 observed, 14 were at the Poto-poto market, 8 at the Talangai market, 12 at Bouémba, 1 each at the Commission and Bourreau markets, 60 at the Moungali market, 25 at the Ouenzé market and 60 at the Total market.

Concerning the question of how the sellers of cloths were distributed in the various markets, it was observed that the sellers of wraps grouped themselves together in a block in all the big markets. We thus saw that at the Total market, there were listed three blocks of wrap sellers, made up respectively of 55, 20 and 12 sellers. In the Ouenzé market, two main groups of 18 and 24 sellers of wraps were listed, to which should be added 4 sellers isolated in a corner of the market. The market at Poto-poto had a block of 13 sellers and a group of 6 sellers. In the other markets, we observed groups of sellers from 2 to 6 and more tables put together.

This preliminary survey of the field covered by this study also enabled us to identify several organizations of wrap sellers. The wrap sellers in the Poto-poto market were formed into a co-operative set up in 1982. It had 19 members – two men and 17 women. It was managed by Madame Marie T. who had been a wrap seller since 1981.

Another co-operative was found in the Total market, with 60 members, which made it the largest. It was managed by Madame Gertrude B. In the other markets, we found organizations that were not, however, as fully structured as those in the two markets mentioned above, but where the wrap sellers still had their presidents. Their role was usually confined to acting as a channel of communication between the market committee and the wrap sellers.

In connection with the object of this study, we noted the communication facilities inside and around the various markets. The work here consisted of listing the Internet cafes and telephone booths in the markets and in the roads and lanes that went round them.

This preliminary work enabled us to put forward two initial conclusions about the degree of ICT penetration. The first was the development at very different rates of the Internet (very slow) and the mobile phone (very fast). The Total market, the largest one in the town, had three Internet cafes; the Moungali and Poto-poto markets had two each, whereas the Talangaï market did not have any. These figures for Internet cafes suggest that the Internet is not yet a very significant factor, particularly since the markets and the areas surrounding them should be ideal places for them to be opened, if only because of the volume of transactions conducted in these areas. The number of telephone kiosks is greater (50 in the Total market, 30 in the Poto-poto market and 28 in the Moungali market), but it is even more interesting to note that most of these kiosks use mobile phones. Several owners said this was because they were more profitable than fixed line telephones.

The second initial conclusion was that the communication centres were more important in the larger markets (Total, Poto-poto, Moungali, Ouenzé and Talangaï). The more outlying markets (Bouémba and Mikalou) were those with the fewest communication centres. This second conclusion led us to suggest that access to ICTs is determined by the level of activity as well as the level of development. In addition to these points, it should be noted that the existence, even at a low level, of these communication centres enabled market traders who did not possess their own means of communication to have access to these tools. This underlines the importance of considering more deeply all the questions surrounding access to ICTs.

The Access of Wrap Sellers to ICTs

The need to approach this theme through questions connected with access can be justified to the extent that globalisation, with ICTs as its vector, is not a linear phenomenon. The inequalities that go with it have encouraged some authors to argue that in the new world of information and communication, ruled by competition and profit, the disadvantaged groups – whether within each society or at an international level – run the risk of being excluded, unless our countries implement clear and imaginative policies so that they can enjoy the results of the on-going revolution. An analysis of questions concerning access within the context of the trade in wraps can provide us with some light on the situation of the men and women who are developing this activity. Three points form the corner stone of this analysis. The first point concerns an evaluation of the degree to which ICTs have penetrated this activity. The second concerns an analysis of what it is that controls access to ICTs, and the third point concerns the constraints inhibiting access to ICTs among the wrap sellers.

The Degree of Access to ICTs Enjoyed by Wrap Sellers

With reference to all the benefits that ICTs are supposed, at least in theory, to provide to the service sector, it has to be said that the degree of access to ICTs enjoyed by wrap sellers is very poor. Our enquiry shows that fewer than 50 per cent of the wrap sellers have a mobile telephone. Put in another way, just over half of the wrap sellers do not yet have mobile phones. Another point is that this overall view does not enable us to detect disparities among the different groups. Indeed, looking at things from this point of view enables us to suggest something that has already been described as the 'masculinisation' of mobile telephones in the wrap trade.

To obtain a clearer view of this phenomenon of 'masculinisation' of mobile telephones in the wrap trade, it is worth considering the way in which mobile phones are acquired. Our enquiry shows that 81.8 per cent of the men had bought their own telephones, while the percentage of women who had done so was only 46.7 per cent. Looking at the provenance of telephones received as gifts, the enquiry showed that 56.7 per cent of wrap sellers had been given telephones by their spouses, 31.03 per cent by their parents, and 10.34 per cent by friends.

A breakdown of the results of the enquiry by groups showed notable disparities between the two groups. The mobile telephones given to men came mainly from parents and friends – up to 50 per cent came from these sources. For women, the telephones received came mainly from spouses (62.96 per cent), followed by parents (29.63 per cent), with friends last of all (7.41 per cent). This set of results gives the first indication of how access to mobile telephones is much easier for men than it is for women.

In considering the Internet, it was decided to use as an indicator the proportion of sellers that had an email address. Concerning the selection of this indicator, it is worth pointing out that unlike the ownership of a computer or of a personal Internet connection, both of them difficult to obtain, an email address can be obtained at a cost of from FCFA 500 to FCFA 750[2].

Someone who does not know how to use a computer can thus use the Internet with the help that is given by the Internet establishments. In spite of this possibility, however, the situation is still more critical for both men and women. The results of our enquiry show that the proportion of wrap sellers with an email address is very low (1.4 per cent). For the women's group, it is even lower, at less than 1 per cent. For the men, it is 6.3 per cent. Once again, more men have access to the Internet. The degree of access to mobile telephones is also low, as it is to the Internet. To improve this level of access, we have to discover what the most significant factors are, both for the individual and in general.

What Determines Access to ICTS among Wrap Sellers

The foregoing analysis shows that the degree of penetration by ICTS, particularly the mobile telephone, is still not very high, given the importance attributed to innovation in this type of activity. In order to work out the most significant deciding factors, that is those factors on which a campaign could be based in order to increase the degree of penetration, a binary logistic model was created. It relates a binary variable 1, when the wrap seller possesses a mobile telephone, and 0 otherwise, and a range of variables that one can put into three categories. The first type of variable concerns demographic aspects. It concerns the age and sex of the seller.

The second set of variables concerns education. It involves the level of education received by the wrap seller and the highest educational qualification the seller has obtained. The third set of variables relates to the activity itself. It concerns the average of daily receipts and where the suppliers, whether local or foreign, are situated.

The results obtained from this estimation model enable us to put forward various points; first the quality of the regression is fairly good: the model's ability to predict is 76 per cent. Concerning the test of probability, the Khi-two (c2) statistics which is 33.787, is significant up to 5 per cent. This result suggests that the negative hypothesis should be ruled out, otherwise there remains a differential coefficient of zero.

Secondly, all the variables used in the analysis are significant up to 5 per cent. One can say that the fact of being a woman has a significant negative impact on the probability of an event, namely that of a seller to acquire a mobile telephone. The level of education also has a significant effect, more so than the other variables, on the probability of having a mobile telephone.

The Constraints Inhibiting Access to ICTs among the Wrap Sellers

Despite the obvious delays suffered by the country in the dissemination of ICTs, some progress has been achieved, particularly in the way the importance of telecommunications infrastructure has been accepted. The efforts in this direction are still inadequate, and a significant proportion of the population is still deprived of access to ICTs, as in the case under study here. Both short and long term problems will be a hindrance to the dissemination of these technologies among disadvantaged social groups. These problems are so interconnected that it is pointless to try to distinguish those that are related to supply and those related to demand. One of these problems is the cost of acquiring the hardware.

As the survey showed, not a single wrap seller had a personal Internet line at home. This is partly due to the basic product. Computer products have a price quite out of the reach of this class of people. A new office computer costs around FCFA 1 million. In addition, to have a personal Internet connection, you have to pay a further FCFA 49,000 every month, something that is not possible for wrap sellers and especially the retailers, whose profit is around FCFA 250 to FCFA 500 for each wrap sold.

There has been a considerable spread of the use of mobile phones, judging by the number of subscribers to the three provider companies. An analysis of the telephone tariffs shows up some other constraints, in particular the impossibility for the telephone companies to provide customers with sets at affordable prices.

The retail sale prices of mobile telephones of FCFA 39,000 or FCFA 55,000, offered by two operators, are not accessible to all social groups. Such prices are high in relation to the income of poor people. The study carried out by the Research Network on Social Policy in West and Central Africa (*Réseau de Recherche sur les Politiques Sociales en Afrique de l'Ouest et du Centre*, RPSA/OC, 1998) shows that the average size of a household in Brazzaville is 6 people. The study estimates the average monthly income per head in a very poor household to be FCFA 31,284, in a poor household FCFA 70,380: and in a household that is not poor FCFA 185,556.

The conclusion one can draw from these figures is that the lowest price of a machine, even during a promotional sale, represents 124.66 per cent of the average monthly income per head in a very poor household. It represents 55.41 per cent of the average monthly income per head in a poor household, and 21.08 per cent of that in a household that is not poor. For a wrap seller belonging to the social group of very poor people, who saves 1/3 of her income[3], that is FCFA 10,428, buying a mobile phone at a price of FCFA 39,000 represents around four months of savings. The same calculation, based on the same hypothesis, for wrap sellers belonging to the poor social group, shows that for them it would represent around two months of savings.

These calculations show how difficult obtaining a mobile phone is for the poorer social groups. One can argue without much risk of being wrong that the explosion in the use of mobile phones involves households that are not poor, which, according to the study mentioned above, represent 56.1 per cent of households in Brazzaville. In other words, the high number of subscribers on the books of the various operators concerns those households that are not poor, where the number of sets is multiplied in order to satisfy the needs of each individual in the household.

Mr Omer I., a consultant with one of the two operators, provides an explanation of why the cost of the telephone is high and why it is hard to reduce it. For him, there is a level of the population consisting of middle ranking officials, traders and students, who cannot afford to buy a set costing more than FCFA 35,000, because of their low purchasing power. However, according to the most recent information he has, a set at the bottom end of the range would cost around FCFA 40,000 when it leaves the factory gate. It appears that even with the costs connected with acquiring a set, the actual set itself might cost less than FCFA 35,000. The logical consequence of this situation is the loss of a considerable proportion of clients who would like to have a set.

For the sets imported from abroad, Mr Omer notes that the cost of the set is fixed at the moment it leaves the factory gate. Hence, obtaining a set abroad could not cost less than FCFA 40,000. Nevertheless in Europe, there are rental agreements that put sets at the disposal of the clients at a small price, while obliging them to subscribe to a particular network for a particular period. This kind of agreement is not possible in our situation for three reasons. In the first place, to oblige the client to stick to a certain network means giving him a blocked set whose frequency corresponds with that of the chosen operator. However, in Brazzaville, there are masses of shops that specialise in selling and unblocking mobile phones. This gives the customer the chance of changing operators for any reason of his own. Next, an operator is delighted to receive a new subscriber, since the health of a mobile phone company depends on the use of the system and not the physical cost of its components. It is the equivalent of the number of subscribers multiplied by each subscriber's average use of his phone. An extra subscriber matters, particularly if the company is listed on the stock exchange. Finally, the rules of the regulatory authority[4] are not very clear on this subject. These rules need amending, so that there could be written agreements among the operators that could protect the interests of each.

This testimony reveals the existence of a further constraint, namely incomplete contracts. Thus, when an operator sells a coded set to a customer, he hopes that he will stick to his network for a certain period. A moral agreement exists between the two. The operator provides the set at a reduced price and hopes to recover the balance from the calls the customer makes from his set.

In a contract between the operator and the customer, there are two kinds of market cost connected with the asymmetry of information. The first is obviously the cost of verification. This comes from the difficulty, if not impossibility, for the operator to be aware of the future conduct of their customers, particularly when they are likely to give an over-optimistic view of their future co-operation with the operator. A hard choice necessarily exists in the mobile telephone market, because the information available is asymmetrical, as the operator, who is making a loan, cannot be sure of the character of the borrower or be aware of the contingencies affecting his future conduct.

The second kind of cost involved is the surveillance or monitoring cost. This comes up when the actions of the customer-borrower, with regard to moral contract, make some follow-up necessary, to ensure that, for whatever reason, he does something that brings into question his promise to stay within the network. The moral angle can find application in the mobile telephone market from the fact that the operators find it impossible or do not have the capacity to exercise any control over the behaviour of their customer-borrowers.

This examination of these questions of access shows that globalization is not a linear process. Not every individual or group of individuals can benefit from its fruits in the same fashion, if only because of lack of equality in the standard of living, organization, etc. This is the case with the wrap sellers, and demonstrates the marginalising of women in access to ICTs, in comparison with that of men. Having discussed the problems connected to access, it is worth going on to deal with the question of how those who do have access to ICTs have used it in the course of their activities. This is the subject of the third part of this study.

The Use of ICTs in the Wrap Trade

The trend in international trade is towards the setting up of telematic networks (Lediberder 1983, Brousseau 1993), which have intensified and accelerated the flow of information in a most impressive way. Being competitive in respect of deadlines and quality is a major aspect of globalization strategies adopted by the various actors in the face of competition. It is vital to gather and handle information, in order to react swiftly in the processes of production and distribution. Such strategic manoeuvring is made possible, mainly thanks to the emergence of ICTs and to their application to the whole of the production and distribution chain. This is why it is essential to evaluate the degree of ICT use in the wrap trade in Brazzaville. This preliminary task will then lead us to an analysis of the channels for transmitting information about this activity.

The Degree of ICT Use in the Wrap Trade in Brazzaville

It is necessary to point out that relations with suppliers have to be considered at three main levels in the oligopoly situation that characterizes the market. The first concerns the few men who are both wholesalers and retailers. They come from West Africa and import the wraps. It is clear that their suppliers are found overseas. Secondly, the retail sellers of wraps, who are mostly women in the Brazzaville markets, obtain their supplies from the West African wholesale sellers, who are their suppliers of wraps from other countries, apart from Congo Kinshasa. Thirdly, there are the wraps from Kinshasa[5] that are delivered by *kinoises*,[6] who are themselves also suppliers of the retail sellers in the Brazzaville markets.

The results of this enquiry, which refers to the sex of the sellers, whether they possess mobile telephones or not and whether they use mobile phones in order to find suppliers, show that contacts with suppliers are made less by telephone, whether the sellers own one or not. Among the women's groups, the proportions are the lowest, never exceeding 30 per cent. With the men, on the other hand, the proportion is of the order of 50 per cent. This shows how men dominate the wrap market. An analysis of the role of ICTs in relations with customers underlines the force of this statement.

An enquiry into two particularly important aspects of relations with customers, namely the announcement to customers of the arrival of wraps and the question of being paid, sheds further light on the lack of equality between men and women in the use of ICTs and on how the men control the activity. The results of the enquiry show how little the wrap sellers make use of mobile phones to contact their customers. The proportion of sellers that use the mobile phone to inform their customers of the arrival of new styles and those who use it in order to get paid by their customers does not exceed 30 per cent. This level is not raised when one considers the women's group.

For the women sellers who do not have mobile phones, the proportions are even lower. They do not exceed 10 per cent in the two cases of relations with customers considered here. Even so, the fact that the percentage is higher than 0 per cent demonstrates that there are some women in the market who do not have telephones but still use telephone kiosks to make contact with their customers.

The proportion of men wrap sellers who use mobile telephones to maintain relations with their customers is higher than that of the women. Even so, the proportion does not exceed 50 per cent. And unlike the women, the difference is not very great between those who do possess a mobile phone and those who do not. These results can more readily be understood from the fact that the men who sell wraps are mostly wholesalers, who feel the need to communicate with the retailers in the different Brazzaville markets, and also the wholesalers'[7] organization that calls for permanent contact with the outside world.

How Information is Circulated in the Brazzaville Wrap Trade

To have a better understanding of the use of ICTs in the wrap trade, it is necessary to see how information circulates. The first task to accomplish this is to list all the agents who take part in this activity. One can distinguish three kinds of agent in the internal market: the wholesaler-retailers, the retailers and the consumers. There are no producers in the area, and the wraps sold in Brazzaville all come from outside. Two kinds of agent can be distinguished on the external front: the suppliers in Congo-Kinshasa and the other external suppliers. The need to distinguish the Kinshasa market from other external markets lies in the fact that Kinshasa, because of its proximity, forms an important outlet and at the same time a source of supply. Through informal networks, the Kinshasa traders sell the Sotexki wraps, which are manufactured in Kinshasa, to the Brazzaville retailers. When they leave to go back to Kinshasa, these traders buy from the wholesaler-retailers the wraps manufactured in China, Côte d'Ivoire, etc. This is because the importation of wraps is banned in the Democratic Republic of Congo, in order to protect the national industry. This analysis has been carried out while drawing a distinction between the vertical and the horizontal circulation of information.

Concerning the circulation of information between the suppliers in Kinshasa and the retailers in Brazzaville, it should be noted that the sellers very often move between the two places and get their information on the spot. The telephone is only used in exceptional circumstances, notably when there are orders for patterns (or motifs) that are not available in the market. An extract from an interview with Mrs Jeannette Y., a seller in the Poto-poto market, gives an insight into the use of the telephone in this kind of case:

On Relations with the Women Traders in Kinshasa

There are three possibilities. The first is when the women traders come to offer us their wraps, and we buy them on the spot. The second possibility is that we provide them with Chinese wraps (sultana), which they sell in Kinshasa, and in return, they bring us Sotexki wraps of the same value. Of course, this kind of partnership is carried on with people we are used to dealing with over the years. The third possibility is that the Kinshasa traders don't find any takers in the market, they sell their wraps to the wholesalers and we go in our turn to these people to get our supplies.

On When there is a big Order

> When I can't fulfil the whole order, I join in with others. You follow? We're here in a co-operative, and I can say that we form one big family, so that we co-operate well together. When we can't fulfil the complete order, we go to the West African wholesalers. And then, if the order is still not fulfilled, I can telephone a partner based in Kinshasa. I give her all the instructions (the designs, the numbers and the delivery date), so that they can help me provide what my customers say they need. I make the buyer put down a deposit – how much depends on the size of the order. It can happen that my partner in Kinshasa can't follow the instructions I am giving about the quality of the wrap. In that case, I send her a letter with a sample of the cloth.

Concerning the circulation of information between wholesalers and retailers, two cases can be discerned. These two cases basically depend on the distance that separates the wholesalers from the retailers. This is the factor that determines how much use is made of ICTs. In this connection, it is worth noting that the twenty or so listed wholesalers are based in the Poto-poto market.

In this market, for example, when a consignment of wraps with new motifs arrives, the wholesalers employ someone whose task it is to spread the information around among the retailers in this market (the first case scenario). To reach markets further away, a telephone call can be made to someone who agrees to spread the news.[8] There is thus a horizontal circulation of information. The information received by one seller or a group of sellers fans out to the other sellers who have not yet been told. Two interviews carried out with two retailers allow us to follow this process:

On the Use of the Mobile Telephone

> Most of the wholesalers we deal with have representatives. They are the people who come and tell us the new wraps have arrived. We then have to go and look at them on the spot (Mrs Jeannette Y., a seller in the Poto-poto market).

> We do use them of course [talking about mobile phones], but you know it doesn't help us very much. The fact that we buy the goods on the spot doesn't help us to gain very much. Even though we may be joined together in a co-operative, we don't have anyone who is really reliable who could go and buy the wraps for us outside, so that we could make a bit more. For example, the profit on one item is between 250 and 500 CFA Francs for Sotexki, Chinoi, wax wraps and the rest (Mrs Julienne N., a seller in the Poto-poto market.)

The circulation of information between the retailers and the customers and between the wholesalers and the retailers does involve some use of the telephone, even if this is at a low level. It is here that a small number of sellers are willing to use the telephone regularly to tell their regular customers, usually workers, about the arrival

of wraps with new motifs. It should be noted that there are rarely more than
three of these regular customers. Generally, the sellers wait for their customers to
come to them, usually in the market. This in itself restricts the use of ICTs in this
form of circulating information.

The circulation of information by mobile telephone between the suppliers in
Kinshasa and the retailers, and between the Kinshasa suppliers and those clients
who are not themselves sellers of wraps, depends on the circumstances. By analyzing
the various interviews with retailers, one can see that the latter had telephone
numbers where they could reach their suppliers when they needed to. It goes
without saying that information between the Kinshasa sellers and the retailers
sometimes passed by mobile phone. As for the passing of information between
the suppliers in Kinshasa and their clients (consumers), communication usually
passed by word of mouth. The mobile phone only had a secondary role.

It is more in the circulation of information between wholesalers and external
partners (the wholesaler-retailers of Kinshasa and other countries) where regular
use is made of mobile telephones. The interview with Mr Camara I. shows how
this is done at this level:

On the Circulation of Information between Partners

> The mobile phone helps us a lot. To take an example, if someone needs a lot of
> wraps, I quote him a wholesale price and I give the order to my supplier. I tell him
> on the phone how many wraps are required. I don't actually go to him to place the
> order. I've got a lot of customers, particularly in Kinshasa. They keep themselves
> up to date over what goods have arrived. If they haven't arrived yet, I tell them
> when they are expected. You know, thanks to the telephone, I keep in touch regularly
> with Europe and Asia. Oh yes, I've got contacts there.

> I keep in touch with the retailers who operate in the markets by telephone. They ask
> me what novelties I've got and when goods are due to arrive. Someone asked me
> this morning for 10 items on the telephone. In the past, he had to get on a bus to
> come here himself. Yes, the mobile phone is very important.

Concerning the circulation of market information, it is essential to have information
about the role of the mobile telephone in the running of the market. To do this,
it is first of all necessary to understand that the different agents who are in the
market all have different interests. The wholesalers want to maximizse their profits
by selling all their stocks of goods, whatever their quality. The retailers also want
to make a profit, but for them to be certain of making it, they have to have high
quality goods that can be readily sold to their customers. Finally, the customers
have their own objective of optimizing their benefit by buying a high quality
product and above all – a speciality of the Brazzaville consumer – a product that
is not too widely in evidence, so that they can be different from other people.

When one takes account of these varying needs, one can see the mobile telephone playing the role almost of an 'auctioneer' (*walras*) in the market.

Just like an auctioneer, the telephone enables information to be passed quickly, so that all the agents in the market are perfectly informed about the different opportunities available to them. In this situation, the wholesaler can quickly pass information on to his likely customers (retailers) in the various markets, and this information is passed on like a wave to all the other sellers almost at once. The presence of seller associations in the various markets adds a bias to the functioning of a market with perfect competition. These associations operate like cartels, in that the sellers place their orders together in bulk, in order to benefit from wholesale prices, and therefore reduce the purchase price of the goods, and once on the market, they decide the minimum price at which they will sell the wraps. The weakness of these cartels arises from the fact that information that has reached the market can also be used by sellers who do not belong to these cartels or associations of wrap sellers. These other sellers, who also want to maximize their profits, can soon set themselves up as an informal group, in order to benefit from being able to buy at wholesale prices.

The advantage of doing this is that these informal groups of around five people on the average can set themselves up within a day, have priority when they go to deal with the wholesalers and can benefit from having a greater choice. Such quick reactions are impossible with associations that comprise more than fifty members. They have to delegate a handful of people to go the wholesalers to collect the motifs and then take them to the other members; then each seller has to make her choice and record her order. Only then can the committee take action and proceed to the actual purchase of the goods. This procedure can take from three to five days, with the risk of some of the motifs no longer being available. This is the first problem of running an association of sellers.

The second problem arises from the fact that the members of the association have a minimum price for the market for each single wrap, based on its quality. The operation of a minimum price is contrary to the principle of a free market, since in a state of perfect competition, the market is supposed to adjust itself in response to the levels of supply and demand. This system of minimum prices also helps the non-members of the associations. These people, somewhat like clandestine passengers, can cut their prices below the level fixed by the associations. This situation is not an unusual one, since the wholesaler-retailers also sell at prices below those of the various associations. This means a reduction in the profit margin, but an increase in overall receipts, together with a speeding up of the rotation of stock, helps to optimize profits. In the long term, this situation could lead to the breaking up of the associations, if they cannot change their operating methods.

The first stage of this analysis shows that even if the mobile telephone can allow complete information to pass between the wholesalers and the retailers, it is rather the opportunist attitudes of the agents that contributes the most to introduce a bias into the operation of a market, which is meant to be in a state of perfect competition, with homogeneous products and uniform buyers, a complete dispersal of both buyers and sellers, complete information for all the actors, with free entry into the market and departure from it. On the contrary, the circulation of information between retailers and customers by mobile telephone does not do anything in itself to allow the market to function in a state of perfect competition.

The first thing to note is that the consumers usually find their information on the spot, by doing a tour of all the retailers and the wholesaler-retailers. In this way, the circulation of information by mobile phone only concerns the regular customers who have probably established special links with the sellers. However, when the customers hear of the arrival of new motifs, there is no tendency to spread this knowledge, if only to stop the wrap they buy finding itself all over the town. There is therefore a holding back of information, and so it is not possible in such conditions to have a market with perfect information. Here again, the mobile telephone in itself cannot play the role of an auctioneer, which is indispensable for the working of a market with perfect competition.

This analysis of the circulation of information leads us to a good understanding of how low the level of use of the mobile telephone and Internet is. It also makes us aware of the marginalization of women, who do not have control over their activity, even though they form the majority participating in it. Lastly, this analysis of the circulation of information shows that it is in the relations between the suppliers and the sellers and in the relations between the suppliers and the external partners that ICTs are most used. This concerns first the relations between the external markets (including Kinshasa) and the wholesalers and, secondly, the relations between the retailers and the wholesalers as well as the suppliers from Kinshasa. Relations between the customers (the consumers) and the other operators, particularly the wholesalers and the suppliers from Kinshasa, are characterized by the use of traditional methods of communication, e.g. by word of mouth.

The Effects of ICTs on the Wrap Trade in Brazzaville

After dealing with the question of the access to and the use made of ICTs in the wrap trade, one might be tempted to think that the latter part of this study is hardly worth undertaking. Indeed, the low level of use of these innovations in the business of selling wraps might leave us with the general impression that its impact is of little significance. Nevertheless, such a conclusion would be premature. Firstly, it would not take into account any possible perception by the wrap sellers that they could thus enhance their profits, by however small an amount. Nor would such a conclusion make any distinction between the effects on relations with customers, on the one hand, and with the supplier, on the other hand. The fact of being greatly or little used does not always justify the importance of the impact on the activity of tools of communication.

The Wraps Sellers' Perception of the Profit They Make from Using ICTs

Despite the low level of access to ICTs and therefore also of its use, the objective here is to find out if the benefits that flow from its use – however small they might be – are noticeable to the wrap sellers. To this end, the wrap sellers were asked to give their points of view on how ICTs had affected the amount of money they received. The results we obtained suggested that fewer than 35 per cent of the wrap sellers admitted that ICTs had helped to increase their sales. This percentage was made up of those who had mobile phones. For those who did not have one, the percentage was under 5 per cent. It was observed that the difference between men and women with mobile phones was not very much, but the sum of the two percentages was still less than 40 per cent. On the other hand, when one looked at the groups of sellers without mobile phones, the proportion went down. This was particularly so with the men (2.74 per cent). These results were minimal with regard to the developments in the second part of this study. Once again, some extracts from conversations with the wrap sellers can explain these results more clearly.

On Whether Mobile Phones have made a Significant Difference to their Activities

> They enable me to talk sometimes to the traders in Kinshasa, when I've got a big order, but even so, I can't say that they have had much impact on my activities (Mrs Jeannette Y., retailer in the Poto-poto market).

> The telephone does help us to make money in our trade. For example, with my partners in Kinshasa, I can find out on the telephone if the goods are ready, if the wraps are available from the factory. In the past, you had to pay for a ticket to go to Kinshasa, but now I can find out at a cost of 300 CFA Francs. You used even have to pay 25,000CFA Francs for a visa to go to Kinshasa... Now with one minute's conversation, you can find out what you want. The mobile phone has also enabled us to extend our activities. Besides making use of them, I can sell lots of other things next to my wraps, such as telephones and their accessories (Mr Camara I., wholesaler).

The reserved attitude of the retailer reflects that of most retailers we met in the markets. As the retailers are the most numerous, it follows that the percentage of sellers who think that the mobile telephone has had a significant effect on their activity is inevitably low. However, the difference between the retailer and the wholesaler reflects also the difference between the levels of use. The second part of this study has shown that the wholesalers use the mobile telephone in their activities more than the retailers do.

As for the Internet, an analysis on these lines is difficult to carry out, since practically none of the wrap sellers used it to carry on their trade. Many of them did not know how to use it, and some had hardly heard of this novelty, as can be seen from the interviews with Mrs Jeannette Y. and Mr Camara I.

Q: Have you ever heard of the Internet?

> I heard about it for the very first time when Koffi Olomidé (a popular singer from the DRC) brought out an album where it was mentioned. I don't exactly know what it is, however (Mrs Jeannette Y., retailer in the Poto-poto market).

> The Internet is important. I haven't yet learnt to use it, but I've heard people talk about it. As trade is slack at present, I'm going to learn how to use it. The Internet, like the telephone is very useful in trade. But the telephone comes first before the Internet (Mr Camara I., wholesaler).

Econometric Analysis of the Effects of Using ICTs on the Wrap Trade

In order to carry out an empirical investigation of the effects of ICTs on the wrap trade, an econometric model was created. The aim was to verify whether the use of ICTs in this activity had had a positive effect on daily sales. An increase in the speed at which information can be handled, which has been made possible by ICTs, ought to be reflected in increased sales. Up till now, these daily sales have been regarded as depending on the number of hours worked each day, and of the experience of the sellers, taking into account how many years they have been engaged in the activity and how much they use ICTs in order to help carry out their trade. The daily sales (endogenous variable) are related to the exogenous variables by a linear-logarithmic function.

The exogenous variables comprised the number of hours which the seller spent each day in this activity, the variable ICT, which had the value 1 when the seller used at least one ICT to contact the customers, and 0 when this was not the case. The variable represented the contact with the suppliers. Like the previous variable, it took the value 1 when the seller used at least one ICT to make contact with the suppliers and 0 when this was not the case.

Working out the equation was done using the data from the research done with the sellers. The statistical problem connected with using this kind of model to make estimates is that of heteroscedasticity (in other words, the lack of constancy of the variation in terms of error). This was resolved by the systematic use of White's Correction in the estimates.

It should be noted that two indicators provide information on the overall quality of the regression: the 'R²' statistic and the Fisher statistic. The statistic 'R²', which indicates the degree of the model's adequacy in data, is at a level which could be considered rather low. This result is not surprising, since the daily receipts also depend on structural variables such as the reduction in the purchasing power of households following devaluation, the reductions in salaries and the impoverishment of households following the wars in 1997 and 1998, which were not taken into account in the specifications for the model. Concerning the Fisher statistic, the probability is very small that the variable coefficients are nil. This leads us to conclude that the model is generally satisfactory at a threshold of 5 per cent.

An analysis of the coefficients suggests that experience and the number of hours worked are significant at a threshold of 5 per cent. By working one hour longer each day, the seller increases her daily receipts by 0.88 per cent. By increasing the number of years worked in this activity by one year (increased experience) the daily receipts would increase by 0.12 per cent.

Concerning the two variables used for noting the effect of ICTs on the wrap trade, the contrasting nature of the two should be noted. The variable 'Contact with the suppliers' had a positive coefficient. This suggests that the use of ICTs by the sellers in their relations with their suppliers had a positive effect on their daily receipts. This result is not surprising in view of the fact that ICTs can enable the sellers to find the motifs that are sought after by the customers very quickly. They can thus obtain supplies and meet the requirements of customers as quickly as possible.

The variable 'Contact with the customers' had a negative coefficient. This suggests that the relations set up by the wrap sellers with their customers through ICT did not match up to the level of their daily receipts, and hence this negative result. It should also be noted that the coefficient is not significant below a threshold of 5 per cent, which leads us to remark that the use of ICTs in relations with the customers had only a marginal effect on daily sales.

The results obtained on the effects of ICTs on the wrap trade reflect the extent of use in relations between the sellers and suppliers, on the one hand, and between the sellers and consumers on the other. ICTs are used to some extent in the first case, while in the second, communication by word of mouth still prevails, which explains the results obtained.

Conclusions and Implications for Policy

At the conclusion of this study, the following conclusions can be drawn at three levels:

- At the level of access, it emerges that the level of access remains low for the whole of the wrap seller group, and is still low when considering the two groups, men and women, together. Despite the low levels of penetration, there was a clear difference between men and women. The proportion of men possessing a mobile telephone was much higher than that of women. The same applies to the Internet.

- At the level of the use of ICT, the first conclusion one can draw from all the analyses is that ICTs are more used between the retailers and the wholesalers and above all between the wholesalers and the external suppliers. Information is very rarely circulated by ICT between the customers and the other operators in the market. Here too, the use of ICTs to pass information among the various operators in the market shows how important are the differences between men (and women), on the one hand, with a mobile telephone and on the other hand, between men and women in each of the situations mentioned above.

- At the level of the effects of ICT on the wrap trade, the first lesson to be learnt from this study is that the proportion of wrap sellers who enjoy benefits from the use of ICT is low both for each group and for the whole. In every case, the results are higher among the men than among the women. The second lesson emerges from the econometric analysis. This shows that it was the use of ICT in relations between the suppliers that had a significant effect on daily receipts. The level of use of ICT in relations with customers was not high enough to throw any light on the daily receipts in this area.

The conclusions drawn at these three levels satisfactorily confirmed the working hypothesis on the differences of access among men or (women), on the one hand, and between men and women, on the other. The same applies for the hypothesis about the limited effects of ICT, which is confirmed as regards the conclusions linked to the effects of ICT on the wrap trade.

It is worth recalling here that the main problem, even more than the use and the effects of ICT, is that of access to ICT by the wrap sellers in general and by the women sellers in particular. They form the great majority of those engaged in this activity, but have no control over it. Access to ICT in the context of globalization is absolutely vital for women. It is a matter of survival in this activity that is so open to the outside world. Otherwise, this activity, however remunerative, becomes for them a simple activity of production and reproduction of hard labour. To be ready and determined to meet this challenge is the only way that is open to the women wrap sellers to get out of a situation of marginalization and exclusion, so that they can have a chance of playing a leading role in the activity. It is not technology in itself that excludes; but on the contrary, it is the methods put in place and the attitudes and state of mind that one sees, which lead to exclusion or marginalization (Babassana 2000).

It follows from what we have just said that the following policies should be formulated on the ways and means of spreading these technologies and the mastering of them by the people in general and by the wrap sellers in particular. There is a leading role for the state, which should define an appropriate strategy and appropriate policies. More precisely, the state and the historic operator should play a major role in the general orientation, the creation of infrastructure and major items of equipment.

The second condition is the setting up of methods or arrangements to enable the general public to have access. These arrangements could include tele-centres and Internet cafes, and the introduction of ICT, particularly the Internet, into the educational system. The different actors should define a policy for multidimensional training, particularly for apprenticeships for computer studies in primary and secondary schools education, and in the framework for further education at all levels.

For the wrap sellers, this involves, on the one hand, making them aware that in order to have control over their activities, they will need more and more to have a command over these new tools for communication. On the other hand, it will be important to reconcile the training programme with the possibilities for the women wrap sellers to be available for it. For the mobile telephone, NGOs, for example, could play a role as agent in setting up an agency relationship between the operator, the wrap sellers and the NGO, so as to facilitate access to this category of possible consumers. As for the Internet, the question remains open: what price could the wrap sellers afford to pay that could make it worthwhile for a trainer to train them, when the willingness to pay remains so very low?

Notes

1. The number of communication points here refers to the number of Internet cafes and telephone kiosks.
2. The price of FCFA 500 is only available to those who can already use the Internet. For this, they have a 30 minute session on the net and can open an electronic mail box. The price of FCFA 750 is for those who cannot use a computer. In effect, they pay a supplement of FCFA 250 for the help they are given in their session on the Internet.
3. This hypothesis implies that the individual must reduce his consumption of food and above all not fall ill, which is not easy for him to do, particularly since good health depends in part on a proper diet.
4. General Direction of the Central Administration of Post and Telecommunication (DGACPT).
5. Through cross-border trade, the women sell the Sotexki wraps, and before returning home, they buy Chinese and other wraps for resale in Kinshasa.
6. The name given to the inhabitants of Kinshasa.

7. The investigations carried out on this point show that the wholesalers do indeed have contacts with external suppliers, who inform them regularly of the prices of wraps. The wholesalers get together and work out what they all need, and then appoint a representative to go and make the purchase. The cost of transporting the goods and clearing them through Customs is met from contributions from all concerned, the size of each contribution depending on the size of each order. The cost of buying the ticket is shared equally among all the wholesalers.

8. It is worth commenting that, there too, the information provided conveys no details. All that is announced is that wraps have arrived, without saying anything about their quality. The sellers have to go themselves to where the wraps are, to find out about their quality.

Bibliography

Adera, E., 2001, 'Experiences in Gender and ICTs for Development: An IDRC Perspective', presented to the National Seminar on Information Related to Women, National Women's Education Center, Japan, 16 March.

Akerlof, G., 1970, 'The Market for Lemons: Quality Uncertainty and the Market Mechanism', *The Quarterly Journal of Economics*, 84, pp. 488 – 500.

Babassana, H., 2000, 'Accélération des nouvelles technologies de l'information et de la communication et émergence et expansion d'une nouvelle économie', paper presented to the Forum of the Congolese week of new technology for information and communication, Brazzaville, 13-17 June 2000, CREP.

Bisilliat, J., 2000, 'Luttes féministes et développement: une perspective historique', *Cahier genre et développement*, le genre un outil nécessaire, l'Harmattan, Paris: AFED, Geneva : EFI, pp. 19 – 29.

Brousseau, E., 1993, 'L'économie des contrats, technologies de l'information et coordination interentreprises', *Economie en liberté*, PUF, pp. 137 – 177.

Cahuc, P., 1993, *La nouvelle microéconomie*, Paris: La découverte.

FNUAP, 2000, 'Vivre ensemble, dans des mondes séparés: hommes et femmes à une époque de changements', United States: Prographics, Inc.

Heckman, J., 1979, 'Sample Selection Bias as a Specification Error', *Conometrica*, Vol. 52, No.3, pp. 542 - 562.

Initiatives Genre et Développement, 2002, ' L'approche genre', http://www.iged-madagascar.org/approche

Jeune Afrique Intelligent, 2000, 'La guerre du téléphone, Congo (Brazzaville)', No. 2076-2077.

Khayat, M., 1994, 'L'échange de données informatisées dans les activités d'exportation des pays du sud: les passages portuaire', Paris: Revue Tiers Monde, PUF, pp. 375 – 390.

Lediberder, A., 1983, *La production des réseaux de télécommunication*, Paris: Economica.

Locoh, T., 1996, ' Changement des rôles masculins et féminins dans la crise: la révolution silencieuse', in Coussy Jean and Vallin Jacques (eds.), *Crise et population en Afrique*, Paris: CEPED, pp. 445 -469.

Marchés tropicaux et méditerranéens, 2904, 6 July 2001.

Marot, C., 2001, 'L'actualité des secteurs', *Marché tropicaux*, Novembre.

Mike, J., 2001, 'Afriboîtes, Télécentre et Cybercafés : Les TIC en Afrique', Coopération Sud, No.1, pp. 112 –127.

PNUD, 2001, 'Mettre les nouvelles technologies au service du développement humain' Global Report on Human Development, De Boeck University.

Raimberg, P., 1995, 'Asymétrie d'information, théorie de l'agence et gestion de l'entreprise', Encyclopédie de gestion, Paris : Economica, pp. 181 – 191.

RSPA/AOC, 1998, 'Alternative stratégique de la lutte contre la pauvreté au Congo', final investigative report, URSPA, RRPS/AOC, CRDI, CRVZ, Brazzaville.

Ricardo–Gomez, J.M. and K. Reilly, 2001, 'Au-delà de la connectivité: l'expérience de l'Amérique Latine et des Caraïbes', *Coopération Sud*, N°1, pp. 128 –142.

Varian Hal. R., 1997, 'Introduction à la microéconomie', Paris, De Boeck University: Nouveau Horizons.

8

The Role of Social Capital in the Establishment and Sustenance of Women's Micro-businesses: A Case Study of Butere-Mumias District, Kenya

Zachary Arochi Kwena

Background

In the fast globalizing world, the importance of raising women's productivity is increasingly being recognized as a critical element in overall poverty reduction and achievement of sustained growth in many developing countries. Globalization as a defining process of the world today has created both opportunities and constraints and, therefore, raised both hope and disillusionment among policy-makers and civil society in the North and South, respectively. The South, and particularly Africa, is left pondering on the viability of globalization in promoting economic growth as initially envisaged (Bunwaree 2002; Khor 2001; Bond 2001). Women have particularly been hard hit and disillusioned by the unforthcoming benefits of globalization (Fall 1999). The disillusionment about the whole process is basically hinged on:

- lack of tangible benefits to most developing countries from opening their economies despite the well-publicized claims of export and import gains;

- economic loses and social dislocation by rapid financial and trade liberalization;

- growing inequalities of wealth and opportunities between developed and developing countries, and;

- the fact that environmental, social and cultural problems are made worse by the workings of global free market economy.

As such, globalization in its real sense has failed to incorporate the needs of women and other poor people who engage in micro-businesses at the base of society. It is a common experience across many developing countries and more so sub-Saharan Africa, to find women engaged in various income-generating micro-business activities in the informal sector to provide for their families (Womenaid International 2001; Keino and Ngau 1996). In Kenya, for instance, participation of women in the informal sector evidently possess potential to alleviate poverty through job-creation and income generation (Kibas 2001; Government of Kenya 1986), yet globalization as a process has made no obvious attempt in integrating efforts by this minority group. Women in rural Kenya engage in various micro-business activities such as running retail shops, market food stores, tailoring shops and selling cloth in market centres which, if well supported by relevant policies at national and international levels, can go a long way in alleviating poverty and bridging women to international trade. This is based on the understanding that it is actual involvement in micro-business that forms the building blocks to international trade.

However, biased benefit emanating from globalization does not seem to support this kind of move. Consequently, this scenario has seen the emergence of the notion of globalization from below to counter globalization (from above). The weight of globalization from below lies in people-to-people cooperation at grassroots level within and subsequently across national borders. The basic argument of globalization from below is for economic integration to start at community level by groups of households integrating their economies to freely support each other economically by pooling resources together, before forming regional blocks that in turn form a national block to integrate globally. The whole idea implicitly tends to define manifestations of social capital, which arguably form the basis of the notion of globalization from below (Fukuyama 1999; Brecher *et al.* 1998). Therefore, the genesis of the notion of globalization from below is indirectly founded on the premise of social capital exemplified by grassroot associations, trust, norms and networks. Women by nature are joiners, that is, they have stronger need to belong to groups (Abrahamsson 1993). As such social capital, which is people's stock of associations, trust, norms and networks that they make reference to help them act collectively and coherently in the interest of development, is well-exhibited in women. An interesting and pertinent question here is how do women exploit this natural endowment of social capital to their own economic advantage?

There is growing empirical evidence that social capital contributes significantly to sustainable development through providing opportunities for poverty alleviation (Woolcock and Narayan 2000; Bates 1999; Kimuyu 1999; Murphy 2002; Sorensen 2001; Heikkinen 2000). Like other forms of capital, social capital is productive, making the achievement of certain end results that in its absence would not be possible (Raffo and Reeves 2000). Business opportunities require that stock of capital be expanded away from traditional financial and human capital to include social capital as well (Scoones 1998). Physical/financial capital is wholly tangible, embodied in observable material form; human capital is less tangible, being embodied in skills and knowledge acquired by an individual while social capital, on the other hand, is far less tangible, existing in relations among persons. Social capital, although far less tangible, is by no means less useful in micro-business performance because it enables business people and communities to carry out their activities in an integrated manner with minimum risks and maximum benefits.

The Problem

One of the limiting factors in the economic advancement of women in business is lack of financial capital (McCormick 1988; Bulow *et al.* 1995; Aleke-Dondo 1991; Womenaid International 2001; Kiiru and Pederson 1996). Intervention measures geared towards the promotion of micro-businesses for poverty alleviation in rural areas has mainly focused on the supply of credit to men who are able to provide collateral, leaving behind more enterprising women traders (Njeru and Njoka 2001; Otunga *et al.* 2001; Kibas 2001; CBS *et al.* 1999). Even in institutions such as the Kenya Women Finance Trust, *Maendeleo Ya Wanawake* and National Council of Women of Kenya, created specifically to serve the needs of women entrepreneurs, ordinary women's access to credit is not all that automatic. The institutions indirectly ask for collaterals in terms of financial deposits up to a certain amount or certain skills or education level. In addition, women in rural areas have a historical perpetual fear of loans from formal financial institutions (CBS *et al.* 1999; Mahinda 1993; Government of Kenya 1989).

Many micro-businesses, especially in rural areas, operate informally without written contracts and receipts. Furthermore, most women carry out their businesses in local markets or shopping centres where they are known and they are, often, prevailed upon by society to give credit. On the basis of this situation within which women operate, how are they able to start and sustain their businesses? What is the role of social capital as the basis of globalization from below in the establishment and sustenance of women's micro-businesses? This study set out to provide answers to these pertinent questions by investigating the role of social capital in the establishment and sustenance of women's micro-businesses in Butere-Mumias District.

Research Objectives

The broad objective of this study was to critically examine the role of social capital as genesis of globalization from below in the establishment and sustenance of women's micro-business in Butere-Mumias District. The specific objectives were to:

- Assess the role of associations in the provision of initial capital for women's micro-businesses;

- Examine the extent to which social trust and norms are important in the sustenance and performance of women's micro-businesses;

- Establish the extent of utilization of networks in the sustenance and performance of women's micro-businesses.

Limitations of the Study

Within the scope of time and resources, primary data collection for the study was limited to four selected market centres in Butere-Mumias District in western Kenya. It is assumed that the findings would somehow reflect the role of social capital in establishment and sustenance of women's micro-business in Butere-Mumias. The concept social capital has arguably been linked to the notion of globalization from below from the fact that they both advocate for social, cultural and economic integration. This link may be contestable for people who do not approach the issue from this perspective. As such, the relevance and acceptability of this paper is limited to people who look at the concept from this perspective. The validity of the results of this study is limited to the extent that information collected from the sampled businesswomen for interviews and focus group discussions was reliable and to some extent representative. The information was collected from a cross-section of businesswomen with different demographic and socio-economic profiles. The results are based on thirty scheduled interviews and three focus group discussions.

Globalization and Micro-businesses

Globalization is not a new process. Over the past five centuries, firms in economically advanced countries have increasingly extended their outreach through trade and production activities (Khor 2001; WTO 2001). However, what is new is the rate of the globalization process necessitated by the factors such as technological development and policies of liberalization that has swept across the world. Globalization as is seen today represents shrinking space, shrinking time and disappearing borders, a situation that is supposedly linking people's lives more deeply, more intensely and more immediately than ever before.

According to Bunwaree (2002) and Seixes da Costa and Desai (2001), globalization has different facets. These are: technological, social, cultural, political and most importantly economic globalisation. Globalization has been seen in terms of technology as 'collapse of space and time', politically as 'rolling back of the state' and economically as 'integration of global economies'. Economic globalization is manifested in the breaking down of national barriers, international spread of trade, financial and production activities and the growing power of transnational corporations and financial institutions based in developed countries. As such, developed countries and their multinational corporations have untold advantages over developing countries, and due to this, economic globalization has turned out to be a very uneven process that does not promise equitable development across the board. Most developing countries have seen their independent policy-making capacity eroded and now subsist on adopting policies made by other entities, which may on balance be detrimental to the countries concerned.

Economically, the 1990s began with the so-called 'Washington Consensus' as the dominant approach to the discourse on developing and transitional economies. The consensus was a series of economic policies that sought to free developing and transitional economies from the dead hand of the State (Fukuyama 2002). These policies were applied with varying degrees of success in many developing countries. The problem with the Washington Consensus was not that it was misdirected, but rather that it was incomplete. One of the ways in which it was incomplete was its failure to take account of social capital in the target countries. The ability to implement liberalizing policies presumed the existence of a competent, strong, and effective state, a series of institutions within which policy change could occur, and the proper cultural predispositions on the part of economic and political actors. The state being referred to is that which effectively em-braced the virtue of social capital manifested in the existence of strong community-based associations, networks, legal framework (norms) and trust in recipient communities. The sole intention of the Liberalizing policies was supposedly to economically enable poor people at grassroots level in target countries. For this to happen these people had to be enterprizing and organised in a particular way.

This omission of recognising the importance of social capital in the implementation of the outcome of the Washington Consensus provided a fertile ground for the birth of the notion of globalization from below (Brecher *et al.* 1998; Brecher 2001). Globalization from below simply champions for attention to be focused on social capital manifested in people's stock of associations, trust, norms and networks to act as an engine for economic growth and subsequently development in its totality. Brecher (2001) argues that the Lilliputian Strategy, in which grassroot groups cooperate within and across national borders to outflank corporations and other centres of power, remains at the core of globalization from below. Multinational corporations have dissolved national borders, broken national barriers and finally disrupted developing countries' trading systems by flooding markets with their own goods. Developing countries have to reorganize themselves from below to counter these bad effects of globalization. Cooperative Bank in Kenya, which is an agglomeration of small grassroot societies, is a good example of how people can form community associations that eventually join up into a big internationally competitive entity.

Proponents of globalization from below were initially united by little beyond their opposition to globalization (from above). However, their common interests go far deeper than that. They share a common interest in putting the world on a safer, saner, and less destructive path than global elites currently offer. Globalization is certainly doing its part to encourage a worldwide backlash in favour of globalization from below. A survey sponsored by the World Economic Forum found that nearly one in two citizens and majorities in half of the 25 countries surveyed support people who take part in peaceful demonstrations against globalization because they are supporting their interests (Brecher 2001; Fall 1999). Globalization is leading millions of people around the world to organize on their own and others' behalf. While globalization may self-destruct through its own internal contradictions, its failure does not guarantee that another, better world can be realized. That depends on the commitment, integrity, wisdom and unity of those who are forging globalization from below.

According to Seixes da Costa and Desai (2001), globalization as a process is driven by both push-up and push-down trends. There is globalization from below (e.g. the proliferation of CBOs, NGOs, etc.) and globalization (emergence of international structures, e.g. WTO). Globalization from below pulls power from the government down to civil society and community, but globalization tends to push power out past national borders to the regions and to the global domain. More importantly, globalization from above seems to be changing the nature of the state and of public policy such that states are playing lesser and lesser role in economic and trade matters. This, however, is not supposed to be the case. Power needs to be bestowed in the hands of people to organize development from bottom upwards.

Social Capital and Micro-business Performance

Social capital as a concept is not new. It dates back to 1916 when it was conceptualized by Hanifan (Woolcock and Narayan 2000; Putnam 1993). It was then suffocated by economic development theories that emphasized modernization and argued that traditional values and institutions were an impediment to development and had to be scrapped. However, there has been rethinking in development theory and practice that has led to the recognition of the importance of social capital in economic development (Barr 1998; Bazan and Schmitz 1997). Social capital has variously been defined in literature. However, the common denominator in all definitions is the aspect of cooperation and networking for mutual benefit of all parties involved. The cooperation and networking is based on social trust and guided by social norms. According to Scoones (1998) and Kahkonen (1999), well-established social capital is able to give rise to financial and human capital through merry-go-round and rotating credit associations. This consequently builds the necessary framework for poverty alleviation in rural areas by enhancing entrepreneurial activities.

Heneveld and Craig (1996), Francis *et al.* (1998) and Gugerty and Kremer (2001) argue that although there is a widespread consensus that social capital is important for development, hardly any research has tried to examine the production of social capital and more specifically the impact of funding or project assistance on the development of social capital in organizations, particularly in developing countries. The results of Gugerty and Kremer's work on the impact of development programmes on the building of social capital among rural women's groups in western Kenya indicate that, at least in the short run, outside funding leads to more turnover among group members and increases entry into groups and group leadership by younger, more educated women, by women employed in the formal sector, and by men. These outcomes are subject to two interpretations: they may simply be an efficient response to the more complex demands on organizations participating in the programme, or they may represent rent-seeking by elites. In either case, the analysis suggests that providing development assistance to indigenous organizations of the disadvantaged may change the characteristics that made these organizations attractive to funders in the first place.

Indigenous organizations of the poor and disadvantaged are often seen as a form of social capital that promotes justice and equality. Baland and Anderson (1999), for example, argue that women's rotating savings and credit associations in Kenya improve women's bargaining position within the household. The policy implications of this are unclear. Many donors are actively trying to support the development of civil society in developing countries through their funding programmes. This funding from governments and nongovernmental organizations (NGOs) could potentially enhance social capital among poor and disadvantaged groups, but could also potentially crowd it out, or lead to the takeover of their organizations by elites.

Murphy (2002), Raffo and Reeves (2000), Putnam (1993) and Coleman (1988) argue that while physical and human capital refer to tools and training that enhance individual productivity, social capital refers to features of social organization such as networks, norms and social trust that facilitate coordination and cooperation for mutual benefit. In other words, while physical and human capital changes materials to tools and equips persons with skills, respectively, that facilitate production, social capital enhances relationships in ways that facilitate positive action. While physical capital is wholly tangible, being embodied in the observable material form; and human capital is less tangible, embodied in the skills and knowledge acquired by individual; social capital is far less tangible, existing in the relations among persons but very important for business performance.

According to Kimuyu (1999), communities possess resources in form of social relations, values and institutions, which can be harnessed for development, and improvement of socio-economic welfare of society. Putnam (1993), using an example from Italian communities, demonstrates that the quality of relationships among people has a significant influence on business pursuits and economic performance. He found that for institutional reasons, some regions in Italy such as Emilia-Romagna and Tuscany prospered while others such as Calabria and Sicily had stagnated. Successful communities had strong norms for reciprocity and strong networks of civic engagement features, which make voluntary cooperation more likely. Similarly, women's strong affinity to associations and networks of civic engagement can be enhanced to promote business activities of women in Butere-Mumias District.

World Bank (2001), Bates (1999) and Coleman (1990) argue that without social capital there can be no economic growth or human well-being and the society at large is likely to collapse. This is because social capital brings about social and cultural coherence that forms a recipe for economic development of any society. For instance, two farmers exchanging tools can get more work done with less physical capital. Similarly, rotating credit associations can generate pools of financial capital for increased entrepreneurial activities. Heikkinen (2000), Ferrand (1998) and Esman and Uphoff (1984) note that in business networks, investment takes place among private individuals that have enduring relationships which result from friendships, kinship, gender, religion or ethnicity. These relationships within groups develop compelling norms, which help members to solve disputes based on social contract. For instance, this relational contracting deters cheating because in choosing to cheat or not to cheat, customers/traders compare the short-term gains of such behaviour and long-term losses related to screening and search costs related to establishing fresh relationship. Therefore, this relationship and networking ensures that when a customer is given goods/services on credit he/she is able to pay back even if there was no formal contract entered between the seller and buyer.

Murphy (2002) and Kahkonen (1999) developed a number of indicators related to village associations, activities, norms and trust to measure social capital. They came up with indicators such as social capital index, density of membership, meeting attendance, participation index, community orientation, number of joint village activities, social interaction index and neighbourhood trust index which, though amorphous, helps to show the density of social capital among people. This study tries to show how these different indicators/measures of social capital relate to the establishment, sustenance and performance of women's micro-businesses in Butere-Mumias District. Granovetter (1985) argues that family, religion and ethnicity play a critical role in initiating business networks, although the latter in such networks are kept in place by business itself. The reason for this is that business relationships are nurtured in business meetings away from family or religious functions. Therefore, the aforementioned agents only facilitate people's meeting and knowing each other. Women are always the majority in such meetings.

This study demonstrates how women turn such opportunities to their own advantage in business.

Involvement of Women in Micro-business

Micro-businesses play a very important role in Kenya's economy. Many of the rural population, especially women, are engaged in micro-businesses as a source of income to supplement other sources (Pedersen 2001; Kibas 2001; Njeru and Njoka 2001; Kinyanjui 1999; CBS *et al.* 1999; Government of Kenya 1997). Consequently, there is a widespread support for the informal sector in Kenya based on its importance and the need to create more jobs. Women, who mostly dominate this sector, have been important partners of men in the development process. They have been major actors in primary production and basic commodity exchange, especially in areas where agriculture and small-scale enterprises form the base of the local economy.

Otunga *et al.* (2001) observe that in most developing countries, up to 80 per cent of the buying and selling of basic commodities, especially in the informal sector, are performed by women. In a historical perspective, they argue that women have been involved in informal trade at least since the time of barter trade. Women in western part of Kenya, which includes the present-day Butere-Mumias District, were involved in the exchange of goods such as pottery, basketry, grains and fish. This, to some extent, means that owing to these women's experience in business, they are able to carry out sustainable business if given a properly enabling environment such as access to initial capital for businesses.

The Government of Kenya (1986, 1997) notes that the contribution of women to economic development has not been adequately highlighted in literature. The documents attribute this to the fact that adequate statistics showing the contribution of women to the development process are lacking. Although the law of Kenya provides for equality between men and women, in practice the latter are still disadvantaged. For instance, employment acts restrict most women from running businesses in their homes or being hawkers although this has been overtaken by the effects of liberalization and women are now engaged, in business activities. Owing to this, some structural and gender-focused efforts, such as those that manifest in women in development programmes, have supported the participation of women in basic income-generating activities through informal sector programmes. These programmes are largely welfare-oriented, operating at subsistence level of production and designed to cater more for enhanced confidence and awareness than to create sustainable profit centres. Such programmes are based on the premise that women can successfully develop themselves using traditional welfare-oriented roles. However, it is clear that women are not a homogenous group but there are distinct classes or strata of women in society. In this connection therefore, many of these programmes have only been taken into effect up to a certain class of women in society, that is the middle class clique of women, leaving unreached the lowest class of women where the poorest of the poor are found.

The Women's Bureau (no date) report that profits made by women in business, as opposed to men, are much more likely to benefit the entire families as the funds are used to purchase food and other health-related supplies rather than the consumer goods which men are likely to purchase. However, despite this, most women who venture into business in the informal sector lack the collateral to enable them secure bank loans to start and/or expand their businesses (Kibas 2001; CBS *et al.* 1999). The major strength of women in the rural areas is their ability to form self-help/income-generating groups and merry-go-rounds such that in the absence of formal loans they are left to depend on their social groups and networks to survive in the business world.

Although there is a presumption that entrepreneurs of both sexes experience similar constraints to business start-up and expansion, the Kenyan social systems are known to be inherently biased against women and thus only give marginal attention to women's needs (Njeru and Njoka 2001). As such, women face problems that are qualitatively different from those encountered by men, with regard, for example, to access to credit, information and training. AFRACA (1983) and Mahinda (1993) argue that constraints to extending credit to rural women are multiple and require careful analysis. On the basis of practical experience, they divide these constraints into three categories, namely: constraints facing women such as lack of technical knowledge, material skills and socio-economic obstacles; constraints facing financial institutions e.g. inadequate funds, lack of supporting services, loan processing; and the constraints facing government such as inadequate extension services, lack of village level infrastructure and lack of foreign exchange. By and large, credit institutions do not reach women due to two facts: one, the institutions are mostly led by male administrators and two, the erroneous perception that women entrepreneurs are small-scale traders without any desire to expand.

Women are usually not involved in full-scale trading, so they tend to concentrate on small business, which require very small capital. Banks find such business unattractive and argue that extending credit to such projects would be overly expensive and a risky venture (Kamunge 1990; Aleke-Dondo 1991). Consequently, banks deny credit to women in petty trade, processing and manufacturing at a micro-scale. Hence women, if anything, have to rely on their associations for finance to start up their businesses. This, to a large extent, explains the observation by Pedersen (2001), Ferrand (1998), Dranchman (1999), Josefa (1999) and McCormick and Pedersen (1996) that micro-businesses, directly or indirectly, employ about two-thirds of the rural population and that worldwide, micro-businesses tend to be dominated by women entrepreneurs. Therefore micro-businesses offer an important source of employment for women that enable them to pave the route to financial independence. This then requires that the dynamics of women entrepreneurs in these businesses are well understood so that a more conducive environment, such as supportive policy framework, is created to encourage more women to start up businesses. As such, this study provides literature on the use of social capital that stands for people's grassroot integration and collective action for economic and social gains. The literature has the ultimate goal of assisting in formulating policies that promote micro-businesses, especially those run by women.

The argument in the first section of this literature review tries to link the notion of globalization from below with the concept of social capital. The link is based on the two concepts being all about integrating people's activities at grassroot level, be it social or economic, for mutual benefit and in the interest of achieving development. As such, this study uses the framework of globalization from below as espoused by Brecher *et al.* (1998) especially in the chapter on 'The power of social movements and its secret' to analysis the role of social capital in assisting the establishment and sustenance of women's micro-businesses. Social capital has been demonstrated to be very important for economic development in any society. The various aspects of social capital, that is, trust, associations, norms and networks manifest more in women than in men. The review also reveals that by nature, women have a greater need to belong to groups/associations and therefore have a greater networking power compared to men. The literature review has also underscored the importance of micro-businesses in Kenya's economy and clearly shown that women in rural areas run most of them. Consequently, this study largely demonstrates how women use social capital to start and sustain their micro-businesses.

Theoretical Considerations

Theoretical orientation of this study is towards group theory. The theory postulates that human beings are members of many groups of which membership may be voluntary, e.g. clubs, societies, associations, political parties or non-voluntary (compulsory) e.g. sex, race, age, neighbourhood, political turmoil (Napier and Gershenfeld 1999; Glen 1975). Various groups/associations have their own social norms that keep members together, strengthening relationships, networking and cooperation. A relationship manifests itself as trust in an exchange situation such that economic agents are confident that parties they are dealing with are seriously interested in sustaining a business interaction. Trust in this case results from repeated success in exchange situations.

Some people have a stronger need to belong to groups (i.e. joiners) than others. Women, for instance, by their nature of being sociable are mostly joiners and they derive a lot of joy and other benefits from it. Voluntary membership of a group/association is determined by a number of interacting factors such as personal, occupation, legal and business. Hence, it is difficult to identify a single clear-cut reason for a person's affiliation with a particular group(s) (Abrahamsson 1993; Glen 1975).

It is common knowledge that membership of an association/group enhances members' acceptability in society. For instance, a person belonging to more than five groups is likely to be more acceptable than one in two or three. Similarly, a business person with membership in several groups is likely to have more friends and therefore attract more customers from the groups in which he/she is a member and also other members are able to get goods/services at subsidized rates and credit. Therefore, group/association membership involves a give and take between an individual and the group (Hirschman 1984). Globalization from below's main premises lies in people cooperating at the lowest level of society, a fact that globalization as we know it today (globalization from above) has failed to take into account. The main tenets of globalization from below exist in the concept of social capital that is manifested in people's stock of associations, trust, norms and networks. By nature women, and more so African women, are well endowed with social capital that they often call on to help them solve their problems.

Conceptually, by virtue of women being joiners and belonging to many associations, they have strong social norms that keep them together, trust in one another and are in good networks. Given this state of affairs, they are able to raise initial capital for their businesses from merry-go-round/rotating credit association, honour their pledges when given credit (are credit-worthy), trust each other and therefore give credit, get market information through their strong networking and follow up on their defaulters and suspend/discriminate against them. In this way, a whole community or region becomes like a small village where every individual's character is known and can be regulated by social exclusion. Consequently, women are able to get initial capital to start business, able to operate a business with less risk and running costs and hence make reasonable profits to be ploughed back for the business to grow.

Methodology

This study used both primary and secondary sources of information. Primary sources used quantitative and qualitative methods of data collection. In quantitative data collection, scheduled interviews were used to gather data on type of business, sources of initial capital, membership in associations, social and business networking, role of trust in running businesses, defaulter arbitration mechanisms and general performance of businesses. The sample size for the study was 30 respondents drawn proportionally, depending on the size of the market or shopping centre. Qualitative methods of data collection made use of Focus Group Discussions (FGDs) with selected businesswomen to follow up on the issues that were not clear or were not captured from quantitative methods of data collection.

Discussions from FGDs were translated and transcribed within 24 hours of completion of each FGD. The resulting transcripts were coded using the programme ATLAS.ti (Muhr 1997) based on the template of topical categories drawn from questions and issues covered in the discussion guides and from the themes emerging from the discussions themselves.

Respondents of the study were selected randomly from women trading, in the markets selected from a list of markets obtained from Butere County Council and Mumias Town Council. At some point, the snowball technique was used. This is where the researcher identifies one respondent and after the interview he/she is asked to name another respondent with similar qualities. Participants of focus group discussions were selected from respondents during interviews and contacts with resource persons. Their selection was dependent upon their wide knowledge of the issues under investigation, their ability to discuss issues freely and lastly willingness to attend discussions.

The first stage in the processing of data for this study consisted of editing, checking for completeness of the questionnaires, verifying the consistency of the responses given and eliminating the questionnaires or responses that are seen as unreliable. Coding and entering the data into the computer SPSS package for analysis then followed. Descriptive analysis such as cross-tabulation, frequencies, percentages, means, standard deviation, minimum and maximum were performed on the data to analyse emerging trends and make deductions appropriately. Recorded data from focus group discussions were transcribed and Analyzed together with notes taken during discussions by use of the ATLAS.ti programme and content analysis techniques.

Secondary sources explored a wide range of documents to collect information and also situate the research theme appropriately in context of other studies. The documents that were reviewed include NGOs' reports on women's micro-businesses, the government's policy documents on support of micro-businesses and especially those run by women. Other documents reviewed were books and academic journals. Owing to the nature the study, data collected was mainly analyzed using descriptive statistics and content analysis and was presented thematically.

Results and Discussions

Background Information of the Businesswomen

This study sought views from businesswomen of diverse backgrounds. The mean age of the businesswomen interviewed was 37 years. The youngest businesswoman was 20 and the oldest 65 years. The dominant age group was 20-24 (23%). The majority of businesswomen (73%) had some formal education. The number of years in formal education ranged from 0 to 16 with the mean of 7. The household size of the businesswomen was between 1 to 15 with an average of 5. On the other hand, the average household income of the businesswomen was KShs.

4900 with huge inter-household differences. The household with the lowest income had a monthly income of KShs. 300 while the highest had KShs. 20000. About 70 per cent of the businesswomen were married with the rest being either single or widowed.

Sources of Initial Financial Capital

The businesswomen were found to trade in a wide range of items. These included: household goods such as utensils, soaps, matchboxes; foodstuffs such as vegetables, fish, meat, maize meal, maize, beans, fruits and clothing materials. Others were engaged in the provision of services such as grinding mill, agricultural extension and hairdressing. However, over half (53%) traded in foodstuffs.

These results agree in a way with Njeru and Njoka (2001) that women entrepreneurs venture mainly into service-oriented businesses such as selling vegetables, fruits, grains, clothes, retain, consumer goods, fuel, hair care, dress making/tailoring, knitting and embroidery. Each businesswoman had reasons for trading in the items she was trading in. The reasons included profitability of items, amount of initial capital available to start the business, frequency of use of items and humanitarian service to community e.g. health services.

On the average, these businesswomen have been in business for at least six years. There are, however, variations within individuals, with some having been in the business for less than one year while others have been in it for twenty years. The majority (29.2%) have been in business for between 1-5 years. It is within the last 6 to 10 years that the economic situation in Kenya has become particularly tough following the World Bank's and International Monetary Fund's (IMF) decision to stop aid until the country met certain conditions including Liberalizing the economy, privatizing public companies and downsizing public workforce (retrenchment), all wrapped under a structural adjustment programme. Retrenchment from both public and private sectors saw many people lose their jobs. Women were particularly hurt by this situation either by them (women) or their husbands losing their source of livelihood. As a result, they (women) had to look for ways through which their family could be sustained financially. This somehow explains why the majority of businesswomen started their business between six to ten years ago.

The source of initial capital varied widely. The sources mentioned included: own savings, rotating credit associations, gift from family members and salary. No woman among the interviewed had obtained a loan or credit from a formal financial institution for initial capital (Table 1). As pointed out by Njeru and Njoka (2001) and Rhyne and Otero (1994), the reasons for the businesswomen not obtaining a loan from formal financial institutions are that, firstly, they had cheaper alternative sources of initial capital and, secondly, they fear getting loans from formal institutions because of the conditions imposed and high interest rates.

Table 1: Sources of Initial Capital

Source of Initial Capital	Frequency	% (Responses)	% (Cases)
Own savings	13	27.7	43.3
Gift from family member	12	25.5	40.0
Rotating credit associations	12	25.5	40.0
Salary	4	8.5	13.3
Retirement benefit	2	4.3	6.7
Loan from friends	2	4.3	6.7
Sale of property	2	4.3	6.7

Source: Field Data, 2002

Among the prominent alternative sources of the initial capital for business was a gift from family members, mostly husbands, parents, siblings, children, uncles and aunts, own savings and rotating credit associations. From the focus group discussions, it emerged that even some of the women who said that their source of initial capital was from their own savings alluded to the fact that the saving was done in merry-go-round/rotating credit associations. This emphasizes the importance of associations, particularly rotating credit, in providing funds for the starting up of micro-businesses by women. The result confirms the observation by Putnam (1993) that rotating credit associations are important not only for sociability but also for small-scale capital formation to start micro-businesses.

Performance of Women's Micro-businesses
The amount of initial capital for the women's micro-businesses ranged from KShs. 50 to KShs.30000. The average was, however, KShs. 24000. Operating capital also varied from KShs. 140 to 60000 with a mean of KShs. 50000. The majority of the businesswomen (76%) reported positive growth in their business. This is depicted clearly from the difference between their initial capital and operating capital. Business growth ranged from 17 per cent to 98 per cent and at least 77 per cent of those that reported business growth had over 50 per cent growth. About 70 per cent of businesswomen who reported positive growth in their business were members of one or more rotating credit associations. This further demonstrates the importance of rotating credit associations in generating initial financial capital for the start of micro-businesses, especially among women.

Of the 24 per cent who had negative growth in their business, only 43 per cent of them were members of rotating credit associations. The reasons for their negative growth were cited as lack of customers due to the poor performance of the economy, high taxation by the local municipal council, lack of enough time devoted to their business due to household chores, and lack of savings due to pressing domestic needs such as school fees and subsistence. Some of these factors agree with what Njeru and Njoka (2001) found in their study on the socio-cultural factors influencing women entrepreneurs' investment patterns in Nairobi. They reported that major constraints facing women's businesses include low returns from business and work pressure due to their domestic chores.

The length of time the businesswomen take to sell their stock (rate of stock turnover) ranged from 1 day to 90 days depending on the type of goods traded in, the number of customers available and the amount of time devoted to the business. However, the average time taken to sell stock is 14 days (2 weeks). As it emerged from the focus group discussions, businesswomen who trade in consumables that are required in households on a day-to-day basis have a higher rate of stock turnover than those trading in goods like clothing and utensils. It is obvious that the rate of stock turnover depends on the number of customers one has. This is closely linked to the extent of the businessperson's social network. It was evident that some businesswomen, especially the newly married, do not open up their businesses for long enough due to domestic chores. Most of them only open in the afternoons after farm work and domestic chores at home. For such businesswomen, the rate of stock turnover was understandably low. When the time taken to sell stock was correlated with membership in associations, it emerged that those who were members of associations tended to sell faster than those who were not members of any association. This point was also stressed during focus group discussions. The participants argued that people who belong to many groups tend to have many more friends and therefore potential customers than those who do not belong to any association. They gave an analogy of the popularity a man with many wives has because of the extended networks of relations and friends among his many in-laws.

Businesswomen's Membership of Associations

Over 70 per cent of businesswomen were members of one or more rotating credit associations. The maximum number of rotating credit association any one individual belonged to was three. About 48 per cent of the women were members of three rotating credit associations. The average membership of each association was 15 with the maximum membership of any one group being 100 and minimum 5. This is in harmony with Kimuyu's (1999) observation that business networks are usually small with strong trust between members. It is, in actual fact, this trust resulting from repeated success in the exchange situation that keeps members of the network together.

Businesswomen who belong to many associations and groups have a bigger radius of trust, that is, circle of people among whom cooperative norms are operative, and as such they are more acceptable (Fukuyama 1999). Such businesswomen are more likely to be successful in business due to the large network of friends and potential customers. The average amount of money contributed in each group is KShs.340 and on average the groups contribute after 18 days. However, the time they take to contribute ranges from 1 day to 30 days (one month) (Table 2). Some of the groups do not necessarily meet, but an appointed treasurer collects contributions from members and hands the whole amount to whoever is scheduled to receive it.

Table 2: Summary of Statistics for Association Members, Contributions and Periods of Contribution

Association	Membership			Amount Contributed			Time Taken to Contribute		
	Mean	Min.	Max.	Mean	Min.	Max.	Mean	Min.	Max.
1st association	17	5	38	278	50	1000	19	3	30
2nd association	13	5	25	261	20	1000	19	1	30
3rd association	12	8	16	484	20	2000	16	7	30

Source: Field Data, 2002

Other than rotating credit associations, the majority of the businesswomen (68%) were also members of other groups. However, these other groups were mostly religious-based such as *Jumuia* (Small Christian Communities) associated with the Catholic Church, Mothers' Unions and *Utulivu* associated with the Anglican Church and Muslim Youth Group. The rest were village development committees and groups. Focus group discussions revealed that membership of these groups/ associations tends to increase the customer catchment area for those businesswomen who are members because of the increased number of friends and potential customers the women have. This is based on the fact that people tend to have business transactions with people they know. This is in agreement with the views of Murphy (2002) that where business networks are ethnically or religiously concentrated, members of ethnic or religious groups tend to socialize and find common acquaintances among themselves and in the long run a beneficial referral system emerges to keep the network concentration. In this way, family, religion and ethnicity play critical roles in initiating business networks but such networks are kept in place by the business itself.

The results of this study on size and composition of associations compare with the views of Putnam (1993) that rotating credit associations vary widely in size, social composition, organization and procedures for determining the payout. The associations reflect not only a general spirit of cooperativeness but also a set of explicit and concrete practices of exchange of capital, which is important in business. Rotating credit associations compare with conventional banks except that while conventional banks loan out money with physical collaterals, rotating credit associations do it with social groups as collaterals. Poor people such as women who lack physical assets to offer as surety in effect pledge their social connections. This is the premise on which the famous Grameen Bank in Bangladesh is based. The bank lends money to groups who offer their social connection as collateral. Thus, in this instance, social capital is leveraged to expand the credit facilities in these communities and improve the efficiency with which markets operate.

The money businesswomen get from rotating credit associations are used for various purposes, depending on the pressing need of the person receiving the money. The majority of the women (45%) plough the money back into the business while about 34 per cent use it to meet domestic needs at home. About 16 per cent of them use the money to pay their children's school fees while a further 5.3 per cent use the money to establish other businesses. Money ploughed back into the business helps the business to grow. This, in fact, to some extent explains why the majority of the businesses run by these women had positive growth. The women argued that rather than struggle to get a loan from formal financial institutions that demands physical collaterals, it is far better to join rotating credit associations and get money to boost their business.

Apart from the businesswomen's membership in associations and other groups providing financial capital to boost their businesses, they also get a host of the benefits from the associations and groups.

As indicated earlier, rotating credit associations form a major source of financial capital among businesswomen to start up or boost business. Apparently, this is the outstanding benefit of the associations for the women. In additions to this, however, other benefits come in the way of association members and their friends becoming customers for the women's businesses. The businesswomen in this case are able to expand their network of friends and potential customers. The businesswomen also get the opportunity to advertise their businesses to association members so that they (association members) can become their customers.

The Role of Norms in Associations and Networks

The quality of the relationships among people has a significant influence on business pursuits and economic performance. Such relationships, in most cases, are sustained by strong norms and dense networks that nurture voluntary cooperation. In accordance with this, each association the businesswomen were members of was found to have rules and regulations to govern its members. The new members were accepted into the association based on these rules. The majority of the businesswomen (39.4%) cited the rule on defaulting as the most important in the association. However, other rules included those on members' punctuality in meetings and contributions, screening of new members for trustworthiness, spending of money given on a worthwhile cause and assisting members in times of need.

Without these norms, for example, it would be difficult for any businesswoman to entrust customers with goods on credit without collateral and/or a written binding contract. It is, therefore, within the well-functioning framework of these norms that businesswomen are able to give credit to customers. They presuppose that a certain amount of goodwill exists to prevent their customers from taking advantage of unforeseen loopholes to default with their money. According to the deliberations of the businesswomen during focus group discussions, norms act to define the boundaries within which members operate. Members who operate with minimum friction with the set norms earn themselves trust in the group as well as in the larger society. As it were, social norms are inculcated and sustained by way of modelling, socialization and sanctions. In the groups/associations and communities where these norms are followed, they have been proved to efficiently restrain opportunism and resolve problems of collective action.

Norms are meant to guard against reputational uncertainty and risk of default by members and create trust and dense networks of reciprocal engagement. As such, social networks allow trust to become transitive and spread such that members of a rotating credit association trust new members because the old members have cleared the new members as trustworthy. In line with this standpoint, Pedersen (2001) rightly argues that micro-enterprises can reduce risks of doing business through collaboration that is effectively sustained by enforcement of either norms, laws or contracts. These norms, laws and contracts are only there to nurture trust that is often extended only to specific groups. While laws and contracts are often enforced by the state, norms are often enforced by relationships and networks. Networks have efficient mechanisms for sharing information such that would-be defaulters are put on surveillance throughout the community. The sharing of information deters defaulting because, in choosing to default or not to default, participants compare short-term gains of such behaviour and long-term losses related to screening and search costs required in establishing a fresh relationship. When the perceived costs are large enough, it is possible to eliminate defaulting completely without legal enforcement.

The Importance of Trust in Business Performance

The importance of trust in business performance can, in part, be summarized by a quotation from Sorensen thus:

> A good trader must be very honest in business because you will get many friends and therefore widen your trading network... Never cheat customers, especially the illiterate village... If you establish yourself as honest old customers will tend to recommend their friends to come to your store (Sorensen 2001:305).

This quotation clearly illustrates the role that trust between traders and customers plays in business transactions. It is the trust traders and their customers have that defines the relationship and the extent of network they engage in. This definitely influences the manner the business is contacted and the availability of such facilities as credit. Trust will facilitate the flow of business information and issuance of credit to customers. In this study, most of the businesswomen (50%) give credit to customers.

The big percentage of businesswomen who give credit mainly results from the fact that their customers are mostly people they know well, either from their village (27%), associations (17%) or religious groups (14%). As such, trust and creditworthiness of these customers is well known to the businesswomen from day-to-day interactions they have in village, associations or religious groups. These results agree with Sorensen (2001) that a trader doing business in the local market is faced with two transactional orders, first, that based on his kinship group where the main axiom is amity and obligation to share, and two, the market sphere that is based on the axiom of individualism and profit maximization. Consequently, in order to handle this intrinsic conflict between individual achievement and the common interests of the kinship group, the local community traders follow economic strategies in which they manipulate and negotiate the principles of both sides through the creation of trust-based and trust-proven trade partnerships. In this case, therefore, traders struggle to locate reliable trading partners based, not on ascribed trust, but earned trust.

Interestingly, there are those businesswomen who sometimes give credit but other times do not give at all. The explanation given for this is that there are specific customers they give credit to while at the same time there are those they never give to, depending on how trustworthy the customer is. Consequently, it is only 30 per cent of the businesswomen who do not give credit at all. The reasons for not giving credit were elaborate. The outstanding reason, however, is untrustworthiness of customers (93%).

The businesswomen observed that there are some customers who cannot be trusted with credit because they hardly fulfil their promises. They argued that the best way to deal with such customers is to lock them out of a credit facility of the business so that every business transaction they undertake is on a cash basis. The women also noted that there are some customers who would only come to buy from the business when they want credit but buy from somewhere else when they have cash money. Such inconsistent/irregular customers are better off if they are denied credit so that they can learn.

Besides the inconsistent customers, the businesswomen also deny credit to customers who take a long time to pay for goods offered on credit. The reason for this is that in most cases the affected businesswomen lack money to restock their business since most of the money is still held up in credit. This is especially so for businesses with a small stock. About 3.7 per cent of the businesswomen do not give credit simply to avoid conflicts with customers because there are those who would not pay until they are taken to the police or the village elder. After such an instance, the relationship rarely returns to normal for business transactions. To avoid all this is to decide not to give credit at all.

Many factors actually determine who the businesswomen give credit. However, the most important factor cited by 30 per cent of the businesswomen is trust. Other important factors are creditworthiness of the customer and the familiarity or the extent to which the customer is known by the trader, consistency/regularity of customers and promptness in debt repayment.

Other than trust lubricating business transactions in micro-business, it also acts as binding and bridging mechanisms in social relations that facilitate information exchange, collective knowledge creation and innovations. This then means that as pointed out by Sorensen (2001) without trust, micro- and small-enterprises cannot collaborate and network, yet they need to do these as a prerequisite for their development. Trust in this case is the belief that the negotiating partner is able and willing to fulfil his obligation. However, the ability of a trusted person to fulfil his/her obligation is guaranteed either by the state or social groups in which he/she is a member.

Consistency of customers and their familiarity or the extent to which they are known by the trader makes them qualify for credit. It is within constant interaction and transaction that traders and customers come to know and trust each other. During one of the focus group discussions, one of the participants argued that trust with customers is a matter of trial and error, but the longer the trader stays with a customer the more the trust builds up. This gives an advantage to those who are members of a rotating credit association, religious group or village in which the trader belongs for they are able to interact on a day-to-day basis and get to either trust or distrust each other.

Arbitration of Debt Defaulters
The handling of debt defaulters was a big issue among the businesswomen. The majority of them (60%) reported that they simply write off the debt and never repeat the same mistake of giving credit to such people again (Table 3). The

reason for this is that they do business in the community where they are known and roughing up a defaulter to pay a debt may not be taken kindly. This issue came out very strongly during focus group discussions. One participant cited an example whereby a businesswoman took a debtor to a police cell and the latter eventually died there. The woman lost face in the entire community to the extent that nobody was buying from her. She finally had to close up her business due to lack of customers. This in a way explains why the option of reporting defaulter to police is unfavourable to many.

Table 3: Ways to Deal with Debt Defaulters

Action taken against Defaulters	Frequency (%)	Responses (%)	Cases
Write off debt	20	45.3	90.9
Expulsion from association	11	25.0	50.0
Arbitration by village committee	9	20.5	27.3
Report to police	4	9.1	18.2

Source: Field Data, 2002

These results tally with the views of Kimuyu (1999) and Putnam (1993) that in most cases, business networks do not depend on the third party, that is, the state (police and local administration) for enforcement of social contracts but rather on social norms. As noted by businesswomen, third-party enforcement of social contracts is expensive and people that rely on it for conflict resolution are likely to be less efficient, more costly and more unpleasant than those where trust is maintained by other means.

The expulsion of the defaulters from an association was another possible step to be taken. This was based on the fact that people belonging to the same association are both bound by norms operating within that association. Furthermore, members are supposed to be trustworthy. A member who is contrary to these expectations raises a lot of questions that can amount to expulsion from the association. However, this is only limited to those who belong to associations. The women argued that it was rare for somebody who is a member of an association to default because, in most cases, members of associations undergo tests for trust and creditworthiness.

Conclusion

This study was on the role of social capital in the establishment and sustenance of women's micro-businesses in Butere-Mumias District. It was intended to draw the attention of policy-makers, non-governmental Organizations (NGOs) and the government to the importance of social capital in the management and performance of women's micro-businesses. From the results of this study, it is evident that social capital, exemplified by associations, trust, norms and networks, is extremely important in the establishment and sustenance of women's micro-businesses.

Stocks of social capital namely associations, trust, norms and networks were found to be self-reinforcing and cumulative virtuous properties that result in an equilibrium with high levels of cooperation, reciprocity, civic engagement and collective well-being among people embracing them. These traits actually define business community where there is trust between trade parties, flow of market information and disciplining of defaulters within the system. The absence of these traits, on the other hand, portrays an unbalanced business community where defection, distrust, shirking, exploitation, isolation, disorder and stagnation is the order of the day. The end result of all these is a suffocating miasma of a vicious cycle for the weak. This situation is clearly exhibited by the process of globalization and its supporting institutions such as the World Trade Organization (WTO), Bretonwood institutions and multinational corporations that have led to the disillusionment of weak parties, mostly countries in Africa.

Social capital holds the potential for enhancing the performance of women's micro-businesses that act as a foundation for the gradual climbing of women to international trade. Policy-makers, as such, need to be more sensitive in the formulation of policies that favour the nurturing and intensification of social capital that has positive implications for the growth of women's micro-businesses.

Bibliography

Abrahamsson, B., 1993, *Why Organizations? How and Why People Organize*, London: Sage Publications.

African Regional Agricultural Credit Association (AFRACA), 1983, 'Women's Programmes in Agricultural Credit and Banking, Report on Policy Makers' Workshop on Women's Agricultural Credit and Banking Programs', held in Nairobi between 14-17 March, 1983.

Aleke-Dondo, E., 1991, 'Survey and Analysis of the Credit Program for Small and Micro-enterprise in Kenya', Nairobi: K-REP.

Baland, J. and Anderson, S., 1999, 'The Economics of Roscas and Intra–household Resource Allocation', Centre for Research in Development Economics, Belgium: University of Namur.

Barr, A., 1998, 'Do Small- and Medium-size Enterprises (SMEs) Network for Growth?' in *Enterprises in Africa: Between Poverty and Growth* by Kenneth, K. and McGrath, S., London: Intermediate Technology Group.

Bates, R., 1999, 'Ethnicity, Capital Formation and Conflict', Social Capital Initiative Working Paper No. 12.

Bazan, L. and Schmitz, H., 1997, 'Social Capital and Export Growth: An Industrial Community in Southern Brazil', IDS Working Paper No. 361, Sussex.

Bond, P., 2001, 'Review of Globalization From Below, http://www.uuhome.de/global/eng/wto059.html

Brecher, J. and Costello, T., 1998, *Global Village or Global Pillage: Economic Reconstruction from Bottom Up,* Cambridge: South End Press.

Brecher, J. and Costello, T., 2001, Global Self-Organization From Below, http://www.zmag.org/content/GlobalEconomics/brecher-costello_may10.cfm

Bulow, D., Van Dambal, E. and Maro, R., 1995, 'Supporting Women Group in Tanzania through Credit: Is this a Strategy for Empowerment?', CDR Working Paper 95.10, Copenhagen: Centre for Development Research.

Bunwaree, S., 2002, 'Export Processing Zones (EPZs), Gender and Globalisation: An African Scenario', paper presented during Gender Institute 2002 1-26 July, Dakar, Senegal.

CBS, ICEG and K-Rep., 1999, 'National micro-and small Enterprises Baseline Survey', unpublished report, Nairobi.

Coleman, J.S., 1988, 'Social Capital in the Creation of Human Capital', in *American Journal of Sociology (Supplement)* 94: 75-108.

Coleman, J.S., 1990, *The Foundations of Social Theory,* Cambridge: Harvard University Press.

Craig, K., 1990, 'The Pride Credit Program, Kenya: An Evaluation Report'.

Dranchman, E., 1999, 'For Some Women, Micro Businesses Pave Route to Financial Independence', http:/www.Atlanta.bizjournals.com/Atlanta/series/1999/02/22/editorials3.htm

Esman, M.J. and Uphoff, N., 1984, *Local Organizations: Intermediaries in Rural Development,* Ithaca: Cornell University Press.

Fall, Y., 1999, 'Globalisation, Its Institutions and African Women's Resistance', in *Gender, Globalization and Resistance* (ed.), by Fall, Y., AAWORD: 75-88.

Ferrand, D.V., 1998, 'Discontinuity and Development: Kenya's Middle-scale Manufacturing Industry', unpublished Ph.D. Thesis, University of Durham.

Francis, P., Agi, S.P.I., Ogoh-Alubo, S., Biu, H.A., Daramola, A.G., Nzewi, U.M. and Shehu, D.J., 1998, 'Hard Lessons: Primary Schools, Community and Social Capital in Nigeria', *World Bank Technical Paper Number 420,* Africa Region Series, Washington DC.

Fukuyama, F., 1999, 'Social Capital and Civil Society', http://www.imf.org/external/pubs/ft/seminar/ 1999/fukuyama.htm.

Fukuyama, F., 2002, 'Social Capital and Development: The Coming Agenda', SAIS Review Vol. XXII, No. 1 (Winter–Spring 2002).

Gittell, M., Ortega-Bustamante, I. and Steffy, T., 1999, 'Women Creating Social Capital and Social Change: A Study of Women-led Community Development Organizations', http://web.gc.cuny.edu/howardsamuels

Glen, F., 1975, *Social Psychology of Organization,* Suffolk: The Chaucer Press.

Government of Kenya, 1986, Sessional paper No. 1 on Renewed Growth for Sustainable Development, Nairobi: Government Printers.

Government of Kenya, 1989, A Strategy for Small Enterprises Development in Kenya, Nairobi: Government Printers.

Government of Kenya, 1997, National Development Plan 1997-2001, Nairobi: Government Printers.

Granovetter, M., 1985, 'Economic Action and Social Structure: The Problem of Embeddedness', in *American Journal of Sociology 91*: 481-510.

Gugerty, M.K., and Kremer, M., 2001, 'Outside Funding of Community Organizations: Benefiting or Displacing the Poor?', http://www.bu.edu/econ/ied/neudc/papers/gugerty-paper.doc

Heikkinen, M., 2000, 'The Social Networks of the Marginal Youth: A Study of Young People's Social Exclusion in Finland', in Journal of Youth Studies, Vol. 3 No. 4, pp. 389-406.

Heneveld, W. and Craig, H., 1996, 'Schools Count: World Bank Project Designs and the Quality of Primary Education in Sub–Saharan Africa', in *World Bank Technical Paper Number 303,* Washington DC: Africa Technical Department Series.

Hirschman, A.O., 1984, 'Getting Ahead Collectively: Grassroots Experiences in Latin America', New York: Pergamon Press, Elmsford.

Josefa, G.F., 1999, 'Gender Dimensions and Dynamics in International Lobbying on Trade and Development', DAWN-South East Asia, http:/www.dawn.org.fj/publications

Kahkonen, S., 1999, 'What Determines the Effectiveness of Community-based Water Projects? Evidence from Central Java, Indonesia on Demand Responsiveness, Service Rules and Social Capital', Social Capital Initiative Working Paper No. 14.

Kamunge, J., 1990, 'Small-scale Enterprise Development: CARS/Kenya's Experience', paper presented at the Small-scale Enterprise Development Workshop, February 20-23, Tunisia.

Keino, K. and Ngau, P.M., 1996, 'The Social Background of Women Entrepreneurs in Nairobi' in *Small Enterprises: Flexibility and Networking in an African Context.* (eds.) McCormick, D. and Pedersen, P.O., Nairobi: Longhorn.

Khor, M., 2001, *Rethinking Globalisation: Critical Issues and Policy Choices,* London: Zed Books Ltd.

Kibas, P.B., 2001, 'Impact of Credit on Women-operated Micro-enterprises in Uasin Gishu District', in Negotiating for Social Space (eds.), Alila, P. and Pedersen, P.O., Stockholm: African World Press.

Kiiru, W.K and Pederson, G.D., 1996, 'Kenya Women Finance Trust: A Case Study of Micro-finance Scheme', African Region No. 70, Washington DC: World Bank.

Kimuyu, P., 1999, 'Institutions Relevant to Commerce and Industry: Moral Norms, Social Capital, Business Systems, the State and the Law', Institute of Policy Analysis and Research (IPAR), DP No. 021/1999.

Kinyanjui, M.N., 1999, 'Employees in Small Enterprises in Nairobi: Job Search and Career Patterns', Working Paper No. 528. Institute for Development Studies (IDS), University of Nairobi.

Mahinda, A.M., 1993, 'Investigation of Factors that Influence the Participation of Women Entrepreneurs in Small Scale Enterprises: A Case Study of Machakos District', Med. Thesis, Kenyatta University.

McCormick, D., 1988, 'Small Enterprises in Nairobi: Golden Opportunity or Dead End?', PhD dissertation, Baltimore: John Hopkins University.

McCormick, D. and Pedersen, K., 1996, *Small Enterprises: Flexibility and Networking in African Context,* Nairobi: Longman.

Muhr, T., 1997, ATLAS.ti, version 4.1, Berlin: Scientific Software Department.

Murphy, J.T., 2002, *Networks, Trust and Innovations in Tanzania's Manufacturing Sector*, in World Development, Pergamon.

Napier, R.W. and Gershenfeld, K.M., 1999, *Group Theory and Experience*, 6th ed., New York: Houghton Mifflin Company.

Njeru, E.H.N. and Njoka, J.M., 2001, 'Women Entrepreneurs in Nairobi: The Socio-cultural Factors Influencing Their Investment Patterns', in Alila, P. and Pedersen, P.O., (eds.), *Negotiating for Social Space*, Stockholm: African World Press.

Otunga, R.N, Opata, G. and Muyia, F.N., 2001, 'Women Entrepreneurs in Eldoret Town: Their Socio-Economic Background and Business Performance', in Alila, P. and Pedersen, P.O., (eds.), *Negotiating for Social Space*, Stockholm: African World Press..

Pedersen, P.O. 2001, 'East African Micro-enterprises Negotiating Social Space: An Introduction', in Alila, P. and Pedersen, P.O., (eds.), *Negotiating for Social Space*, Stockholm: African World Press., pp. 1-24.

Putnam, R.D., 1993, *Making Democracy Work: Civic Traditions in Modern Italy*, New Jersey: Princeton University Press.

Raffo, C. and Reeves, M., 2000, 'Youth Transitions and Social Exclusion: Developments in Social Capital Theory', in Journal of Youth Studies, Vol. 3, No. 2, pp. 147-166.

Rhyne, E. and Otero, M., 1994, 'Financial Services to Micro-Enterprises: Principles and Institutions', in *The New World of Micro-Enterprises Finance*, West Hartford: Kumarian Press.

Scoones, I., 1998, 'Sustainable Rural Livelihoods: A Framework for Analysis', IDS Working Paper No. 72.

Seixes da Costa, F. and Desai, N., 2001, 'Globalization and the State', Report of 56th Session of the United Nations General Assembly on Globalization and the State, Washington DC.

Sorensen, P., 2001, 'Trust-A Cornerstone in Trade: The Economic Universe of the Iganga Maize Traders in Uganda', in Alila, P. and Pedersen, P.O., (eds.) *Negotiating for Social Space*, Stockholm: African World Press, pp. 304-327.

Swamy, A., Grootaert, C. and Oh, G., 1999, 'Local Institutions and Service Delivery in Burkina Faso', World Bank, Local Levels Institutions Working Paper No.8.

Womenaid International., 2001, 'Financing Women's Entrepreneurial Activities', briefing paper No. Mc/BP.01. http://www.womenaid.org/press/info/microcredit/micro.html

Women's Bureau (no date), 'Women Entrepreneurship Development in Kenya', Task Group Meeting held between 2-5 September 1991, organized by the Women's Bureau.

Woolcock, W. and Narayan, D., 2000, 'Social Capital: Implications for Development Theory, Research and Policy', *World Bank Research Observer* Vol. 15 (2).

World Bank, 2001, *Developing Social Capital*, Technical Paper No. 324, Washington DC: World Bank.

World Trade Organization (WTO), 2001, 'State and Globalization', http://www.wto.org/info/global.html.

9

Gender, Trade Liberalization and the Multilateral Trading System: Towards an African Perspective

Zo Randriamaro

The gender dimensions of trade policies and institutions have attracted increased attention from different stakeholders, including activists and researchers. Most of the attention has focused on the impact of trade policies in terms of income and formal employment, and most of the analyses have been done by researchers from the North, on the basis of data that include a minority of African country case studies, while African women remain largely absent from the debate over trade policies and their gender dimensions.

This first session therefore aims to respond to a central question: why is an African perspective needed in the analysis of the gender dimensions of trade liberalization and the multilateral trading system (MTS)? The session is divided into four parts that seek to respond to the different aspects of this question. The first part provides a retrospective on the history of the General Agreement on Tariffs and Trade (GATT) and the World Trade Organization (WTO) in order to identify some of the determining factors of Africa's position in the MTS. The second part examines the prevailing trade theory with its assumptions and myths and their gender implications. The third and fourth parts provide a critical overview of the main issues raised by the existing literature on gender and trade, and by the current approaches to gender mainstreaming in the WTO.

The 'Shadow' History of the Multilateral Trading System: *From GATT to the WTO*

An important justification for an African perspective in the analysis of trade liberalization and the MTS derives from the history of GATT and the establishment of the WTO. This history – which is usually untold by the mainstream discourse on trade liberalization – shows that African countries have been integrated into the multilateral trading system without any kind of meaningful participation, and under peculiar conditions that define their position in the global trading arrangements.

The fundamental principle of the MTS, the Most Favoured Nation (MFN) principle, is a European concept that was constructed in the mercantilist period of the 19th century, namely with the Anglo-French trade treaty of 1860. As a leading industrial power together with Britain during the post-Second World War period, the US played a central role in the conception and formulation of the MTS. The origins of the GATT go back to the discussions and agreements between the US and Britain about the post-war economic system (Dam 1970:12). This was mainly done based on their own priorities, namely the need to ensure a ready supply of cheap raw materials and expanding markets for manufactured goods. Thus,

> During and immediately after the war, the two governments advocated the worldwide reduction of tariffs, the removal of trade barriers and 'equal access to the markets and raw materials of the world'. Their discussions focused on the 'removal' of restrictions to trade by others, and there is very little reference in the discussions to the problems that would be faced by the 'underdeveloped' (TWN 2001:24).

From the establishment of the GATT in 1947 up to now, the developing countries have confronted barriers placed on the export products interesting to them by the developed countries. Despite the numerous attempts to address their complaint, many of the trade barriers identified in the 1960s against exports of the developing countries remained in 2001 (Raghavan 2001). The sectors of agriculture and textiles, which are of particular interest to African countries, provide typical examples of such barriers.

The history of the MTS shows that trading rules actually work as a system for the regulation of the exercise of power within which weaker countries have actually served the interests of powerful trading nations. As the trading system is based on power by nature, these nations have the power – i.e. the political clout, but also the market size and the capacity to produce goods and services for trade – to define both the rules in the trade agreements and the processes at the WTO. This is important for the appreciation of the power relations and the domination of weaker nations and the weaker sections of their populations within a system which proclaims to be rule-based.

The decisive influence of the US and major trading nations, together with the imbalances against and lack of participation of developing countries, are entrenched features of the MTS. The measures that have been taken to redress these imbalances are not legally binding and supposed to be implemented as a 'best-endeavour effort', without any contractual rights and obligations (Raghavan 2001). The major premise used to induce developing countries to accept the establishment of the

WTO, following the Uruguay Round of trade negotiations (URA), was that this would put an end to US unilateralism by establishing a multilateral 'rules-based' system, past and recent history of international trade demonstrates the continuation of US unilateralism.

The US unilateralism has been closely associated with the key role of transnational corporations in shaping the trade agenda, agreements and rules. This influence of transnational corporations is reflected in the evolution of the relationships between the developed and developing countries within the trading system: after the Kennedy Round in 1964-67 'the developed countries became interested in breaking into the markets of the developing world. This objective became even more evident in the Uruguay Round, preparations for which took place in the early 1980s' (TWN 2001:31). This development coincides with the decline in manufacturing profits during the 1960s in the North, which led to the switch of productive reinvestment into financial assets by big companies and to the start of their search for new markets, cheaper inputs and labour. The pressure on developing countries to liberalize not only trade but also investment is linked to the influence of transnational companies in the US and other industrial countries.

In particular, the influence of the negotiation of the North American Free Trade Agreement (NAFTA) during the same period as the URA, together with continued pressure by the US since 1982 (TWN 2001:31), resulted in the extension of the GATT system to areas such as intellectual property, services and investment measures after the conclusion of the URA and the establishment of the WTO in 1995. In this context, the WTO represents the product of a political process which has involved 'intense lobbying by specific exporters groups in the United States and Europe or of specific compromises between such groups and other domestic groups' (Rodrik 2001:34). This implies that there is very little space for development concerns and goals in the MTS which has primarily been designed to enforce policies in the interest of major trading nations at the global level.

The Political Economy of Trade Liberalization in Africa

The first phase of the GERA programme (1996-1999) was aimed at studying the impact of structural adjustment programmes (SAPs) on women and gender relations in Africa. The findings of the research carried out by GERA and other researchers largely confirm that economic reforms have been a major cause of increased poverty and social inequality by region and along class lines, and that SAPs worsened the situation of African women (GERA Programme 2000).

It is important to see the continuity between SAPs and current trade and investment policies. Indeed, trade liberalization is an essential component of SAPs. During the last two decades, trade policy reform and foreign investment have become key elements of the internal policy changes and strategies aimed at consolidating the structural adjustment reforms in African countries. A further step in the pursuit of SAPs and post-adjustment policies emerged with the contemporary global regime for the regulation of international trade, especially as brought into being by the URA. With the emergence of the WTO, most regional and national trade regulations are now defined within an intergovernmental framework. What before were simply rules about the import and export of products of different national economies have been transformed into instruments shaping national policy and domestic economic structures.

Furthermore, there is rising concern about their undermining effects on international commitments and domestic laws and policies that have been adopted in order to protect fundamental rights and freedoms (Olaka-Onyango and Udagama 2001).

Both the US Africa Growth and Opportunity Act (AGOA) and the Cotonou Agreement seek to underpin relationships with Africa on a new agenda of trade and investment liberalization. The bilateral arrangements established between African countries and their trading 'partners' of the North imply similar effects, especially since these bilateral 'partners' are mostly the former colonizers and still have an important influence on the economies of their ex-colonies.

Of note is the fact that most African countries have undertaken trade liberalization under structural adjustment, as part of the conditions under SAPs. This position is very different from that of the developed countries who freely initiated the process of trade liberalization in the context of regional trade agreements and the WTO. Combined with the lack of inclusiveness and transparency of the WTO, this power differential enables developed countries to impose rules and obligations on developing countries.

Moreover, the convergence between the IMF, the WB and the WTO has created not only a dominant discourse promoting the trade liberalization agenda, but also cross-related conditions through mechanisms such as the IMF Poverty Reduction and Growth Facility (PRGF) and the World Bank-led Poverty Reduction Strategy Paper (PRSP) mechanism, both of which reproduce the conditions of SAPs. The Integrated Framework for Technical Assistance which is meant to ensure the integration of trade and development involves the combined efforts of the IMF, World Bank and WTO along with other UN agencies.

Just like SAPs, the implementation of the WTO agreements is 'one of the key factors exacerbating economic problems (especially in the agricultural sector) in many places. Many developing countries, and especially the small island developing states (SIDS) and LDCs, are in far worse straits after implementing these agreements' (Williams 2001). Most importantly, like SAPs, these agreements threaten the realization of the right to development of African nations, as well as the social rights of poor women and men among their population.

Thus, the gender dimensions of the analysis of SAPs which focused on the relationships between globalization, macroeconomic policy, development and poverty remain critical for an African perspective on gender and trade liberalization, particularly in relation to the interconnections between trade and macroeconomic policies imposed by the IFIs. Such analysis should also consider the human rights implications of trade agreements and rules.

Since trade is about the exchange of goods and services, the ability of a country to benefit from the trading system fundamentally depends on its productive capacity and, correlatively, on its resource endowments. In this regard,

> One of the most important sources of inequalities in resource endowments is the history of colonization that shaped and is shaping trade patterns and relations between developed and developing nations. It cannot be denied that developed countries have been able to grow fast using their higher endowments of capital, technology and skills and this level of growth is built on their past exploitation of their colonies. The developing countries, on the other hand, have been convinced that they should specialize in labour-intensive production (because that is where their comparative advantage lies) without any concrete proposals on how to increase capital, skills and technology, which is the basis for real and continued growth (Durano 1999).

It is important to recognize that 'a major reason why the world trading system has not been working beneficially for developing countries is because their main way of participating in the system has been to export commodities, whose prices have been declining, and thus their terms of trade have been deteriorating' (TWN 2001:51).

It is equally important to recognize that there is a definite link between the history of colonization and racism, and global economic realities. Neoliberalism and current processes of globalization are built upon a history of discriminatory and exploitative policies and practices, especially against women.

Overarching Issues from a Gender Perspective

Just as inequalities and power relations shape the relationships between the participating nations within the MTS, gender relations constitute a structuring factor of the relationship between trade policies and their outcomes. Trade policies affect men and women differently, and generate different responses from men and women due to pre-existing gender inequalities in access to and ownership of resources such as land, capital, credit, education, health, time and income, as well as in access to power and decision-making, alongside the sexual division of labour which assigns the unpaid reproductive labour to women. From a gender perspective, trade liberalization and the international trading system raise a number of overarching issues at different levels.

In an environment characterized by the features that have been described in previous sections:

> The relevant comparative advantage of developing countries would seem to lie in cheap labour. Increasingly, that cheap labour is female labour, which is systematically underpaid. Over-reliance on such a strategy in the medium to long run is likely to trap both women workers, and the countries which depend on a low-wage growth strategy, in a perpetual swirl of debt and dependency (Williams 2001).

Moreover, feminist economists draw attention to the fact that gender inequalities in wages and working conditions have been found to contribute positively to growth in semi-industrialized countries, which means that export successes and growth in such countries come at the expense of gender equality and women's rights. They underline that using gender inequality as an instrument of international competition may result in long-term adverse effects on the terms of trade of developing countries (Cagatay 2001).

Despite the fact that the export-led, market-based and private sector-driven growth that multilateral trade arrangements seek to promote depends to a large extent on women's labour in both the production and reproduction spheres, women are excluded from macroeconomic policy making and processes. Not only are they under-represented in macro-level institutions such as the WTO, but multilateral arrangements related to trade and investment have been devised with complete disregard of gender considerations, based on the implicit assumption that such considerations are not relevant at the macro level. Therefore, these arrangements tend to reinforce gender inequalities, thereby affecting women's ability to move between sectors even when opportunities exist.

Gender inequalities also have an impact on trade performance. This is the reason why gender-blind trading arrangements that have been designed by governments in order to promote growth by moving labour to tradable sectors actually aggravate the constraints that prevent women from moving into these sectors. Empirical evidence from many African countries shows that their exports are severely constrained by gender inequalities in command and control over income and assets, including land and credit.

Women and small producers are subject to a constant insecurity due to continuous changes in international market conditions. In Africa, women and small producers are singularly vulnerable to such insecurity, because of the absence of any form of compensatory social protection. In particular, with respect to the subsistence agricultural subsector which has already been weakened by the liberalization of agricultural policy due to increases in the price of imports and withdrawal of subsidies, current trade policies raise the issue of food security in general, and the issue of women's unequal status as producers and consumers in particular.

With regards to the meso level i.e. institutions and markets, the new policy orientation removed and delegitimized the public policy instruments that could be used in addressing women's economic subordination. Moreover, as most African countries lack national consensus-building institutions that can guarantee the convergence between the interests of different social groups and actors, the interests canvassed in international trade negotiations are often those selected by governments without the participation of women, other vulnerable groups or the mass of the population. This has major implications:

- The first implication is related to the multiple disempowerment of African women in the context of international trading and financial arrangements: an internal disempowerment due to their overall economic subordination and lack of participation in decision-making processes at the national level, and an external disempowerment brought about by the biases against African countries in international trading and financial arrangements.

- The second implication pertains to the dynamics of power relations, in particular the interplay between internal and external relations of domination: indeed, the internal disempowerment of women and other marginalized groups enables to a large extent the perpetuation of the inequitable trading and financial arrangements, and subsequently, the domination of powerful countries' interests.

This also raises the issue of the role of the state and national institutions in such a context.

Some political scientists call for attention to the combined effects of trade arrangements and other economic reforms on the re-conceptualization of the notion of 'governance', including not only the re-definition of the role of the state, but also the political processes and spaces within African nations. These analysts point to the far-reaching consequences of the institutional reforms brought about by current trade and economic policies, notably the increased tightening of the political space for democratic participation. This is due to the imposition through the proposed institutional reforms of the concept of 'horizontal accountability', promoting the balance between the different governmental institutions in order to contribute to a 'self-restraining state' at the expense of a 'vertical accountability' of policy-makers to citizens and their elected representatives. Shrinking political spaces have implications on women's participation in governance which is already very low, as well as for their efforts and struggles.

In addition, each type of trade arrangement comes with a specific set of parameters that determine the impact of the related policies on different social groups and genders, namely through their consequences on the legal and regulatory institutions that have been established by the different nations. Gender activists point to many gender-biased provisions in the content of trade commitments themselves, and to their possible interactions with formal and informal laws and norms that determine women's condition and position in a particular country or location, as well as with institutional and practical factors that influence the enforcement of laws.

Of particular importance for women are the changes brought about by trading arrangements in the definition of the so-called non-tariff barriers to trade (NTBs), as in recent years, TNCs have begun to use regional trade agreements and the WTO to expand the definition of NTBs to all national laws and measures that they do not benefit from. For example, special incentives such as low-cost loans, tax credits or training provided to women under affirmative action laws could potentially be challenged as an 'unfair barrier to trade' under the Subsidies and Countervailing Measures (SCM) agreement.

The consumption dynamic impulsed by trade liberalization, notably through the attempts of TNCs to expand and deepen markets, involves the manipulation of sex, sexuality and gender identity, together with the reinforcement of gender stereotypes by advertising and marketing campaigns. A very common example of this trade-based sexual exploitation of women and girls is the selling of the 'exotic' image of beautiful and hospitable local women to promote tourism in African countries. A more disturbing one is the expansion of sex tourism in many African countries.

With respect to employment, liberalization policies have led to increased unemployment and informalization of work in most African countries (GERA Programme 2000). Together with the changes in production relations, namely the growing number of home-based and temporary workers – the majority of which are women – and the various forms of increased pressure on workers within the workplace, this development raises critical issues about the sustainability of women's livelihoods and their rights as workers, in a context where the reduced fiscal capacity of states does not allow for effective safety nets or other forms of social protection.

At the level of the households, national trade and investment policies have resulted in additional constraints and burdens on women. In addition to the fact that they bear most of the costs of the reduction of public spending in social services, including in terms of increased reproductive work, price liberalization has forced poor women to reduce their food consumption and to increase their unpaid work – often on family farms and family-owned businesses – in order to provide for their families. Devaluation of the exchange rate has had a similar negative effect, especially on women involved in the services sector. Because imported food often out-competes domestic crops mainly produced and traded by women, the liberalization of imports has had an adverse impact both on women's revenue and on domestic food production.

These realities have been masked by the new economic orthodoxy which justifies post-adjustment policies and legitimizes the subordination of women in several ways:

- by overlooking the differences in both entitlements and constraints between men and women;
- by building on the assumption that women's work is free and infinitely elastic, and that they will therefore continue to supply their unpaid contribution to the care and reproduction of society in the 'global village';
- by reinforcing the gender stereotypes that perpetuate women's subordination;
- by providing the rationale for consolidating the economic reforms undertaken under SAPs, regardless of their deleterious effects on women and gender relations;
- by imputing all the adverse effects of current trade and investment policies to the African nation states themselves, not to these policies or to the market;
- by defining most social policies and regulations that are especially important for women as 'trade barriers' to be eliminated.

For African women, these issues suggest the urgent need to transform the economic model underlying the international trade regime, because of the structural and political biases that undermine gender equality and disempower women in the economy.

The Conventional Theory and Associated Myths of 'Free Trade'

The Assumptions of the Conventional Trade Theory

The principle of comparative advantage is one of the pillars of the conventional trade theory. According to this principle, countries should specialize in producing the goods they are relatively more efficient at producing, and then trade with other countries that are relatively more efficient at producing the other goods needed. Free trade without the interference of governments benefits everyone because it allows countries to specialize in producing what they are good at and then exchange it in the world market. Thus, in the theory of comparative advantage, gains from trade result from the sum of specialization and free trade.

Free trade theories make a number of explicit and implicit assumptions:

1. Full employment, obviously an unrealistic assumption for African economies.
2. Resources are fixed, and are perfect substitutes, i.e. that everything used in one type of production can be automatically re-deployed to another type of production, thereby ignoring the costs of the re-training of workers and investment in different types of technology, etc., which are most likely to reduce the gains from trade.

3. Producers do not move between countries, in other words, that there is free movement of goods and services, but no free movement of production. This assumption is particularly unrealistic in the context of globalization, as evidenced in the current organization of production at the global level.

4. Factors are mobile across sectors and there is perfect competition: such an assumption ignores the structural constraints that do not allow for the mobility of factors, especially labour. In particular, it ignores a number of factors, including the gender division of labour, the lack of economic and social infrastructure and access to information, which inhibit women's ability to respond to economic incentives and opportunities offered by trade.

5. International prices adjust automatically: there is ample evidence that rapid trade liberalization led to trade deficits in developing countries as exports stayed flat or did not keep pace with rising imports (UNCTAD 1999). Moreover, the practices of the major trading powers show that these promoters of free trade themselves use non-market pricing systems.

Most importantly, the theory of comparative advantage is silent on the distribution of the gains from trade, thereby making the assumption that benefits from trade will trickle down to everybody alike as a result of growth and increased total income of participating countries: to business owners, as well as to workers and consumers, both men and women. It ignores the reality that this distribution is part of a political process within which benefits from trade often accrue only to the business owners who can make increased profits, while workers and communities become worse off.

The assumption made by the conventional theory of the convergence of factor prices that would lead to lower prices in domestic markets and, subsequently, increase consumers' purchasing power has been invalidated by research, namely by a study commissioned by the WTO on the relation between trade and poverty which found that:

> There is no 'tendency of catch up convergence' in respect to income; rather, incomes tend to be diverging within each segment of global income. Whenever convergence tendency was observed, this was among lower income countries and reflected the relatively better off among the poor countries slipping backwards (downward convergence) (Williams 2001:4).

Feminist economists[1] (Cagatay 2001) have provided a critique of the mainstream trade theory (also known as the neo-classical, neo-liberal theory) in terms of its distributive effects. According to this theory, if the two factors of production are unskilled and skilled labour, in developing countries whose comparative advantage is assumed to be in goods that make intensive use of unskilled labour, the wage differentials between the two types of labour should close with trade liberalization. The opposite should take place in developed countries.

If the two factors of production are capital and labour, trade liberalization should reduce the return on capital while increasing it on labour in developing countries. The opposite should occur in developed countries. This implies that trade liberalization should be equity-enhancing in developing countries while being disequalizing in developed countries. However, studies have found that in many developing countries, disparities between skilled and unskilled workers have increased.

Regarding the analysis of the gendered impact of international trade, it is argued that the central question should be whether trade reform and emerging patterns of trade perpetuate, accentuate or erode existing gender inequalities. A related question is whether there is a change in gender-based power relations within households, communities and the society at large.

The responses to these questions should consider:

a) changing patterns and conditions of work, including paid and unpaid work
b) changes in gender gaps in wages, earnings, patterns of ownership and control over assets
c) changes in consumption patterns by gender
d) changes in use of technology by men and women
e) changes in public provisioning of services and their gendered impacts
f) gender-differentiated empowerment implications of trade flows.

With respect to the gender, trade and poverty nexus, it is underscored that the assessment of trade policies should not focus on market-based criteria such as income and consumption and 'whether they maximize flows of goods and services, but in terms of whether they further desired social outcomes such as equity, social inclusion, freedom from poverty, development of human capabilities, protection of human rights, democratic governance and environmental sustainability' and 'incorporate power and power relations within and across nations' (Cagatay 2001:12).

Gender, Trade and Employment

Authors such as Standing (1989a and b) have argued that in the current context of intensified global competition, supply-side macroeconomics and deregulation, employers have tried to establish a more 'flexible' labour force by substituting female workers, with lower reservation wages, for men. This argument is an important part of the debate over core labour standards and workers' rights. It points to the general context of macroeconomic and labour market policies within which the feminization of employment takes place.

This context is characterized by the increasing erosion of workers' rights and the power of traditional trade unions vis-à-vis capital, due to the triumph of neo-liberal policies. Market liberalization policies and the increased mobility of capital have contributed to this erosion of workers' rights, as labour market deregulation was justified in the name of achieving international competitiveness.

In general, studies on export-oriented countries show that although trade liberalization seems to favour women in terms of employment, the 'competitive advantage' of women as workers lies in the inferiority of their conditions of employment in terms of earnings as well as health and safety conditions. Indeed, much of women's trade-related gains in employment have taken place in EPZs and the informal sector where conditions of work are very poor. In many establishments, practices of sexual harassment and pregnancy tests have been reported.

It is important to recognize that there are also winners and losers among women. The celebrated increase in women's employment under trade liberalization policies is real in the aggregate, but at the same time, some women have also lost their jobs because of import competition and the sectoral reallocation of work. Such loss of employment has mostly happened in informal work, small firms and among low-skilled workers where poor women dominate.

Moreover, trade liberalization makes it difficult to achieve gender equity in wages at the national level. At the heart of this dilemma is the fact that women in different countries are segregated into a relatively narrow range of occupations, and through trade, they compete with each other. Trade liberalization provides an incentive for the repression of wages.

Therefore, the claims about women's gains from trade in terms of employment call for closer examination in the case of Africa. Such claims must be assessed against the context and conditions within which women integrate into the formal labour market. Given the expansion of the informal sector in most African countries, special attention should also be paid to the impact of trade policies on this sector.

Myths and Realities

The mainstream discourse on the benefits of trade openness in developing countries has generated a significant number of myths that have informed the design of trade policies at different levels. Among these is the misconception that free trade is the major cause of economic growth in today's developed countries. The historical evidence shows that during their own development and industrialization process, these countries protected their domestic industries behind tariff walls. Tariff liberalization took place only when the home industries were sufficiently strong or efficient to stand up to competition from imports. For instance, the US, who is the major promoter of free trade today, began its industrialization behind rising tariff barriers at the end of its Civil War (Handlin 1947, cited in TWN 2001:23).

This evidence also contradicts the theory of comparative advantage, as it demonstrates that what is presented as the 'natural' comparative advantage of developed countries in terms of capital investment, technology, know-how, etc., is actually a 'constructed advantage' that developing countries should also be able to develop, at least in principle. Some analysts underline that the development of newly-industrialized countries such as Taiwan, South Korea and Singapore is the outcome of a specific type of comparative advantage based on the government's protection of and support to domestic industries until they were able to compete internationally (TWN 2001, Rodrik 2001).

The most recent analyses of the links between the openness of economies and growth rate demonstrate that 'there is no convincing evidence that trade liberalization is predictably associated with subsequent economic growth' (Rodrik 2001), as the increase in growth rates can be attributed to other macroeconomic policies related to exchange rates, technology or exports promotion. Furthermore, country case studies show that 'employment growth has generally been slow to dismal and rising primary income disparity (in some cases over and above the already high levels of income inequality) has been the rule' (Taylor 2001, cited in Cagatay 2001:17).

Similarly, the reality in African countries dismantles the myth of the 'trickle-down' effect of trade liberalization policies. There is no evidence of such a trickle-down; on the contrary, studies on the impact of SAPs show that trade liberalization has increased inequalities along gender and class lines because of its differentiated impact on the various social groups (GERA Programme 2000).

The myth that gains from trade accrue to nationals and that consumers determine the type of commodities that are produced and traded is undermined by the overwhelming evidence that most of the time nationals do not have the ownership of resources or subsequently of the benefits from trade. The large majority of the owners are foreigners, and nationals participate in trade mainly as workers and consumers. Advertising and marketing campaigns at the global scale have entailed significant changes in the behaviour of consumers, including the creation of certain needs within people's psyches and a culture of gender stereotyping by the advertising industry (Durano ibid).

The widespread myth that governments do not intervene in trade has occulted the fact that the promotion of free trade has actually required a great deal of governments' intervention. The deregulation of the labour market and financial sector, as well as the promotion of export-led industrialization which relies on women's labour, are examples of such intervention.

Last but not least, it has been underlined that 'free trade theories have always been advanced by the major developed countries to further their own interests' (TWN 2001:23). It appears that the mainstream trade theory and the 'free trade' rhetoric are used to legitimize the system of rules which governs the WTO and reflects the balance of power among its member countries. These rules do not reflect free trade for all products, nor has 'free trade' been practised by the major trading parties in areas that are crucial for African countries.

Critical Overview of the Literature[2]

This brief review of the literature on gender and trade starts from the position that for trade to be meaningful, it has to deliver some growth, not just to a country, but also to all its citizens, especially the most disadvantaged. Trade policies should both protect and strengthen the capacity of nations and their citizens to address issues of poverty and social exclusion. Growth should be socially equitable and environmentally sustainable.

Conceptual Issues Identified in the Literature

There is a general agreement that trade liberalization is experienced differently by different social groups. However, in terms of gender analysis, the neo-liberal analysis ignores the issues of other social groups and focuses mainly on the gender dimensions. On the other hand, those who adopt a political economy approach tend to address the intersection between gender, class, region, among others with a strong focus on gender. It is interesting that the majority of the analysis is of the view that trade and investment liberalization either perpetuates or exacerbates, but does not address, gender inequalities.

It has been argued by a minority that trade liberalization has been helpful to women because of their increased labour force participation in certain parts of the world, and this in turn has reduced the wage differentials between men and women. However, this view has been strongly challenged in the sense that it ignores the conditions under which they integrate the labour force, and the fact that the reduction in the wage gap is more a result of the downward trend of wages, rather than an increase in women's wages.

Among the arguments deployed in support of the dominant view that trade liberalization policies have been detrimental to women as a social group is the fact that trade liberalization in general, and the WTO rules in particular, ignore the gender inequalities that prevent women from benefiting from opportunities they may represent. Another argument is that trade liberalization policies themselves perpetuate or exacerbate gender inequalities and even create new ones. For instance, those who think that the only problem with the rules is that women are not able to participate in trade focus on expanding the ways in which women can also take advantage of the situation. On the other hand, those who contend that the rules themselves are problematic and exacerbate inequalities focus on reforming those rules and challenging the fundamental structures and assumptions underlying the system of rules. These different arguments have different implications not only for the research but also for the discussion about the different attitudes that activists have taken towards the WTO.

Some of the analyses have focused on the micro-level impacts, as social implications are easier to track at the micro level. Feminist economists have called attention to the importance of three levels of analysis:

- the micro level, which focuses on the household and intra-household processes and relations;

- the meso level, which focuses on formal and informal institutions such as the markets and the State, the laws, norms and practices; and

- the macro level, which focuses on the monetary, fiscal and exchange rate policies, prices, etc.

The focus on the interconnections between these different levels provides for a more comprehensive analysis of the gender dimensions of trade policies. For instance, at the meso level, the argument is made that some of the perceptions about women's work, which persist despite of international conventions such as the Convention for the Elimination of all Forms of Discrimination Against Women (CEDAW) and the Beijing Platform for Action, have been reinforced by trade policies. One such perception is that women's reproductive and domestic responsibilities are seen as their primary function. In spite of more than 20 years of gender equality activism, their productive activities are always discounted. Their income is considered as secondary and supplementary to the income of the male breadwinner. These perceptions are reinforced by trade policies which build on the assumption that women's unpaid labour is in unlimited supply.

Central Findings of the Impact of Trade and Investment Liberalization on Women and Gender Equality

Some of the studies on the impact of export-oriented industrialization on the gender composition of the labour force have found that women's participation has risen globally, but that differences exist not only between developed and developing countries, but also between Africa and the rest of the world. Many of the gains made by women have taken place in the EPZs, sub-contracting chains and the informal sector where working conditions are characterized by long hours, instability and insecurity of employment, unhealthy working conditions as well as low pay. Combined with the issue of de-industrialization and the growing informalization of work, this situation means that the gains women have made have to be offset against more problematic losses to them.

In the area of agriculture, the gains have been much less beneficial to Africa and all its small farmers, particularly women farmers. One reason is the removal of subsidies for agricultural production, which has posed major threats to food security and micro enterprises. For many African women whose labour has increased in export agriculture, the benefits have not come directly to them, mainly because they are not the owners of the cash crops. It has been argued that this preference of cash crops over food crops is discriminatory against women who do not benefit from government support for their food production. In addition, their work in the cash crop production has reduced the time available for their food crops.

Regarding the issue of import competition, it has been argued that large and medium scale producers may benefit from trade and investment liberalization. Since women tend to be small marginal farmers, these benefits are not likely to affect them. Whilst trade reforms can create new markets – for instance, for the celebrated non-traditional export crops discussed below – it is important to remember that it also destroys some of the traditional ones.

It is often argued that non-traditional agricultural exports (NTAEs) generate significant revenues, and therefore represent a potential area of comparative advantage for African countries. It is also argued that the promotion of this sector will allow for a more equitable internal distribution of the total benefits from trade on gender lines, redressing the bias against women elsewhere in agriculture. However, there is little evidence of their gendered outcomes in the context of the current provisions under the AoA. Already, one can tell that gender biases limit African women's access to productive resources and their rights in land, and thus the incentive and capacity for devoting resources to the production of NTAEs.

One of the indicators that has been used for the success of liberalization has been the increase in household incomes. Gender analysts have pointed out that this does not necessarily improve the nutritional status of women and children. In places where self-employment and unpaid family labour are more prevalent, the lack of control over resources such as land and capital is a critical issue for women.

The gender impact of the collapse of commodity prices around Africa has to be verified. This has notably affected government revenue as well as household incomes. In particular, the reduction of government spending in social services has increased women's reproductive work and reduced their leisure time, as women have had to take up more responsibilities in the areas of health care and education. Last but not the least, liberalization and the reduction of the state's participation in productive work have also meant that the state has not been in a position to implement some of the promises that it has made to women in the Beijing PFA and other international conventions.

This review of the impacts of trade liberalization, as discussed in the literature, points out that many claims in the gender and trade literature are very preliminary and need further work. It also points to the overwhelming focus of this literature on the impact of trade policies on incomes and formal employment, which tends to overlook other elements that are important for gender equity and sustainable human development in the African setting. These elements can be best identified through contextualized and country-specific studies.

Trade Policy-making Institutions and Processes

The focus on trade policy-making institutions and processes is a very large issue in the current debate about trade and investment policy because it goes to the heart of the rights of citizens to participate in decisions which affect their lives in very profound ways. Trade policy is made at three levels: national, regional and international levels. Therefore, any analysis of trade and investment policy-making institutions and processes needs to look at all three levels and how they are interconnected.

National trade policy is the remit of the executive arm of governments. It is the executive which makes most of the important trade policies. Legislators play a less fundamental role, such as ratification. This means that there is bureaucratic control of trade policy decision-making. It is interesting that this has been rationalized as an attempt to depoliticise trade and investment policy making so that national as opposed to partisan interests can be served. The assumption that the executive and the bureaucrats will serve the national interests – or that there is one agreed-upon national interest – is hotly contested, but also largely undermined by the vehemence of free-trade protestors around the world.

This mode of decision-making raises fundamental questions about the transparency and inclusiveness of the processes: who can participate and how. For example, the private sector, in spite of all its complaints, does better than many citizens' groups in the participation in trade and investment policy decision-making. In this regard, it is important to acknowledge that the large number of women who work in an informal sector trade are not considered part of the private sector. The GERA study in Uganda showed very clearly that the stratum of people who are considered to be part of the private sector are the medium and large scale operators who tend to group in elite institutions such as the Private Enterprise Foundation funded by the World Bank and the (GERA Programme 2000).

The sections of the population where many women traders are involved in trade and investment work are not part of the groups which participate in trade and investment policy decision-making. Civil society activists do not have a place at the table as such, and whatever is done with them is seen as consultation and always comes at a much later stage in decision-making. Even with the regional trade institutions such as ECOWAS, COMESA and SADC, the distance between citizens and decision-making bodies has been heavily criticized. In order to bridge this gap, it is important to analyse the decision-making mechanisms within those institutions in the same way as national trade policies: who is participating and how, who is outside the processes and how are they excluded.

The Major Approaches for Addressing Gender Issues in the WTO

This section aims to provide insights into the existing landscape and options put forward by gender activists and researchers for gender mainstreaming into the WTO. The current status of the debate on gender issues and the WTO among women's organizations and networks, along with their different approaches to mainstreaming gender into the WTO are discussed, with a view to identifying some possible options for the definition of an African perspective.

The Status of the Debate

It is important to situate the debate in the context of the evolution within the women's movement, so as to identify the key players and the different interests that are involved. The debate on how to address gender issues in the WTO was institutionalized with the creation of a global Informal Working Group on Gender and Trade which developed out of the Women's Caucus at the first ministerial conference of the WTO in Singapore in 1996. At that time, this group gathered a majority of Northern women's organizations and networks, and a few from the South. African women were noticeably under-represented. This group shares a common concern about the impact of trade liberalization on women and a wish to ensure that a gender analysis is built into trade policy-making and associated decision-making, procedures and organizations.

The main issue of the debate is not about the principle of the integration of a gender perspective into the WTO's work. It is rather about whether WTO policies should encompass social issues such as labour and gender. The controversy within the women's movement revolves around the same issues as the general debate on the link between trade and labour standards, and has produced a North/South divide among women's organizations.

Broadly speaking, the Northern groups support linkage, while Southern groups oppose it. There is no consensus on the institutional channels through which gender considerations should be integrated into the WTO, and whether this is the best or most effective way to promote gender equality in trade and the human rights of women as workers.

An underlying issue is the interpretation of the concept of gender mainstreaming by the various participants in the debate. On the one hand, many of these participants have adopted the technical and result-oriented approach, promoted by the World Bank and some donor agencies, which tends to overlook the underlying causes of gender inequalities, including many assumptions of economic and development models. On the other hand, there are those who want to challenge the structures and assumptions of the prevailing economic and development paradigm that underpins the MTS and current trade policies, and perpetuates women's subordination.

While the debate continues, it is clear that the issues at stake are larger than the integration of gender into the WTO agreements and processes, touching among others, on the issue of national capacity and resources to effectively realize women's rights; the issue of continuing protectionism in industrialized countries' markets which are critical to developing countries, and involve women's labour; as well as on the issue of subsidies for agriculture in developed countries, which make it particularly difficult for female African producers to maintain their livelihoods.

The Different Approaches to Gender Mainstreaming into the WTO

a) The Adaptive Approach

The proponents of an adaptive approach consider that trade is a given phenomenon and that women have to understand the rules of trade in order to adapt them. Mainstreaming gender into major trade institutions such as the WTO is therefore a matter of urgency. The majority of the proponents of this adaptive approach are organizations from the North. Most of them are members of the IWGGT mentioned above, which currently includes about 30 organizations.

This group has defined its priorities as follows:

* promotion of gender awareness in trade issues
* integration of gender perspectives into all levels of WTO work
* promotion of the availability of gender-disaggregated data for trade analysis
* making visible the gender-trade links in trade analysis.

The IWGGT has chosen as an entry point the country reports produced by the Trade Policy Review Mechanism of the WTO. It has developed an analysis that can be used to include gender in the TPR process in order to identify potential opportunities and threats for women's well-being as well as for other vulnerable groups.

A major problem with this approach is that the main purpose of the TPRM is not to assess the impact of trade agreements and rules, but the compliance of the concerned country with these and the extent to which it has met its commitments. In addition, because of the power relations that determine the WTO processes, such impact assessment could potentially be distorted into a process that could be used to serve other interests than those of women and vulnerable groups. Therefore, the fundamental problem related to power relations in the MTS limits considerably the efficacy of this approach in promoting gender equality and women's empowerment in trade.

b) The Alternative Approach

Critics of the adaptive approach are mainly organizations from the South. They point to the implicit endorsement of existing WTO rules and agreements with their imbalances and biases that this approach implies. In particular, it is underlined that this approach implies the recognition that free trade is basically good, and that the issue at stake is merely how to ensure that women will take advantage of its opportunities. It is also argued that its focus is too narrow, thereby overlooking the larger framework of trade.

These critics advocate an alternative approach which aims at developing alternatives to current WTO agreements and rules, as well as to the overall trade agenda, because they are inherently biased against the interests of developing countries and vulnerable groups within them, including women.

Proponents of the alternative approach, focus on the conceptual framework underlying current trade policies and institutions. While they agree on some objectives of the adaptive approach, such as women's participation in decision-making in the WTO, their main argument against the adaptive approach is that it does not address the conceptual issues related to the prevailing neo-liberal paradigm in the WTO.

In-between these two approaches are organizations that seek to combine the two approaches. An example of such a combination is provided by the International Gender and Trade Network, who has produced a number of papers for addressing gender issues in the WTO, while supporting research and economic literacy on trade at the regional level to promote alternatives.

c) Emerging Approaches

A new approach to gender mainstreaming in trade has emerged with the conceptual shift in the most recent analysis of gender and trade (Cagatay 2001). This new paradigm goes beyond the traditional 'winners and losers' analysis of mainstream trade theory to incorporate the social content of trade policies, as well as human development and rights-based approaches.

It emphasizes the need for a contextualized understanding of the interactions between gender inequalities and trade policies, and for a democratization of policy-making. It evaluates trade policies not in terms of flows of goods and services, but in terms of equity, social inclusion, poverty, human capabilities, human rights, democratic governance and environmental sustainability.

While this emerging approach includes various elements of the adaptive approach, it broadens its scope to include policy measures such as debt cancellation, increased aid flows, elimination of protectionism against developing countries exports and monitoring of TNCs. This approach also suggests that regional trade agreements offer a possibility for the promotion of workers' rights and securing female workers' rights in particular.

General Framework of an African Perspective

The prevailing approaches are not contextualized and do not therefore incorporate African specificities. The lack of an African perspective on the issue of gender mainstreaming into the WTO is an important concern, as African women are largely absent in a debate that has important implications for them.

First of all, responding appropriately to this issue requires asking the right questions. Therefore, the first step in that direction is the development of a coherent analysis from an African perspective, in order to clearly articulate the interests of African women in the debate. The second step is the definition of a framework for ensuring, not only that women gain from trade liberalization, but also that the structural causes of their economic subordination are addressed.

Such a framework needs to take into account the distributive effects of trade policies on African economies, as well as the interaction between trade liberalization and other types of economic reforms and policies, and the extent to which this general context is empowering or disempowering, because women's empowerment in trade also depends on the general economic and political conjuncture in which they integrate into the trading system.

Most importantly, the political economy of trade and development in Africa needs to be factored in such a framework. In particular, it is critically important to acknowledge the multiple disempowerment of African women in international trading arrangements, as this implies that the problem is not only about the WTO agreements and rules, but also about the role of international financial institutions and TNCs, as well as the state and institutions at the national level.

Furthermore, African gender researchers and activists need to re-claim the concept of gender mainstreaming so that it plays the role of a political tool for women's empowerment, instead of a technical device for legitimizing inequitable trade and economic policies. Just like the conventional trade theory, the prevailing approach for addressing the gender implications and impact of trade policies should be critically evaluated and challenged. As a first step in this direction, the intersections between gender, class, race, ethnicity and other forms of identity should be incorporated into the analysis.

In conclusion, an African perspective on the gender dimensions of trade liberalization and the MTS requires a thorough understanding of the way in which inequalities are created and maintained by the global economic system. In particular, it needs to recognize that this system encourages structural discrimination against women and the poor. Ultimately therefore, it must seek to transform the paradigms and structures of the global economy.

Notes

1. The rest of this subsection, as well as the following subsection, refer to the background paper by Nilufer Cagatay on *Trade, Gender and Poverty*.
2. This section draws heavily on the presentation made by Dzodzi Tsikata on 'Trade and Investment Policy in Africa: A Gender Analysis' at the GERA Regional Training Workshop on Gender, Trade and Investment in Africa, 27 June-5 July 2001 in Accra.

Bibliography

Cagatay, N., 2001, *Trade, Gender and Poverty*, Background Paper, New York: UNDP.

Dam, K. W., 1970, The GATT: Law and International Economic Organization, Chicago: University of Chicago Press.

Durano, M., 1999, *Gender Issues in International Trade*, International Gender and Trade Network.

GERA Programme 2000, *Demanding Dignity: Women Confronting Economic Reforms in Africa*, edited by Dzodzi Tsikata and Joanna Kerr with Cathy Blacklock and Jocelyne Laforce, The North-South Institute and Third World Network-Africa.

Olaka-Onyango and Udagama, 2001, 'Globalization and Its Impact on the Full Enjoyment of Human Rights', Progress report to the UN Sub-Commission on the Promotion and Protection of Human Rights, 53rd Session, 2 August 2001. E/CN.4/Sub.2/2001/10.

Raghavan, C., 2001, 'Historical Evolution and Changing Perceptions of the Trading System', Unpublished paper, Geneva.

Rodrik, D., 2001, 'The Gl obal Governance of Trade As If Development Really Mattered', Background Paper, New York: UNDP.

Standing, G., 1989a, *Global Feminisation Through Flexible Labour,* World Development 17, No 7.

Standing, G., 1989b, *Global Feminisation Through Flexible Labour: A Theme Revisited,* World Development 17, No 7.

Third World Network, 2001, 'The Multilateral Trading System: A Development Perspective', Background Paper, New York: UNDP.

Tsikata, D., 2001, 'Trade and Investment Policy in Africa: A Gender Analysis', Presentation at the GERA Regional Training Workshop on Gender, Trade and Investment in Africa, 27 June- 5 July 2001, Accra.

UNCTAD, 1999, *Trade and Development Report*, Geneva.

Williams, M., 2001, 'Imbalances, Inequities and the WTO Mantra', DAWN Discussion Paper II on the WTO.

www.ingramcontent.com/pod-product-compliance
Lightning Source LLC
Chambersburg PA
CBHW060038030426

42334CB00019B/2392